How to get
RICH REWARDS
in *Real Estate*
in *3 Years*

By 40 Aussie and Kiwi investors who have already done it!

How to get RICH REWARDS in Real Estate in 3 Years

By 40 Aussie and Kiwi investors who have already done it!

PHIL JONES

Best-selling author of *Real Money Real Estate*

With **ANDREA CRABB**

RICHMASTERY

Disclaimer

Although every effort has been made to ensure the accuracy of information contained in this book, Richmastery Limited holds no responsibility for the correctness of contributed material, or for any negative consequences resulting from the use of this book.

Published by Richmastery Limited
www.richmastery.com
Phil Jones – Director

Packaged for Richmastery Limited by Renaissance Publishing,
PO Box 36 206, Northcote, Auckland
Distributed in New Zealand by Celebrity Books,
Private Box 302 750, North Harbour, Auckland

ISBN 0-9582669-0-5

© 2005 Phil Jones and Andrea Crabb
The authors assert their moral rights in the work.

First published 2005
10 9 8 7 6 5 4 3 2 1

Printed through Bookbuilders, Hong Kong

*The authors would like to acknowledge the
courage, generosity, honesty and goodwill of all
the contributors in this book. Their stories are
truly inspirational and were shared in the hope
that they would motivate, educate
and help others on the journey to
financial freedom.*

Contents

Introduction

So you want to get rich in three years?

What better way than to learn from the successes, strategies, tips and processes that 40 of some of New Zealand and Australia's most successful real estate investors have used to amass significant rewards in less than three years!

And why would you want to do this? So you can replicate their success and enjoy real rewards from real estate yourself.

Investors who experience success so rarely choose to share it with others.

That is why this book is so special: it contains not 5, not 10, not 20, or 30, but 40 individual investors baring their souls and sharing their most intimate investing secrets just for you.

How to Get Rich Rewards in Real Estate in 3 Years is a celebration of tall poppies; average investors achieving exceptional results and who have the guts, honesty, desire and compassion to share their stories with you so you can be empowered to create your own success.

All the investors in this book are richer for investing in real estate because it has enriched their lives, their freedoms and their bank accounts. Every story has unique lessons and often it is not about the outcome an investor produced but where they came from to achieve it.

So, in order to prepare you for the sizzling investing meat by 40 investors in this book and the 400-plus tips they share, let's break a few chains.

Break the chains of slavery — get a life!

I am bewildered by the number of Aussies and Kiwis who choose slavery over freedom every day. We have been conditioned en masse by the media, government, bosses, family and friends that we MUST work every day for a living.

We have become conditioned slaves, accepting the polluted mantra of our society that only freaks, geeks and criminals STOP WORK and RETIRE EARLY and as we are not one of those crazies, our destiny is to work, work, work!

Every day people slave for others like blind mice frantically racing hard on the work treadmill in the hope they achieve a better life. Yet without realising it, *most are just turning the same wheel and running on the spot.*

Of even further amusement are the thousands that congregate in pubs, clubs, bars and lottery outlets whittling away their pay packets in order to escape the meaninglessness of their predicable and unfulfilled work wheel lives.

But here's the game breaker: have you ever been to a football match? This just blows me away. Here thousands of people hustle into a stadium from miles around to spend a not too insignificant amount of money on seats to watch 30 odd guys kick a pill around.

Now don't get me wrong, I love sport and the rivalry between Australia and New Zealand makes the games even sweeter, but let's just stop and think for a moment. Thousands of people are prepared to invest their hard earned cash in a short sports fix that delivers **no tangible financial outcome**, yet in the same week few of those very same people are prepared to invest either their time or money in some form of financial education that could have a life changing and long term benefit on their lives.

Our priorities are *screwed!* Most people are poor because they believe that's all they ever will be. So they live in the matrix and perpetuate the lie that has been told to them.

My dear friends it's time to WAKE UP and take off the blindfold you have been wearing! Step out of the matrix and realise that your life can be what you want it to be. A life of slavery in work does not have to be your allotted outcome. The joy of true financial freedom through real estate is a realistic and achievable outcome, if you choose.

Doing it hard or doing it easy — your choice!

Most people work to age 60, retire for seven years, then DIE. I just don't get it; what is the point of working for 60 years to enjoy seven and then die? That just sounds crazy, and yet that is what most of us do.

The good news is ... there is a better way, an infinitely better way.

I suggest you get a good financial real estate education and work seven to 10 years building a lifetime property portfolio so you can retire for 60 years.

Now what sounds better, *work for 60 and retire for seven, or work for seven and retire for 60?*

The answer is obvious to most of us, yet few people actually follow through and choose the obvious and easy outcome. Most people in our society go off-road, take the hard route and blow their money on trivia rather than investing in themselves and their future to create long term security and financial freedom.

The 40 investors in this book and myself have all made conscious decisions to build a solid real estate portfolio over a few years so we can enjoy the long term rewards and time freedom that property creates. Our collective hope is that you will have the wisdom, foresight and initiative to do the same.

Success leaves clues for others to follow

Throughout the stories in this book there are several common themes running through them all. They are:

- The investors have had direct contact with Richmastery. The positive influence of the Richmastery organisation in New Zealand and Australia is undeniable, evidenced and clearly documented in this powerful and inspirational book.

    The significant and direct benefits that thousands of Australasian investors have experienced as a result of their interaction and use of

Richmastery website, staff, programmes, educational resources and training is confirmed in chapter after chapter of this book and demonstrated constantly by the quiet multiplication of our graduates' net worth and through the monthly success stories archived on our website, www.richmastery.com.

● All investors attribute a significant portion of their personal and financial transformations directly to the real estate education they sought and received.

● All investors in this book have followed real estate investing principles or strategies that have been taught by Richmastery since its inception in 2001.

Overwhelmingly this book has two clear messages:

● *If they can do it, so can I*
The people featured in this book are not gifted, special or different from you; they include solo mums, church ministers and mechanics. There are no freaks or geeks and the testimony of the investors' success in this book should inspire and empower you to realise that you too can achieve similar results if you follow a similar investing path.

The message of this book is simple – you do not have to be a genius to win at the real estate game, you just have to follow the process and enjoy the results, and anyone can do it!

● *Education is the key to real estate investing success*
The explosive, radical and some times incredible financial transformations achieved by most of the investors in this book all started with one critical ingredient of gunpowder that catapulted their dreams into reality.

The gunpowder is not a magic formula, it's an obvious formula: *a quality real estate education.*

The education was the spark that lit the fire ... that resulted in massive financial outcomes for most of the property investors in this book. The pivot point for change for investors to morph from average to exceptional in short periods of time was the pure and simple power of *real estate knowledge* gained through education.

Education or ignorance?

The more education you put in,
the greater investing results you get out!

It never ceases to amaze me the number of people who willingly blow hundreds of thousands of dollars blindly buying investment property that is a total loser because they won't spend a few thousand getting an education that would save them tens of thousands in the first place. Or people that refuse to invest in their own education and stall their own property investing progress as a result.

Where is the sense in saving $5 to lose $10? Ignorance is madness!

Real estate investing is a business and it needs to be treated with the reverence and seriousness it deserves. If you are going to work for a number of years building your future lifetime income stream, isn't it a good idea to take some time and invest in yourself to ensure you do it well? After all, what's your greatest investment? What can give you more cash flow, more capital growth and greater returns than any piece of dirt? Answer: Yourself – invest in yourself with education.

 If you fail to plan, you are planning to fail.

Your Success is directly proportional to your Knowledge

and

Your Momentum is directly proportional to Education.

No Knowledge, No Education = No Success, No Momentum

Pretty simple stuff; it's just that most investors don't do it! They would rather save the 25 cents and lose $5 than spend the 25 cents and make the $5. Tight fisted investors punish themselves with their own ignorance and the opportunities they miss.

In life you get out exactly what you are prepared to put in. If you don't put petrol in the car the car won't go; if you don't feed your body it dies; if you don't feed your mind it fails and your investments may fail with it.

 The most expensive advice you can ever get is free advice from a poor person!

Filling the knowledge bank

When you went to school how did you learn?
How do our schools, universities and colleges teach the nation's children?
How do almost all serious professional trades like doctors, dentists, mechanics and lawyers learn?

Answer: We learn by direct interaction with a teacher or master who has more knowledge on the subject than the students being taught.

This most basic principle has been a fundamental part of our society for hundreds of years. The value of a teacher's direct interaction with students is well documented and well known and is clearly established as the most effective and beneficial learning process available. That's why we use it across the nation!

> We do not have students turning up to schools with **no teachers** and a security guard handing out textbooks as students arrive and collecting them again at 3 pm before they go home. And if we did this there would be a massive public outcry from homes across the country because the process would significantly disadvantage and fail large portions of students unnecessarily.

My point is this, books provide valuable resources for real estate investors but they are *one-dimensional learning instruments* that *cannot* talk back. They *cannot* answer your questions, they *cannot* provide expanded clarification on difficult points and they cannot show you how the principle that is taught directly relates to your specific and unique circumstances or spend extra time with you helping you understand the issues as needed.

There is no substitute for the multi-dimensional education gained from a live interactive real estate seminar or event where investors can benefit from a proven learning experience that enables the curriculum to be absorbed and personalised to the audience.

None of us would allow a surgeon who had just read a textbook to operate on us, nor would we want to drive in a car with someone who just got their licence by reading the road code but had never driven a vehicle before.

And so it is that interaction, clarification of questions and practical application of the skills to do the job are all fundamental components needed to establish competence and success in any role whether it be surgery or property investing.

For this reason I sincerely recommend investors attend live real estate educational events. The value gained and information gleaned from these events can often be significantly more beneficial than a one-dimensional book.

Knowledge is power

Many of the investors featured in this book credit much of their success to their attendance at the Richmastery Property Academy. This is an intensive three day course of over 40 hours featuring over 25 speakers that is only run once or twice a year.

It's no coincidence that the success of many investors in this book is directly or indirectly linked to the education they received at the Richmastery Property Academy. This was never our intention when commencing the research for this book, but it has developed as an obvious and natural outcome.

Success and education are intertwined and, as a natural consequence, Richmastery's education of investors forms an important part of many investors' stories in this book. Knowledge is power!

My life changed radically as a result of knowledge I gained and applied from a speaker at a seminar. My personal success, like those in this book, came from the time someone else devoted to teach and empower us.

Looking back, I see my life would have been so different if I hadn't received the 'wake up call' and 'information' I needed to stop being an employee and start taking control of my financial destiny. In my journey since those early days I have refined, distilled and significantly added to that raw knowledge that was given to me and feel a desire and obligation to share with others the gems, tools and strategies that have changed my life.

Richmastery Ltd was established as the vehicle that would enable me to provide investors with greater access to the education and knowledge that positively affected my financial outcomes and which could do the same for you.

The Richmastery regional office network, with local experts, mentors, support staff and educators in each area, provides you with a much higher level of service, support and access than one person like me personally ever could. For me the delivery of the message is important, not the person who delivers it.

As a result, in the last few years Richmastery has become one of the fastest growing wealth education companies in Australasia. Our success is due to a few simple factors:

- We stand behind everything we do with a 100% money back guarantee.
- What we teach works and people get real results.
- Each of our regional branch office directors practises what we preach.
- We are here for the long haul not the short sprint.
- We have a range of services that have been developed to help investors achieve their goals no matter where they are in their investing life cycle.
- It's about our clients' outcomes, not individuals' personalities.

As a result, I am blessed to have been a small part of a company that changes and empowers investors' lives for the better. There is no greater reward than each day reading new success stories on the Richmastery website from investors who have taken the tools we have given them and created sensational outcomes for themselves.

 Success is created, it does not just happen.

If it's time you propelled your success to the next level and started turbocharging your investing, maybe it's time you considered attending the Richmastery Property Academy or register for the FREE newsletter on our website and we'll send you a $249 real estate investing pack for FREE.

Bookings for the Richmastery Property Academy are limited. For more information go to www.richmastery.com or the colour section at the end of this book.

 It's not what you know that's holding you back but what you don't know!

You think education is expensive, try ignorance!

 Real estate investing is the key to financial freedom. You just will never get free if you don't get in the game.

The power to change

Richmastery provides Real People, Real Strategies, Real Results that *give you the power to change* and this book is stacked full of real life examples of real people who have achieved dramatic financial transformations.

Each investor has achieved their result because of the strategies they have acquired through education and the action and passion they have harnessed to drive them to an exciting new destination. The good news is you can do the same!

They have each faced their own challenges and conquered more than a few demons, but their determination to escape the 'work wheel' has resulted in a new outcome, a brighter future, and more fun days in the sun.

In life it's not what happens to you but how you choose to respond to it that matters.

May this book, inspire, empower and educate you to seek out a quality financial real estate education and start the exciting journey towards true long term financial freedom through property investing as it has for thousands of other successful real estate investors across New Zealand and Australia.

 It's not where you start but where you finish that counts.

Successful investing!

Phil Jones

Living the dream

'We set a goal of becoming successful property investors. A year on, we're living that dream.
— Jonelle Phillips and Jane Foote, Auckland, NZ

B oth professional working women in their own right, Jane and Jonelle began investing in property in mid 2004 and, together, have built an impressive portfolio of residential rental property worth $6 million and still building. Through meticulous planning, patience and sheer determination, the pair made more than $1.1 million in equity in just under seven months and now benefit from more than 90 rental income streams.

New beginnings

As qualified management accountants, the pair met early in their careers while working for one of the top financial consultancies in Auckland. Over the years, Jonelle and Jane sought different career challenges and quickly moved up the ranks to executive positions. In 2003, Jane went to work for Jonelle as Financial Controller for a privately owned group of companies of which Jonelle had progressed to General Manager. While the work was challenging, both were forced to rethink their futures with the group as their positions became untenable under the current executive structure. In early 2004, both decided to take a risk and do something for themselves so they could be in complete charge of their own destinies.

'This was the turning point in our careers,' says Jonelle. 'We realised we had spent a lot of time making other people wealthy and now it was time to focus on ourselves.'

The plan was to work together as management consultants in the interim until they could make property investment their full time focus.

'It's probably one of the biggest decisions we have ever made in our lives – getting out of our comfort zones and trying something different. In saying that, it's also one of the best decisions we have ever made,' says Jane.

Saying goodbye to 'safe' careers and regular incomes was no easy feat, particularly given Jonelle and her husband had just purchased a second business and a new home and Jane was about to get married.

In May 2004, the pair attended the Richmastery Property Academy in Auckland. 'This was well timed as it helped us identify our strengths and weaknesses and learn about new areas we needed to focus on,' says Jane.

Planning is key

The day after attending the academy, Jonelle and Jane carried out an intensive full day of planning in order to map out their path to success.

'You would never drive a car in a strange country without a road map so why would you begin an investing career without a proper plan? It was imperative that we sit down and map out our vision, goals, objectives and financial future first,' says Jonelle.

The women created a strategic plan that consisted of strategies and financial goals for the following 6, 12, 18 and 24 months. Their vision was: *To build significant property portfolios for long term investment and wealth creation and to replace our employment incomes within a two year period, combined with financial freedom, from a property portfolio with total annual earnings of over $1 million (mixture of equity and cash flow).*'

'Our objective was to aim high so we achieved high,' says Jane.

The pair knew their strategies needed to concentrate on where they were both starting from financially and what exactly they needed to purchase to achieve their set goals within the required timeframes.

Purchasing rules

Jane and Jonelle also developed strict purchasing rules to complement their plan and assist them in reaching their investment goals. 'Our purchasing rules are our absolute minimum criteria for measuring the viability of every property purchase. We never compromise any of our rules as that would mean compromising our whole plan and, more importantly, our future. If it doesn't fit our criteria, we move on to the next one,' says Jonelle.

Jonelle and Jane's purchasing rules include:

1. Always ensure your deposit (usually 20%+) can be recycled out within six months by adding value to the property and its total annual cash flow earnings (gross income).

Jane: 'Buying under valuation is absolutely imperative. If you buy a property at 13% below valuation, whereby your deposit is 20% on settlement, you need to be confident you can add value to the property and its cash flow earnings by at least 7% within a 12 week period in order to gain your full deposit back and be able to move on to the next purchase.

2. Purchase solely on the numbers and, in particular, on positive pre-tax cash flow rather than solely the after tax cash flow.

Jonelle: 'After tax cash flow is considered to be just a bonus for us as no one can determine what the government's going to do with the current legislation. Bank it, but don't rely on it!'

3. Cash flow or capital growth properties?

Jane: 'It all depends on your circumstances as to the ratio of purchasing cash flow to capital growth properties. Our aim was to focus on cash flow properties only in the first 12 months in order to replace our incomes.'

4. Acceptable property returns

Cash flow properties: Minimum return of not less than 1.5% above the current interest rate for the property, i.e. a 7.5% fixed interest rate would require a 9% return. Cash flow properties must be positive before and after tax cash flow.

Capital growth properties: Minimum return of not less than 1.5% below the current interest rate for the property. Capital growth properties must be positive after tax cash flow only.

Jonelle: 'This is non-negotiable for us as it ensures we receive positive before and after tax cash flow every time. Even if the numbers came in at less than 0.1% under these rules, we would still walk away or negotiate harder.

'Sticking to these rules ultimately ensures we still have some headroom should the rental market change dramatically.'

The pair say their strategic plan has now become a monitoring tool for them that measures their results against their goals on a regular basis.

'Our plan has helped us focus on our goals and has completely eliminated the scattergun approach. In just six months, we had already met our 12 month goals so we were able to re-forecast our expectations and achieve even more,' says Jonelle.

And the results?

In just under seven months, Jonelle and Jane have:

- Purchased 52 properties, with 90 separate income streams.
- Purchased, on average, at 13–15% below the registered valuations.
- Purchased property with an average net return of 10%+ (after property costs are deducted from income).
- Focused on positive pre-tax, as well as positive after-tax, cash flow.
- Purchased properties with multiple income streams on one or a number of titles.
- Only purchased property where they could add further value – whether it be adding additional rooms, making cosmetic improvements or simply furnishing the houses. Any planned improvements were carefully researched to ensure works would add value to the overall earning capacity of the properties – to annual gross rentals. This is the key with refinancing.

Case study: Buying right and adding value

One of the properties Jonelle and Jane purchased was a block of units in the Manawatu, lower North Island.

'It was an ideal investment as it had multiple income streams from two old villas and 12 self contained units (eight studio flats and four two-bedroom units). It had formerly been a motel and was based centrally,' says Jane.

Growing up in Palmerston North, Jonelle knew the area well but hadn't lived there for well over 10 years.

'We researched the area thoroughly by talking to a range of people including various agents, property managers and locals in order to find out what things were renting for, market values for different property types, what the renting population currently was in the area, future business growth and

Our Manawatu investment: two villas and 12 self contained units, giving multiple income streams and a 9.4% return.

what the capitalisation rates were, etc,' says Jonelle.

The capitalisation rate is the risk factor taken into account in the valuation and is determined by a number of factors, which may include:

- Current economic factors, e.g. interest rates, consumer confidence etc
- The state of the property: is it new or run down?
- Location: is it centrally located or out of the way?
- The length of the tenancies: the longer they are the lower the risk.
- Is it near community facilities such as bus routes, schools and shops?
- The quality of the construction and products used to build the property.

'Capitalisation rates vary greatly from property to property depending on these factors. It also has a bearing on the level of borrowing you can achieve so it is a very important factor and your research is absolutely key,' says Jane.

Structuring the finance was also critical to the success of the deal.

'Normally, for properties of this size, banks would only lend around 65% of the purchase price,' says Jonelle. 'Fortunately for us, the property was situated on six different titles at three different addresses, so we were able to split up the addresses and titles and take these to different banks to get 80% residential funding, rather than having the property classified as commercial.'

The pair also negotiated with the vendors hard and purchased the property for 14% below valuation. The property required refurbishment and a few structural changes to bring its value up, to recycle their deposit.

The property was fully rented when the pair bought the property and was providing them with an income stream of more than $40,000 in pre-tax cash flow or a 9.4% net return.

'The refurbishment is being carried out in stages and, prior to it commencing, we wanted to get buy-in from all the tenants in the block. We have done a lot of work with them, talking to them about our plans and they are just as excited as we are about the refurbishment,' says Jonelle.

Given a property like this is usually valued on its rental income, the pair say the refurbishment will mean they will be able to substantially increase the rents once it is complete, which will increase the value of the property and also allow them to recycle their deposit out.

'We have been extremely mindful of not over-capitalising on refurbishments so our general rule is that for every \$1 spent on refurbishment, you should be able to recover \$4 in value added to the property,' says Jane.

So what have been the main contributors to Jane and Jonelle's success?

'We've always had HUGE dreams – and we define success as turning these dreams into reality,' says Jonelle. 'It's also important to stick to your goals. You also have to have confidence in yourself and not get scared of all the zeros! As long as the numbers stack up, then it's workable,' she says.

The pair agrees that gaining the necessary knowledge and tools is also a big contributor to success.

'We're continually learning and gaining more knowledge,' says Jane. 'You never stop learning and we continue to learn new things every day from just getting out there and doing it.

'Planning our road map was also critical to our success as it ensured we were both being realistic with what we could achieve within the set timeframes,' says Jonelle.

'And of course, most importantly, we took action! We had the determination and motivation to succeed and this has helped us overcome many fears along the way. We have experienced some exciting highs and some very forgettable lows, which were sometimes both in one day,' says Jane.

Lessons learnt

Jonelle and Jane say many valuable lessons have been learnt along the way and their office even sports a corkboard with a range of key lessons pinned to it to remind them of these every day.

'There are days when we experience a complete roller-coaster ride,' says Jonelle. 'We've often found this has been due to a lack of understanding from others, like a bank or vendor, so our challenge has always been to find a solution. Hurdles can always be overcome if you think hard enough.

'If you've done your due diligence and the property stacks up, then challenge how things are done; don't ever give up,' she says.

Another big lesson the pair have learned is to always check the documentation properly.

'One of our biggest lessons occurred early on in our investing career when we went to sign a bank document and discovered all the details in it were completely wrong – from the negotiated interest rate to the type and term of the loan. If we had signed that documentation without checking it, it would have cost us thousands and, in fact, would have made the deal unviable.'

The pair also says that it is critical to never just accept a verbal bank acceptance of a loan.

'It's extremely important that your loan is properly signed off by the credit department of the bank prior to going unconditional. Don't ever just take people's word for it,' says Jane.

Another key lesson for Jonelle and Jane was the importance of taking photos of the property and the chattels prior to settlement.

'We were about to settle on a significant property which, when we first viewed it, featured new appliances and electronic equipment,' says Jane.

'On settlement day, we discovered many of these items had been replaced with old chattels. Luckily, Jonelle had taken some digital photos during our original visit so we were able to hold settlement up until the vendor returned the items we had agreed would accompany the property.'

'One of our key mottos now is, "Always be awake, because if you're asleep, nobody will wake you",' says Jonelle. 'You always have to have your wits about you and ensure you understand exactly what the agreement includes, otherwise it can cost you dearly.'

 **Success is a journey, not a destination.**

JONELLE AND JANE'S TOP TIPS

1. Get the knowledge: education is everything and no one should ever stop learning.
2. Plan a realistic road map for yourself, tailored for your personal situation.
3. Learn from your mistakes but don't let them set you back.
4. Don't allow hurdles to get in your way: there is always a solution!
5. Set your investing rules and stick to them; don't compromise them by letting your emotions take over.
6. Become an expert on an area, by understanding the capital growth rates, population growth, current residential market values and growth of surrounding industry and facilities.
7. Concentrate on only one or two areas at a time: avoid the scattergun approach.
8. Travel to the location during due diligence (if out of town): get out there and talk to people who know the area.
9. For credibility's sake, know what you are talking about! Even if you are scared, act confident (particularly around real estate agents) otherwise no one will take you seriously.
10. Surround yourself with a good network of people who understand what you are trying to achieve. Get rid of those that don't measure up!
11. Get the support of your partner. They need to understand and believe in what you are doing as well in order for you to succeed.
12. Always verify and understand everything yourself: never rely solely on what others tell you.
13. Do whatever it takes! Set yourself some goals and make sure you put in the necessary time to reach them.
14. Celebrate your successes, even the little ones, and, more importantly, make sure you have fun along the way!
15. Face your fears and overcome them,
16. And finally ... GET OUT THERE AND DO IT!

A Special Reward

To help you get the most out of this book we provide you with the following four Special Rewards. Please make sure you use them and enjoy them.

The goal in providing you with these free additional resources is to encourage you to continue the positive real estate investing journey you have started by reading this book.

1. FREE Bonus Chapters

In addition to this book there are at least five bonus chapters that are available for you to read or download from our website. These chapters are essential reading and will further equip you with an array of powerful tools to help polish and improve your investing. To access these bonus chapters go to: **www.richmastery.com/getrichbonus**

2. FREE Online Investor Support

We invite you to join the Richmastery Forums at our website **www.richmastery.com**. This is a live, fun internet meeting place used by thousands of other investors (and many of the investors in this book) to meet, chat, support, share information and help one another achieve investing success.

We strongly recommend you participate in this investing community, which is designed to help support and further your investing results.

3. FREE Property Analysis Software

The number one tool that EVERY successful investor should be using is Property Analysis Software. It's a critical decision making tool that can save you thousands and make you thousands. To download a free 14 day trial of the software many investors in this book use and recommend, go to: **www.reviq.com**

Note: Many of the investors in this book refer to the Richmastery software; this software is now known as ReVIQ.

4. FREE Live Event

We want to give you two tickets valued at $79.90 to Richmastery's four hour How to Profit from Property Live Event so you can build on the exciting knowledge you gain from this book. If you would rather watch the DVD of this evening, we have arranged $20 off the price of this for you. To get your FREE tickets and DVD discount go to: **www.richmastery.com/getrichbonus**

One property a fortnight

I live with my wife Yoland and our family in Mt Roskill in central Auckland. We have been married for 33 years. We have two children: Karen (32) and Jared (29). Karen's fiancé, Jason Joe, and Jared's partner, Jennifer Lim, live with us too.

I started investing in property way back in the late 1960s when I was 21 and Yoland was 19. I found it impossible in those days to find any information on how to invest. I bought, held and sold many properties. I tried 'wrapping' and experienced the infamous rent freeze of the late 1970s and the massive interest rates rises in the 80s.

The long and short of it is that I made many mistakes and wish I knew then what I know today having had the benefit of the Richmastery education. My motto now is 'Never sell'.

Penthouse pains

For the first time in my working life in 1995 I found myself in the position where I didn't own any property except my family home and after three years I decided I wanted to buy an investment property again. So in 1998 I bought the penthouse suite in the Metro Apartment Building in Wakefield Street, right in the heart of Auckland CBD. I paid $250k for it and put down a deposit of $35k to purchase it off the plan. I bought it on emotion. My idea was that because the casino was being built nearby that it had the potential to make money.

Under the agreement with the developers, finance on the property was guaranteed to 85% plus 9% rental return. After two years it went unconditional. Another year later the developer went into liquidation and I was required to settle on the contract. However, the banks refused to loan 85% and I was told the market had changed and that I had to put down a 55% deposit ($137k). I chose to walk away from the deal and lost my deposit of $35k. The developers went bankrupt and the property was sold off to an overseas investor for $180k through tenders. I was fortunate not to be sued for the balance.

Franchising

Having lost the Metro penthouse apartment in 2001, I was quite upset and had virtually decided to give up the property game forever.

I decided it was easier to just put money into my business, The Tofu Shop, and to just open up new retail branches. My first shop was sold as a license, with the owner operator paying a weekly flat fee for the name. Then I received a good offer on one of my other shops and that's when I decided to get serious about selling my businesses as franchises.

I learnt about franchising and understanding franchises was the start of my understanding about passive cash flow, time and leverage. I now have eight shops, five that I own personally and operate through managers and three that are currently franchised.

> From then on I realised that through the leveraging of time and passive income was the only way to really make a massive amount of money. My knowledge of leverage has become integral to my property investing business today.

Back to property with a vengeance

It wasn't until my son-in-law Jason encouraged me to buy a rental property that he had found in Onehunga, a suburb of Auckland, in 2002 that I began property investing again. Ironically, in January 1999 I had talked Jason and my daughter Karen into putting their savings into a rental investment while saving for their first home (today, six years later, they now have 17 properties).

I raised $180k against the equity of my own home in the form of a

This two bedroom Onehunga flat was my first purchase after almost giving the whole game away.

revolving credit account and in October 2002 bought a two bedroom flat in a block of eight with a full basement at 4/394 Onehunga Mall for $192k. I spent $6000 on renovations and rented it for $310 per week.

Encouraged by my success on the very first deal, after three months I refinanced the Onehunga Mall property and topped up the mortgage. I still had $140k in the revolving credit account. Jason found me another place, which I bought in February 2003. It was a three bedroom house at 256 Mt Wellington Highway. It was valued at $195k and I got it for $185k. I settled in early April 2003 and spent three months doing it up (which I now know is way too long).

In early March 2003 I attended the Richmastery Profit from Property evening seminar at the Sheraton Hotel in Auckland with my son Jared, his partner Jennifer and my son-in-law Jason. I loved it; it was like after 30 years I had finally found a course that would teach me the information I had been searching for – the nuts and bolts of property investing. All four of us signed up that night to attend the Richmastery Property Academy in May.

Soon afterwards I bought a property in Malone Road. It was advertised at $139k and I got it for $137k. I wasn't a very good negotiator at that stage. I was in a panic to buy as the market was starting to move. Today this place has a value of $210k and I have yet to do anything to it.

My fourth property was at 1/269 Mt Wellington Highway. I purchased it for $140k; it was valued at $148k and is now worth $180k. It rents for $260 per week.

Next I bought my fifth property at 2/112 Owairaka Avenue, Mt Albert, for $180k as a private sale from one of my staff. I arranged a long settlement with a $1000 deposit. I signed the deal in March to settle on 27 June 2003. I spent $3000 on renovation, and today the estimated market value is $245k. It currently rents for $295 per week.

I purchased my sixth property on 24 April 2003, a three bedroom house at 267 Mt Wellington Highway, with settlement due 6 June 2003. It was advertised earlier for two months at $220k. It was a mess, full of bikies, with motorcycles parts everywhere inside. I saw the tenants move out and it was re-advertised at $205k. The vendors were divorced and neither party wanted to keep it. I put in an offer of $175k and got it for $186k as they just wanted a quick sale. I renovated it and converted the extra large bedroom into two rooms with a hallway in the middle, creating a fourth bedroom. I also added a toilet and tiled the bathroom, put in a concrete drive and shared the cost with the neighbours. I painted it inside and out, and put a new fence railing on the terrace. In total I spent $13k. Its current valuation is now $290k, and I rent it out for $370 per week.

One property a fortnight

I attended the Richmastery Property Academy in May along with my son Jared, and his partner Jennifer, who also had one property each by now, plus my son-in-law Jason. In the 12 months following the academy I purchased a further 18 properties, increasing my total portfolio value to a whopping $4.6 million. In the 18 months since I had started investing again I gained equity of $1.68 million and the net profit from rentals before tax is $101k per annum.

> I came out of the Richmastery Property Academy and started to buy property at the rate of one a fortnight because after 30 years of searching for the correct knowledge and tools on property investment I was finally armed with all the resources I needed.

During the 1970s and 80s and even the 90s there were very few books about investing. I had attended a seminar by Bob Jones in 1980 and had read his book, *Jones on Property*. I had also read Olly Newland's books and the Rydges publication *Investing in Real Estate Wealth*. This was originally my

I spent $6000 renovating the Onehunga flat, including redecorating the lounge and kitchen. It rented for $310 per week. The success of this property gave me lots of confidence.

bible but in reality it never told you about the pitfalls, the skills of negotiation needed and the resources to buy from. The books just told you someone's story and not the nuts and bolts.

The bank and finance companies would advise you to pay off your mortgage as fast as possible through principal and interest. My lawyer would consistently ask how I would ever own the property outright if I kept rolling over, topping up and increasing my mortgages. It seemed that no one really knew how to benefit from the property cycles apart from saying properties would double approximately every eight to 10 years. No one talked about how it was done, and even getting a mentor was impossible. I now put it all down to learning and experience.

Sharper skills, better knowledge

After completing the Richmastery Property Academy, suddenly things like my buying and negotiating skills changed. Before the academy if a place was advertised at $200k I thought offering 10% below was enough and then you would end up buying it for about 5% below. I've since learnt to go in an offer at about 25% below market value and end up at 10 to 15% below. This meant if a vendor was asking for $200k, I would start my offer at around $150k.

The more properties I bought, the sharper I got with my negotiating. I'd use all the different clauses suggested at the Richmastery Property Academy. Things like long term settlements, cash offers (within a shorter period), finance

Three bedroom house at 256 Mt Wellington Highway. I spent far too long renovating it.

clauses, subject to valuation and builder's reports; these clauses would give me an out if a place didn't value up; LIM (Land Information Memorandum) reports could be used to renegotiate prices afterwards if anything was untoward; QV (Quotable Value) online was a major source of information to give me market values of a place I was considering and places surrounding it. I gained a fairly accurate idea of values so if a bargain came up I knew the value even before I saw it.

I contacted an agent from Barfoot and Thompson, Jane Wang, through whom I had purchased three of my properties, told her I wanted to buy 10 more houses to ensure her support and to show I was serious. She was very good at her job so I built a rapport with her. Jane went on to become the 'Top Rookie Salesperson of the Year 2004'. The fortunate part of this relationship was that I showed her how to become an investor herself, something that is important to all property investors when building a team of experts around you.

I became an expert in buying in the suburb of Mt Wellington, in particular Sylvia Park about 20 minutes' drive from downtown Auckland and right near the motorway entrance.

This whole Mt Wellington Highway area is a fantastic rental investment area as it is near where the proposed Sylvia Park Shopping Centre is being built. Excavations of the area are already in the advanced stages and values are continuing to climb. It also will be near the new motorway corridor. So naturally I decided that this was an area I would continue to buy into. I also believe Otara and Otahuhu are great areas to buy in.

When I purchase properties I always use 'Ron Hoy Fong and/or nominee', and never use the name of my LAQC as that alerts the vendor that an investor is buying it.

Revaluing to recycle

At this stage I was running out of funds from all my deposits and discovered due to the property boom and do-ups that I did that I could recycle my equity by topping up my mortgages. I had all the properties revalued, recycled my equity, and transferred the additional funds back into my revolving credit account to reduce interest payments on unused funds – another trick I had learnt through Richmastery. I also raised an additional $100k revolving credit over the investment properties with the ASB from all the new values.

A friend told me about a property at 41 Albrecht Street in Mt Roskill. It was an immaculate three bedroom house but had no curtains. There were some problems with the garage that had yet to be permitted on the plans because it was on the boundary line. The previous owners had subdivided the land and had placed the garage right on the adjoining boundary. As a result two previous prospective buyers had pulled out as it wasn't legal. The cost to have the garage permitted on the plans was $5000 so I took this into account with a low offer.

They had dropped the asking price from $239k to $219k. I offered $205k and they accepted it. It rents for $350 per week and the current valuation is $293k.

The eighth property I purchased was in Barbary Avenue in Kelston. My mortgage broker sold it to me. He thought he was being clever and that he was getting over valuation, asking $149k. I saw it as another do-up. I used the Richmastery analysis computer software to check out the rental return. I told him he was asking too much and paid $138,500 after getting him to drop $10k. I spent $6000 on renovations, replaced the carpet, a new kitchen bench, new toilet, security light and generally tidied it up. I rented it out for $280 per week, which is a 10% return. It is now valued at $210k.

My ninth purchase was in Parker Road, Otara. It was a three bedroom house with a double garage converted into a sleep-out; it had power but no water. One of Jason's real estate agents told me about the house and said it was on the market for a quick sale for $110k and would not accept any offers. He told me I would need to be able to settle in three days. I spent $9000 doing renovations as it needed a total interior repaint, new stove, curtains, carpets, vinyl, changed light fittings, power points and door handles; I relined the bathroom and put in a new mirror. The registered valuation at the time of purchase was $121k. In February 2004 it was valued at $150k but today is likely to be worth as much as $175k. It rents for $260 per week.

Number 10 was a unit (No. 3) in a block on the Mt Wellington Highway. It settled at the end of June 2003. I got it for $120,200. They were asking $130k. It was a multi-offer but I had the highest bid by $200 because I always use small amounts in my offers. It is rented out for $240 per week and the market value today would be $180k.

The next purchase (my eleventh) was the next door unit (No. 4) in the same block. I purchased this in June with a delayed settlement for 12 September 2003. I got it for $120k. It rents for $245 per week. Once I owned both the units I was able to create new access for No. 4 and had this area concreted. The current QV online valuation is $170k each.

In August, 2003 I purchased another flat in a block on the Mt Wellington Highway. They were asking $150k and I got it for $140k; it is now worth $180k. It is rented for $260 per week.

Creating a crash

By this stage I was buying many properties at below valuation, because of this the registered valuer kept referring to recent sales in the area that happened to be my own properties as well.

Effectively I was creating a mini property crash in the Mt Wellington area that I was investing in, while the rest of the country was enjoying a 20% capital growth. This in one way gave me the advantage of buying further properties below real values, but on the other hand hindered me when I wanted to recycle equity because I couldn't get the values to increase after renovations. So the solution to this in the end was to buy in another area and allow other purchasers to push sales prices up in the neighborhood.

For all the deals I put down 20% deposit from recycled equity of previous places and raised the 80% from the bank. My mortgage broker would arrange my finances and my loyalty to them and the banks only lasted as long as loans were being approved. Finding the mortgage funds is a very important part of investing, so when the mortgage broker, who is a very important part of your team of experts, can no longer help, then seek another.

Buying fast

The next two properties I bought were at 70 and 70a Jolson Road, Mt Wellington. I signed them up on 10 August with settlement on 10 October. It was a two bedroom with an attached three bedroom minor dwelling and a separate sleep-out, all renting for $500 per week. I created a third bedroom in the original two bedroom dwelling so it now also has three bedrooms.

I paid $250,500 for the property and spent $10k on doing it up including the kitchen and a new wall for the third room. The kitchen cost about $4000 and I did some other tidy up work on all the places. I rent out the three places for a total of $610 per week.

I purchased my fifteenth property at 1/295 Mt Wellington Highway from a motivated vendor because two previous sales agreements had fallen over. I picked it up for $180k and it was valued at $199k at the time of purchase. I didn't need to do any work to it and rented it out for $310 per week.

I then bought 2/27 Mataroa Road, Mt Wellington, overlooking the water. I got it for $155k, which is what they were asking even though it was worth $180k. The offer was made in October 2003 and settled in April 2004. The real estate agent made the offer at 2 am because the vendor worked nights; they were motivated sellers because they had been waiting for five months for an offer. It was advertised for a month at the time when it was first listed but the agents had since moved on to promote other properties and left it sitting as an old listing in their books. I rented this for $285 per week.

The next place (my seventeenth) I bought was 256a Mt Wellington Highway at an auction in October 2003; it never reached its reserve price. I knew the value of $240k beforehand so put in a successful cash offer of $225k with a long term settlement in March 2004. It is a house two doors away from food outlets and next to the proposed Sylvia Park Shopping Centre, so it could potentially become offices one day. It is now rented for $345 per week.

Renovated kitchen at 256 Mt Wellington Highway.

Watch out for dummy bidders at auctions; these people are unethical bidders because their sole purpose is to push the bidding price upwards without going over the reserve price themselves. Stick to any rules you may have and know limits and avoid being emotional and you will avoid overpaying for the property.

The next purchase was 4/45 Kingsway Avenue in Sandringham, an up and coming inner city suburb of Auckland. At this stage I was told not to buy any more in Mt Wellington to avoid having all my eggs in one basket. I bought it on 21 November for $295k with a settlement on 30 January. I readjusted my goal from passive income only properties to include some capital growth properties in a capital growth area. It rents for $295 per week.

Number 19 on

By now my borrowings were reaching close to $3 million and the banks were considering me as 'rent reliant'. Personal income was no longer being taken into account as part of the equation when applying for loans and all rentals had to be sufficient to cover all expenses on investments. In hindsight I should have been stricter on my buying rules by sticking to a 10% minimum return before tax. As a result of this I found myself going into penalty interest because of delayed settlements and actually lost my deposit of $20k on a place at 9 Shale Road, Massey, on which I had intended to build a minor dwelling. My real loss on this place was around $75k because market value on the place has since increased considerably. Fortunately, my nephew

Anthony Hoy Fong, whom I was mentoring at the time, took over the deposit and was able to raise 90% finance because it was his first investment property. It was a blow for me to lose it but I am glad it has stayed in the family and not gone back to the vendor, who was an investor and had only owned the place for six months. When the minor dwelling is completed the return will be $620 per week on a $275k investment plus an estimated market value of $380k.

Number 19 was a private sale which I signed up on 18 January 2004 with settlement in early April. It was a three bedroom home at 267b Mt Wellington Highway. I offered $180k and got it for $195k; it was valued at $230k at time of purchase. I made $50k on it when I settled, and a further $50k since. I spent $8000 on renovations and today it rents for $350 per week. Today you are lucky to find a three bedroom house in Mt Wellington for less than $280k.

My twentieth property was 2/269 Mt Wellington Highway, which I purchased for $155k two days later on 20 January 2004. This was in the block where I already owned units 1 and 5 so I now have control over the whole block. I arranged a private sale with the vendor. He wanted $155k but it was only worth $150k so I arranged a long settlement and he stayed there rent free until settlement in July 2004. At the time of settlement the value had risen to $180k.

 With all my renovations in the previous 10 months I had students help me paint them. The work on this place cost $2500 and is now rented for $260 per week.

Next I purchased units 4, 6 and 9, in a block of 10 units at 99 Avenue Road, Otahuhu (which featured on TV3's *House Traps* programme). The asking price was $129k for each unit. I successfully negotiated a price of $105k per unit. They were disgusting but I could see the potential beyond the cockroaches, damaged walls, rubbish and leaves covering the outdoor area and the general mess. These deals settled on 6 August 2004 and are rented for $210 to $230 per week, giving 10% pre-tax returns. The registered valuation was $119k, but the market value is $125k to $130k. Prior to settlement I reassigned Unit 4 to my nephew Anthony and Unit 9 to Jane Wang, my real estate agent, who has helped me to find so many hot deals.

297 Mt Wellington Highway: before re-laying driveway.

Goals set

My main aim is to reach my goal of $200k per year passive income from properties within five years before retirement. Once I've achieved that I will start to look mainly for capital growth properties. I'm still good for another 1.5 property cycles in my working life as I am now 56.

In the flat market, which we have now, it will probably take me another two years to reach $200k per annum in passive income. The recent boom cycle has ended so it will now take longer to recycle my equity. Hopefully, then I will start to enjoy investing in capital growth properties, which have a longer investment cycle of eight to 10 years.

I am still involved in much of the renovations myself and have just leveraged my time by getting the help of student friends. I work about 20 to 30 hours on renovations each week and about 10–20 hours on my business. I am a JP, have been awarded a Queen's Service Medal, am heavily involved in community work and am the chairman and president of several Chinese related organisations.

When I am on a high I find that I achieve a lot more. I'm at peace now with where I am at in life, my daughter and son are in good relationships and in just one year my children and I have purchased $10 million of property. Imagine what we can achieve in the next 10 years.

We are well and truly established at this stage. It has been really rewarding for me and I love helping other young people who have no idea about

297 Mt Wellington Highway: after re-laying driveway.

property to start on their own journey. All I do is repeat to them what I have learnt over the past year.

I am sharing my knowledge by running seminars through Richmastery and have also made my own DVD (see colour section at the end of this book). I am a workaholic but if I had known what I knew now at 21 years of age, I would have been very rich today; that's why I want to share my knowledge and help others who are starting out.

Goal setting and mentoring are very important in achieving your goals. Everyone in their lives should have goals based on their place in life. At my stage of life I am concerned about passive income. However, if you are young I believe you can focus on some passive income and some high capital growth properties, as you will be earning an income for some time. At middle age when you have a better income, that is the time to really focus on capital growth properties and then when you are older focus on passive income.

I always keep in mind when I am investing where the market is at, whether it is falling or rising, and take this into account with the offers I make. I was more flexible on the 15–20% below market value rule in a rising market, but in a flat market you have to negotiate hard and create your own capital gain by adding value. Do your own renovations and make sure things look fantastic for the valuer and remember, if the numbers don't work, don't buy!

TOP TEN TIPS

1. Become an expert in an area then you'll see the bargains when they come up. Know the rental returns you can expect so you can make a fast educated decision.

2. Renovations create instant capital gain. Look for the best house in the street, understand its value and potential and then negotiate and buy the worst house.

3. When purchasing use your personal name and or nominee as it creates the impression to the vendor that you are a home buyer rather than an investor. Always appear to be an eager buyer to the real estate agent. A positive buyer conditions the agent to keep pushing for the price you want.

4. You make money on properties when you buy them at a low wholesale price and then get them valued up to retail.

5. Understand simple skills of negotiation. Know how to make a silent close by playing on a person's ego. If you know how the agent or vendor is working on you then you are not going to be conditioned yourself.

6. Follow the 6 Ds: deceased, deadlines, divorced, d-bank, desperate, dummy and, now, developers.

7. Get pre-approval of finance because you can make a cash offer, an extremely good bargaining tool. Cash is king. It can be possible to get another 5% further down on the price even after you have made an offer.

8. Never be afraid to walk away from a deal. A way to avoid getting too emotional is to have two or three deals on the go at once.

9. Buy time with long settlements and try to get early access.

10. Take action and put in offers even if they are stupid ones; you never know why a vendor may accept them. Remember the Number One Rule: buy only on the numbers and never on emotion (use the Richmastery Analysis software to crunch the numbers).

Chapter 2

Positive crossroads

'It really is magic — dreams really do come true.'
— **Michael and Annette Harris,**
Bribie Island, Sunshine Coast, AUS

Michael and I have been together for 12 years, and we live on Bribie Island on Queensland's Sunshine Coast, an hour's drive north of Brisbane. When we met Michael had six grown up children from a previous marriage and I had three. We also had our own businesses. I had a coffee shop that I had owned for three and a half years and Michael had a mattress manufacturing company. He had worked in that company for 11 years and taken it over from the owner three years earlier.

I had a home of my own and had always wanted to live on a 25 acre property and when I met Michael he lived on a 30 acre property. We both had always been interested in real estate and Michael had worked in that field for a short while.

Before meeting the boys from Richmastery Australia we had purchased three investment properties in Wyong, New South Wales, near where we lived. One was a duplex that we intended to keep for a rental return, one was a house we intended to renovate and sell and the other was a new home that we had built, as a new spec home for resale.

A hectic schedule

In late 1993 I sold the coffee shop and for the next five years worked for two large bedding retailers as well as having two businesses of my own. I then joined a large corporate that made polyurethane foam, Joyce Foam Products,

39

working in marketing. For three years I commuted to Liverpool in Western Sydney each day. I travelled two and a half hours each way per day, as we were living in Wyong.

Michael sold his mattress company in 1997, and went on the road as a freelance furniture agent, setting up a business called Harris Furniture Agencies. He was covering most of New South Wales and did 80,000 km a year on average in travel for his job.

After speaking to our accountant, just before we built the spec house we started a company called Harris Property Developments, as his advice was that to buy and sell within the company would be to our advantage financially.

In 2000, because of the excessive travelling I was doing to get to work we bought a house at Narellan in Western Sydney, only 20 minutes from my work. My brother needed rental accommodation in that area also, so we rented the house to him at a nominal rent and I stayed there a few nights a week. We bought the house for $170k. It was a three bedroom brick and tile, the worst house in the best street. The vendors were divorcees and had run out of money to finish it off. It was a new house but had no driveway or gardens. We added a carport, gardens, back patio and then sold it 13 months later for $238k.

Michael was diagnosed with throat cancer in March 2001. This was such a shock to us both we decided we had to have a change of lifestyle. We had led such hectic lives for many years and it was now telling on our health.

Change of focus

I gave my job away and Michael retired from being a furniture rep. Our property investment was only part time so we needed another income stream. We decided to open a retail bedding shop in Maitland, New South Wales, 80 km north of Wyong and 50 minutes' drive from where we lived. We invested $150k for stock and $50k for fittings in cash and began the process of opening the store.

Michael found out he needed surgery and when he was having this I rented a house as close as possible to the new business and opened the shop myself in May 2001. We called it the Maitland Mattress Market. While we experienced some very tough months on a personal level during this period, the business grew rapidly, which was very rewarding.

Michael had an aggressive cancer and had to have radiation treatment for six weeks. It took him a long time to recover; he lost a lot of weight and strength. It made us look at life totally differently, now we don't let the stupidities of life get in our way anymore.

In the course of setting up the bedding business, we joined our local Business Enterprise Centre (BEC) in mid 2001. In May we received an email from them advising us that there was an evening real estate seminar being held in Cessnock. I persuaded Michael to go along.

So in March 2003 we attended the Richmastery Profit from Property seminar, and what a terrific evening that turned out to be! We learnt that negative gearing was not the way to go, which was what we had been doing with all our properties to that point. We were also inspired to invest in real estate in a more profitable way and maybe even make our living from doing so.

From what started out an inexpensive evening, we were so enthused we purchased a Club Richmastery membership, a number of books and a ticket to the three day Richmastery Property Academy being held in Sydney in August 2003. After coming away from the meeting having paid $3000 for the academy tickets, while I knew it was something I really wanted to do, Michael was skeptical and we both wondered if we had done the right thing. Later, it proved to be one of the best things we have ever done together.

Even then, both Michael and I were so motivated by the presentation and content of the Richmastery Profit from Property seminar that the next day we started looking for positive cash flow properties on the internet.

We both went to the bank and created an interest only line of credit against Michael's 30 acres farm in the Yarramalong Valley, on the Central Coast of New South Wales, which he'd bought for $90k; it was now worth $600k.

While watching the *Today* show one morning we saw a broadcast from Rockhampton in celebration of Beef Week; we were rather impressed by the look of the city. We checked it out on the internet and we saw we could buy properties as cheaply as $50k each. We later found these to be flood prone, but nonetheless we found some very good properties between $80k and $100k.

Seven properties in six weeks

The result was over the next six weeks we purchased seven properties in Rockhampton, something we would not have done before the three hours we had spent at the Richmastery Profit from Property seminar evening in Cessnock. There was no way in the world we would have bought a property on the internet before.

Michael got on well with the real estate agent in Rockhampton, Linda, and purchased the first of many properties from her. It was a five bedroom house in Western Street with a swimming pool. It was timber, two storied and well presented. The vendors were asking $155k; we paid $145k. We thought it seemed cheap. We rented it for $200 per week, which meant it was not such a good deal after all.

Michael decided to go up to Rockhampton to take a look. While he was there he checked out an old duplex for $83k returning $180 per week, but we missed out on this one. Later, Michael called home and was like a kid in a sweet shop. He had bought a brick duplex in Halligan Street. It was a two by two-bedroom, returning $250 per week. We purchased it for $152k; they were asking $160k but as we were cash buyers due to the line of credit we'd arranged we were able to negotiate a discount.

We also bought another duplex that we'd seen on the internet in Anne Street, two two-bedroom units. We got this one for $111k and rented these out for a total of $220 per week. In the end we also got the first duplex Michael had missed out on as the first sale fell over. The buyers hadn't been able to arrange finance and the same vendor had been buying a house next door as well. So we picked up both these deals.

They were in Fitzroy Street; we got the duplex for $83k. It was a two by two-bedroom that rented for $180 per week (which is more than 10% return). The next door property was a three bedroom house that we purchased for $75k that rents for $135 per week.

New line of credit

We then created a new line of credit against two of our original properties in Wyong. The duplex was now worth $450k (bought for $293k in 1999). And the first investment home was now valued at around $300k (bought for $153k).

We continued looking on the internet in the evenings now that we had more money to spend.

The next purchase in Rockhampton was a three bedroom Queenslander in Norton Street, with double garage. The vendors were asking $110k and we got it for $104k and rented it for $170 per week, so it takes care of itself.

We bought all the Rockhampton properties through LJ Hooker and they managed them for us initially. However, they don't now as they didn't find tenants for them quickly enough when they became vacant. So we called other letting agents in Rockhampton and gave them the opportunity to find tenants themselves. Now the properties are under four different property managers and we haven't had much down time at all.

The Anne Street unit hasn't had a good rental record, but we've since renovated it and spent $3000 on new floor coverings and a paint job. I organised this to be done by tradespeople, aided by the property mangers, and it has now been rented on a regular basis.

Annette's brother's marriage had failed and we'd promised him one of our houses in Rockhampton, but found the agent had let our spare house. So in July 2003 we bought a two bedroom house for $80k in Miles Street for him to live in. We had a double garage built for his purposes, which also added to the value of the property; it's now valued at $120k.

We did all this from what we learnt at the Richmastery Profit from Property seminar at Cessnock – that was the motivating force behind it.

I then attended the Richmastery Property Academy in Sydney in August 2003. It was the best experience I have ever had. From the very start it was full on, interesting, challenging and enlightening. The speakers were all so enthused about real estate and how to buy right, but they were also enthused about life. The team of people helping were not only helpful but were an inspiration as they were out there, into doing deals and living life to the full. I became very excited as to what Michael and I could achieve with the knowledge I had gained in those three days.

The rules changed a few times during the three days and I learned the hard way that life is a challenge and you have to go with it or pay the price and at the academy that meant paying the fine, so I was a few dollars out of pocket, but my mind was filled with knowledge and wisdom.

On the last day I had a visit with Lisa, our mortgage broker, and after she offered some information regarding our financial status, I was blown away: she said with our assets we could borrow up to $2 million. I couldn't wait to get out of the course to call Michael.

WOW. I rang Michael very excited and said to him, 'You know that Jaguar car you were dreaming about, well go and order it.' We laughed but we can now see that with Richmastery as our mentors we can and have achieved so much.

In May 2003 we put Michael's farm on the market. It went to auction but didn't sell. When the agent's contract ran out we went to another agent, who found us a buyer at $625k (we owed about $100k on it) but we wanted a delayed settlement so we sold it in November 2003 and it settled in January 2004.

A lifestyle change

Michael had always wanted to move to Queensland, and I hadn't been keen as all the family are in New South Wales. But we had arranged to take a week off work for a much needed holiday at Burleigh Heads in Queensland and Michael convinced me to take an extra week off to go to Brisbane and show me around.

A friend and his wife invited us to stay for a night at their place on Bribie Island, an hour's drive north of Brisbane. We stayed three nights and totally fell in love with Bribie and the surrounding area. We also fell in love with a house. We could not look inside as the vendors were away on holiday overseas, but the position and what we could see through the windows convinced us to buy. We had no cheque book but decided to buy it so we put $100 down and signed a contract.

We offered $625k, which was their asking price; it was a hot market and the owners were overseas. We also asked for a delayed settlement as the farm was not settling until January 2004. They accepted and the agent faxed them

Our Bribie Island home. We've borrowed heaps against its improved value.

the deal. The next day the agent said, 'Congratulations, you've bought a house,' and Pacific Drive, Bribie Island, Queensland was to be our new home. When we bought it, we had to go home and sell our retail bedding business in Maitland, so we rented out the house in Bribie Island to the vendors for six months as they were building on Bribie Island, a bonus for both of us.

We sold the bedding business in September 2003, which enabled us to make our lifestyle change.

We bought another house on Bribie Island, not long after we had bought our own. We had some real estate brochures sent to us and found a house we liked the look of. It was owned by an older couple who desperately wanted to get into a retirement village and were going to miss out and would have needed a bridging loan. Their asking price was $260k, we offered $230k cash with a quick settlement as we had our line of credit again in place and they took it. It's just around the corner from us, and is a three bedroom brick and tile house; this was to be our first reno job done in our retirement from normal 9 to 5 employment.

Michael's 89-year-old father had indicated he would like to move to Bribie with us, after going to Bribie for a holiday and loving the place as well. So Michael's father bought the house off us for the same price as we paid for it.

In September 2003 we finally moved to our canal front home on Bribie Island. We have never regretted the move and though we live so far from family we still see each other quite often and more quality time is spent together. We have spent seven months renovating our Island home, which

Two bedroom house in Rockhampton bought for Annette's brother for $80k in 2003. We added a double garage; it's now valued at $120k.

has been a very stressful time, living with renovations going on around you for so long. But we are now on the home stretch and it is looking beautiful. The most important thing is we bought our home for $625k, have spent $100k on the renovation and in two years it is now worth $1.1 million – more value to borrow against, Yahoo.

Ready to go again

We joined the Richmastery Personal Property Mentoring Programme soon after moving to Queensland and completing the Richmastery Property Academy. We found this most beneficial in terms of being able to talk to our mentors face to face and also the expert guest speakers that are invited to most of the meetings. Plus we got a lot from the interaction of other like minded people that are members of our group.

We went to our local bank, Suncorp, to see the loans manager and she said we could borrow $2 million on the value of the properties we owned, but a week later she said, 'I'm sorry, we can't loan you anything because you don't have any income stream.' We needed a 9 to 5 job to borrow any money. Then we called Lisa (our mortgage broker) again. She's not interested in what you earn, it's what security you've got, so we were away again.

After settling in to our new home we purchased a further canal front property on Bribie Island in Voyager Drive for $615k. This settled in January 2004 and we aimed to renovate and sell it quickly. The tenant still had until May left on his fixed term lease, so we told him he could move out whenever he found somewhere else as he was only paying $290 per week and we wanted to renovate.

He moved out in April and we spent a month renovating it. We put in new carpet, painted the bathroom, bought a new dishwasher. We got a bobcat in and cleared the front yard, put in new turf, gardens and flowers, painted the front wooden fence the same cream as the house. We moved the pontoon from our home to the Voyager Drive property. We personally sold our smaller pontoon to our business Harris Property Developments and had it moved and power and water put on to it. We then sold the house for $720k five months later, making a gross profit of $105k. With the proceeds we were able to buy a new and bigger pontoon for our house.

Being members of Club Richmastery we are sent emails every day giving us real estate deals that they have procured on their members' behalf at very good prices. In March of 2004 we purchased, through the Richmastery website, a block of eight units in Emerald (Central Queensland) for $595k and a finder's fee of $3995. This was a cash flow positive deal. We sent for their due diligence kit, went through it and liked what we saw. We talked to our mortgage broker and got finance sorted out. The rent at the time was $1100 per week. We have since renovated two of the flats, painted, redone bathrooms, put down new vinyl flooring, recarpeted and spent about $15k in total. We have now increased the rents to $1300 per week.

A commercial leap

I had never been to see all of our properties in Rockhampton and Emerald, so we made the six hour drive to Rocky and stayed with my brother in our rented house there. We checked on our properties, and were very impressed with Rockhampton, a lovely large country city. We then made the three hour drive to Emerald, a mining town west of Rockhampton.

While we were in Emerald the real estate agent showed us around the town and pointed out two blocks of units that are expected to come on the market shortly; they were owned by the mine department.

The agent then asked us if we'd ever be interested in commercial property. We said we may be, depending on what it was. He showed us a hardware and timber complex situated on two acres of land, which was on the market for $1.5 million, showing an 11% return. It was a fantastic package with a retail store as well as three large storage sheds where they made frames for houses. As we were driving home we talked about what a great deal that would be but we'd never be able to afford it. However, during the three hour drive back to Rockhampton the deal grew on us.

Michael made the first call to Lisa (our mortgage broker) on the way home and she put us on to another broker who specialises in commercial deals, the Balmain NB. The next day we drove back to Emerald and exchanged contracts on the deal subject to valuations, council compliance and finance. The property is part of a big hardware group called Home Hardware. The rent return is $160k per annum and repayments are $109k per annum. Rates are $4000 per annum and insurance is about $1000.

Because of Richmastery, and all we had learnt from them, we spent $2.1 million in Emerald.

A rewarding path

We recently strata titled the duplex in Wyong, which was valued at $600k. It cost us $7000 to do this but has added between $50k and 100k to the value. Our plan is to sell it and we should now get between $650k and $700k.

Our net worth is now $5 million; our total loans are $2.7 million, meaning we have created equity of $2.3 million in just a couple of years. Our after tax cash flow is close to $2000 per week.

So, as you can see, in the short space of time since we first attended the Richmastery Profit from Property seminar we have been very proactive in increasing our real estate portfolio. There are many crossroads in life that may lead one in a totally different direction from the normal path; some of these crossroads may lead one to a much fuller, rewarding and happier life. The chance meeting with Richmastery at Cessnock for us is one of those positive crossroads. Richmastery lives up to its name and is also a hugely inspirational organisation.

It's amazing to think it was only 18 months ago that the idea of collecting the old age pension was not something we wanted to get involved in, and needless to say we are now fully self funded retirees. We were always wondering what we were going to do to sustain our lifestyle. Now we have dolphins swim past our front door and we have a boat at the bottom of the garden. We took my granddaughter out on the boat the other day and baked scones on the way – this kind of lifestyle was what we always wanted but it always seemed out of reach. It really is magic – dreams really do come true.

TOP TEN TIPS

1. Create the pyramid; build your wealth by balancing positive cash flow for income with more expensive capital growth properties.
2. Don't procrastinate — there's no point learning if you're not going to take action.
3. Take calculated risks and do your due diligence; but you must take your first step.
4. Do the numbers.
5. Always use interest only mortgages for investment properties so your money goes as far as it can.
6. Borrow against your own home for investment because homes are liabilities.
7. Educate yourselves. Without going to the Richmastery Profit from Property seminar and the Richmastery Property Academy we wouldn't be where we are today.
8. Read widely — we subscribe to *Australian Property Investor* magazine.
9. Learn from other people — the Richmastery Personal Property Mentoring Programme was fantastic as our mentoring group fed off each other. It was great to be around positive people — remember negativity breeds negativity.
10. Window shop on the internet for property; it's an amazing resource.

Chapter 3

Securing a future

'Our personal growth has been huge and our financial security is compounding every day.'
— **Roger and Sandy Bruys,**
Whakatane, NZ

I live with my husband Roger and our two children in Whakatane, a coastal town in the Bay of Plenty with a population of 17,000, four hours' drive from Auckland. Whakatane is my husband's hometown; I am originally from Adelaide, Australia.

Roger and I met at Police College in Adelaide in 1986. We got married in April 1988 and returned to New Zealand to live in Auckland in November 1989. Roger joined the New Zealand Police Force. I got a job with the Accident Compensation Corporation, a government agency, as a client officer, and I still work for ACC part time. In September 1998 Roger got transferred to Whakatane and we moved back to his hometown where his family live.

We decided to buy a house. We looked at several, and we liked two houses and played one vendor off against the other. In late 1998, the market was peaking. In the end we purchased a four bedroom bungalow on a 1200 square metre section on Sullivan's Lake, 3 km from the centre of town. The vendors were asking $172k and we got it for $160k.

Looking for long term passive income

Since 2000 we had been toying with the idea of property investing but did not know how to start. Roger's colleague was always talking about how to make money but he always seemed to have work-intensive ideas. We wanted to provide a better future for ourselves and our children.

For the last 10 to 15 years both Roger and I have watched older friends and family, who thought they were prepared for retirement, discover that the savings or retirement plan they had was insufficient. We did not want this to become our reality.

Our current reality is also complicated by having a disabled child who will be dependent on us in some way for life. It scares the hell out of us to think our daughter, who is autistic, will have no means of generating income once we are gone and so for her (as well as for our son) we want long term passive income that can be passed onto both of them.

In April 2003 Roger attended a local property investment seminar: Richmastery Profit from Property. He was sold. That night when he came home we talked for hours about what we wanted in life and decided that we had found the tool to achieve wealth. Roger felt that a light had gone on for him that night. The seminar gave him the building blocks of how to go out and do the deals and get positive cash flow passive income properties.

We established that we had little equity or money in cash. All our money was tied up in our family home and the market was just starting to peak. To free up our money we decided to sell our house. Although many say never sell, we decided we would to give us some cash to move forward.

We had bought our home for $160k with 10% deposit and, after five years and huge hours of our hard work and money that we put into doing it up, the valuation only came in at $185k. But as our home had a unique lakeside location we felt its valuation was low compared to what people were willing to pay for it and we were proved right.

The house sold prior to auction for $40k more than the registered valuation. The lady who bought it paid $225k and our reserve at auction was going to be $200k ($15k more than the registered valuation). We arranged a six month delayed settlement so the purchaser could sell her house. However, because we had the unconditional sale and purchase contract for the house at $225k we were able to raise $75k equity against our home (our mortgage was about $139k).

We used this newly created equity to buy two properties, one for us to renovate and then rent out, and a two on one property. We set up an LAQC. This was to be the start of a very exciting phase for us.

Changing structures

The two on one property was on Bridge Street, Whakatane, just around the corner from our home. It was a two bedroom weatherboard house with a single bedroom flat at the rear. We purchased it for $155k in May 2003; it had been listed at $169k. We rented both places out for a total of $290 per week.

We immediately had it revalued at $170k so were able to recycle our deposit. We never had to do any work to this house. But we did end up selling it in July 2004 for $215k to clear some personal debt, credit cards and HPs, and to re-adjust our debt to equity ratio.

The power of this recycled equity was amazing – in just one deal we had made the equity to buy our next house. Quite different from our first home which we had slogged our guts out on it for five years, spent every spare cent on it and only sold for $225k. We had paid $160k and probably easily spent $40k on it plus our time and effort, all for a meagre $25k gain in five years.

The do-up we bought was in Noel Mills Place, Whakatane. The vendor was on transfer for his job and the property was listed at $270k in a market that was about to boom. We offered $240k. The negotiations came to a stalemate and the vendors wouldn't budge and we wouldn't budge, then he actually had to leave for the job and the emotional pull came on because his wife and family were left behind and they buckled. We managed to purchase it after a lot of negotiation for $240k, in September 2003. This house valued up immediately to $260k and we moved into it.

We rented the house in Noel Mills Place to ourselves because we had been told by our accountant that it was okay to do this, as long as you paid market rent. However, after Roger attended the Richmastery Property Academy in May 2004 and had a meeting following this with structures and asset planning expert Mathew Gilligan from Gilligan Rowe and Associates in Auckland, a presenter at the academy, we discovered that this could be seen as borderline tax avoidance.

We've now restructured things: we set up a trust and the house, which is now our family home, will be shifted into the trust. To do this we have to discharge the mortgage for the house out of the LAQC and then shift it into the family trust and then they will run a gifting programme. The beauty of this is that they can shift the majority of debt on the family home onto our property portfolio and increase our tax rebates across the portfolio.

> Although it cost us around $8000 (tax deductible) to restructure, because we are planning on owning millions of dollars worth of property that is nothing. It has been a costly mistake not having our structure right from the beginning. However, you have to change your mindset and be prepared to spend the money to do things properly.

Setting investment rules

In September 2003 I attended the same Richmastery Profit from Property seminar that Roger had attended in April. That night we bought the Richmastery Property Investor software package.

> The fact we had both attended the Richmastery seminar helped us to set our investing rules. It also gave us confidence to go in low with offers and to walk away if the property did not meet our criteria. It must have worked because in the nine months since Roger attended the initial seminar we had achieved seven income streams.
>
> Our rules were to buy a minimum of two for ones, meaning that for every $100k invested we must receive $200 per week in rent, with at least a 10% return on purchase (yield) and to buy on figures not emotions. When purchasing a property we never pay more than $1000 deposit on anything.

Early on we had decided that while we were both still employed and very busy – and with a special needs child – we would invest within 30 minutes' drive of our hometown. Then, once one of us has exited our employment, to undertake full time property investing we would look further afield.

Our third investment property was shown to us by Stu from the local branch of Harcourts, who has since become one of our favourite real estate agents. It was one of two houses going up for mortgagee auction in Edgecumbe, a small town 15 minutes from Whakatane. Both properties were to be auctioned on 15 December 2003.

Edgecumbe appealed to us because we knew that Whakatane was booming, as was the rest of the country, but Edgecumbe had not yet been bitten by the boom bug. This was December 2003. Our theory was that with house prices rising rents would also rise, forcing renters to outlying towns – the pebble in the pond effect. Our money was on Edgecumbe to boom early in the new year. The timing of the auction was perfect.

The first one was expected to go for the mid to high $40ks but it went for $66k so we pulled out real quick. On the second one the bidding started at $30k. We wouldn't go higher and the house was passed in, failing to meet the bank's reserve of $45k. We negotiated a purchase price of $33k. With an 80% mortgage our personal input was $6700 – it was a steal! The government valuation was $61k.

The house was situated in Kowhai Street in Edgecumbe. It was very rundown and very bright; every room had different colours in it and the purple patterned carpet was not good for anyone with a hangover. The tenant was cooking on a gas burner as the stove did not work and was washing her clothes outside using the garden hose to fill the machine as there were no taps inside. But it was structurally sound.

'Stealing houses from banks'

The sitting tenant was paying $130 per week rent. One week after settlement the tenant did a midnight run. Some people would have seen this as a setback but we used it as a positive opportunity to start renovations on the property. As the tenant had left unexpectedly we knew that at least three weeks' rent would be due to us through the tenant's bond. This enabled us to renovate the property while still effectively collecting rent.

The pre-renovation valuation two days later was $45k, an instant gain of accessible equity of $9200. We redrew this equity to pay for renovations, bearing in mind we still had only put in $6700 of our money. Effectively the bank and the tenant were paying for the renovation.

The James Street unit. After $4800 of renovations it was valued at $108k, a gain of $23k after expenses.

Due to Roger having recently had back surgery, we decided that all the work would be done by professionals. The total cost of the renovation and incidentals were $12,586.08. This included an exterior and interior repaint, new carpet and vinyl, a new stove, landscaping, a new washing line and other repairs.

By doing the renovations we achieved a rental increase from $130 to $160 per week. Our mortgage was now at $36k. The latest valuation at April 2004 was $80k, an increase in value of $44k and the market has gone up since then (so the value is now closer to $100k). We are really proud of this deal. Not bad for beginners!

The local valuer who valued it rang and said, 'We hear you've been stealing houses from banks.' That was a nice feeling. You know you've got a bargain if the valuer says that.

We started looking for more properties but decent deals were hard to find; we made a few offers but as the market was booming, some agents wouldn't even present our low offers.

Three houses in one day

Finally we made progress. We looked at a two bedroom unit in James Street, Whakatane. It is situated about 1.5 km from the centre of town, right by schools and a supermarket. The vendor was asking $86k. The agent said the vendor's son was living in it and it needed a bit of work and that it had been on the market a year before at $95k. We knew the unit next door had sold for $105k. We went and had a look and it did need a lot of work. The carpet was good, but there was a broken window in the lounge and the agent suggested we knock $5000 off so we said round it down to $80k. The vendor agreed. It was to settle on 9 June 2004.

We had an early access clause in our contract to do it up but their solicitor argued that paint and paper doesn't constitute repairs, so our solicitor went head to head with him and we won. So we got early access and all the work was done before we settled.

We then discovered during the due diligence period that the flat had less land than the other flats in the block, so the agent said knock them down to $79k. The vendor agreed. The bank advanced us $79,500.

The renovations included an interior and exterior paint, replacing all the windows plus a new stove, a total cost $4800. It valued up to $108k, a gain of $23k after expenses. We rented it for $165 per week.

> While Roger was signing this agreement on the boot of the agent's car she said that she had just listed another one. So he checked that out and made an offer on that too. Then, she said she had another one and we bought that too. It just snowballed. Three in one day!

The second house we bought that day was a four bedroom house at Watarawi Place in Awatapu, a suburb of Whakatane, with a separate bedsit, a fully self contained unit. The vendor was asking $169k. After much haggling we got it for $155k. We rent it for $360 per week, $240 per week for the house and $120 per week for the unit, all providing positive cash flow.

The third house was in Kawerau, a town some 30 km from Whakatane. I recognised the address as a home that a colleague of Roger's had owned 10 years earlier, so we'd been into the house before and knew it was a nice place. It was 260 square metres and had five bedrooms and three bathrooms; it was listed at $79k and had only come on the market that day. Roger made an offer of $67k and I went out to take a look at it. The real estate agent was astonished that we had made an offer on a house without seeing it. When we went out there, I sat in the car and the agent was mortified that I didn't look inside. But as we were buying on the figures I did not need to see the inside. We put an offer of $68k on paper. They came back at $73k and we went to $70,500. It settled at $71k. We then got it valued at $90k. The rent then was $160 per week but this has now increased to $175 per week – another positive cash flow property. We settled on 25 June and have not needed to do any work to it.

Decreasing debt to equity ratio

Roger attended the Richmastery Property Academy just after we purchased this one and we still had settlement on the other two properties pending. He went with his brother-in-law Steve Hall, who had become very interested in what we were doing. The academy really reaffirmed that we were doing the right thing for us. The most important aspect of the academy was about structures, and how we hadn't set things up properly first.

> At the Richmastery Property Academy, Roger bought the Cash Flow game. We really enjoy playing it. It showed us about debt reduction and how fast you can eliminate personal debt so that one of us will be able to leave work. We felt we needed to decrease our debt to equity ratio.

So we decided to sell the Bridge Street house. We told the agent we had decided this from playing a board game and she couldn't believe it! We sold it on 21 July and paid off all our personal debt.

A local real estate agent, Shirley from LJ Hooker, who has sold us a lot of the properties, lives in Taneatua. There's no or little employment there now, although there is rumoured to be a cannery going in there, for a large food company. The place is rough and well known for local gangs.

We heard that a local councillor was going to sell a portfolio of houses for an average price of $45k and we decided that we were going to buy all of them but he pulled out. However, we did end up buying one that he did want to sell. This was a two bedroom weatherboard home, on a cross leased site, a half share of 1000 square metres. We purchased it for $43k and it is renting for $140 per week. Then Stu (our favourite agent from Harcourts) said one of their agents owned the other half of the cross lease and wanted to get rid of it, so she gifted it to us for one dollar! We bought the tenant some

The Taneatua home, purchased for $43k and renting at $140 per week.

new curtains, and are now looking for a relocatable house to move onto the $1 section.

Next we bought two houses in Hotene Street in Awatapu, Whakatane. Awatapu was badly flooded in July 2004, making national news, but these two houses were not affected. The first one, a two bedroom house on a cross leased site, we bought in early September 2004 for $80k, and it settled a month later. The vendor was asking $94k. It is now valued at $87k and is rented for $160 per week. The tenants have been there for eight years. Then on 23 September we offered $67,500 for a second house in Awatapu. The vendors were asking $85k; we got it for $73k. This house had the tenants from hell who were hoarders and we asked for vacant possession. It settled on 26 November 2004 and is now rented for $170.

> We recently tried to negotiate a deal on 10 fully renovated three bedroom houses in Tokoroa, owned by a property development group in Napier. They were asking $984k with a registered valuation of $898k. We offered them $795k then $805k. The agent said we could buy them at $840k so we then made an offer for $820k. However, the vendors decided that $820k was too low and tried to negotiate higher. We walked away.

We use the Professionals as property managers. From our experience they are really good; we feel they can see that we are serious investors with respect for our customer – the tenant – so they look after us. We have never deferred maintenance and when anything is identified we will take action immediately.

We now have no personal debt other than our home mortgage. Our home is now worth between $380k and $460k.

Doing the basics right

We couldn't have achieved what we have achieved without doing the Richmastery educational seminars. It comes down to the basics: KISS – keep it simple stupid, and the personal development they teach.

We've read many books; some that stand out are: *Real Money Real Estate* by Phil Jones; *You Need a Rocket* by Martin Ayles; *Building Wealth Through Investment Property* by Jan Somers and Dolf De Roos; *Feel the Fear and Do It Anyway* by Susan Jeffers; *First Things First* by Stephen Covey; and most of Robert Kiyosaki's books. *Real Estate Investors' Secrets* by Graeme Fowler is a favourite. We also subscribe to *Kiwi Property Investor* (KPI) magazine (available through www.richmastery.com).

We entered our Edgecumbe property into KPI's Action Challenge run by Martin Ayles and KPI to see how we compared. We won the competition and in February 2005 we were flown to Adelaide, Australia to spend the day with Martin Ayles and have one day of personal mentoring. The day was wonderful and we learned a lot.

Our personal growth has been huge and our future financial security is being established and compounding each and every day. When we bought that first investment property, if someone moved out of the flat we were worried. Now it's a breeze, due to the power of numbers and having eight

The Taneatua house's neighbouring section — which we got for just $1! We'll put a relocatable home on it.

This Hotene Street house was in Awatapu, an area of Whakatane flooded in 2004 — but this one wasn't affected. We bought it for $80k and it rents for $160 per week.

income streams. If one or two are vacant for short periods of time, the total positive cash flow, although slightly reduced, is still positive.

We have realised there's another way; you don't have to work for someone else until you are 65. The only downside is that we are slowly becoming unemployable! Or is that an upside? Our job satisfaction has dropped. Roger's job in the police is very negative every day. Both of us could not see a way out of being an employee, and had resigned ourselves to the fact that we were fortunate enough to have good jobs. Now our motivation to be good employees and strive to please the boss has decreased.

The positive gains have been enormous and have had a huge impact in relation to who we are and how we treat others. We deal with our kids differently on a day to day basis, do things for people because they are nice things to do, not with any agenda or tally sheet, and we give to charity.

At first we bombarded our friends with talk about it but we have learned to remember it's not everyone's cup of tea so we have consciously tried to stop talking about it. Now we will only talk about our properties if asked. We always keep in mind what Phil Jones said at the academy: 'What other people think of us is none of our business.'

We have also started using the surplus cash flow that we are generating: we have a cleaner, we go out more often and have more time without the kids and more quality time with them. It has enriched our lives, and it has not been difficult.

In just 14 months we have created a total portfolio value (including our own home) of $1.148 million, with total mortgages of (including our own home) of $745k, making our total equity $403k. Our total after tax cash flow is $542 per week ($28,184 per year).

TOP TEN TIPS

1. Read anything about real estate, money and personal growth.
2. Socialise with like-minded people.
3. Treat tenants well.
4. Property managers — have a good one.
5. Decrease personal debt.
6. Write your goals or outcomes down — be specific and tick them off.
7. Don't waste time doing work someone else can do.
8. Stick to your rules.
9. Celebrate your successes.
10. Property investing is simple. Don't make it difficult!

Chapter 4

Develop for profit

I realised there was a whole world of possibilities out there ... things that my parents, school or university hadn't taught me.'
— **Dr Ruth Edwards**, Goulburn, AUS

I live in Goulburn, a rural town of 20,000 people in New South Wales. It is situated just under two hours' drive from Sydney and 50 minutes' drive from Canberra.

I am 34 and married with no children. My husband, Justin, is 39. I am a medical doctor and my husband is a surveyor. I am disillusioned with Western medicine and with people not taking responsibility for their own health and happiness. I have a doctor's surgery that I established four years ago. I plan to expand it into a Wellness Centre to offer ways of preventing illness.

I am now looking at internet marketing and property investment as a way of diversifying my income. I guess I've had an interest in investing for a long time. When I was first working I remember being sold income protection insurance and super schemes, and realised when the agents showed me the figures that superannuation wouldn't take care of me. I couldn't rely on it like my parents had. It was this that planted the investing seed in my brain. Before that I hadn't really thought about my financial future. I had just been focusing on medicine, studying and what area of medicine I wanted to work in.

Living by others' rules

It took me until I was 29 years old to buy my first home, which was in Goulburn. Unfortunately, I bought it in my own name, which is not recommended in my career as there is a higher risk of litigation. Before I bought it I had been renting a house for $170 per week. When my flatmate moved out, it prompted me to work out that if I bought a house for $120k, it would only cost me $165 per week to repay it on a 25 year P & I (principal and interest) loan. So I thought, 'Why am I paying off my landlord's mortgage when I could be paying off my own?'

Prior to that time, I hadn't bought my own house because I was under the illusion that you had to know where you were going to settle down first. I was living my life under all these other people's rules, which I had subconsciously absorbed over the years.

> Another thing I wondered was why I didn't buy my investment property before I bought my own house. It was due to another one of these rules that you absorb: the rule was that you buy your own home first, pay it off, and then you buy your investment property.

I purchased my first home for $112,500 in December 1999. It was an old three bedroom federation home, built in 1890, with a gorgeous garden, one bathroom, and carport on a quarter acre lot (960 square metres). I fell in love with the garden and the house with its cute little veranda. I put down a 10% deposit and borrowed 90% on a P & I loan, so I had to pay mortgage insurance. We renovated it extensively and spent about $200k on it. We added a dining room, lounge, study and laundry, upgraded the kitchen and rebuilt the bathroom. It's now worth $520k. My husband and I still live there.

The next thing I did was buy a cottage for my doctor's surgery, so I could stop seeing my patients in the front room of my home! I purchased this for $100k in January 2003. I spent $14k painting and adding heritage-style timber on the front veranda. It's now worth $220k and houses my medical business. It's also in my own name (unfortunately, I didn't know anything about structures for asset protection then).

Consolidating my knowledge

Many years ago, one of my GP mentors suggested reading Robert Kiyosaki's *Rich Dad, Poor Dad* to learn about investment and passive income. I had it on my bookshelf for years but could never be bothered to read it. Then one day when I was off sick I saw it lying there and told myself that I'd read the first chapter and if it didn't get me in by then it would go back on the shelf for another five years! I read the first chapter and couldn't put it down. That was in 2002 and after that I began reading many books about property investment. Other great books I have read are *Psycho-cybernetics* by Maxwell Maltz and *The e-myth* by Michael Gerber.

I had always had the idea that by the time I was 30 I would be retired, but I didn't read the first book until I was 32. I was nowhere near to being able to retire. I felt I'd been really slack and hadn't planned for my retirement at all. Now I think back: if only I had read it a couple of years earlier before the boom had started, and not at the tail end of it! Oh well ... better late than never!

I spent about a year reading all sorts of investment books to saturate my mind. However, although I knew my brain was full of knowledge, I was too scared to act. I didn't know where to start. My fears were holding me back.

I realised this when I attended the Richmastery Property Academy in Sydney in August 2003. This was a major breakthrough for me. I actually stumbled across the academy by accident (thank God!). I was having a meeting with my credit union manager about getting some banking services for my business and there was this new guy with the company. He was talking like an investor not a banker. He recommended I read *Real Money Real Estate* by Phil Jones. So I did. After that I looked up the Richmastery website mentioned in the book, and that's how I found out about Richmastery's courses. I knew I needed to do something to apply all my knowledge.

> What I got out of the Richmastery Property Academy was confidence and inspiration, and a consolidation of my knowledge. I felt like they had walked me through, in baby steps, the many ways of becoming wealthy through investing in property. It felt like a compete package from people that had already done it for themselves.

The Richmastery Property Academy is the best thing I have ever done in terms of personal growth seminars. I came back from the three days having had very little sleep. I remember driving back home from Sydney. I left the city at 7 pm, after a 4 am start, and I was so pumped I had this silly grin from ear to ear and my mind was racing. I had the music going at top volume and I was thinking about all these strategies for building wealth through real estate. I decided to also join the 12 month Richmastery Personal Property Mentoring Programme, which has also been a fantastic help to my investing.

When I arrived back in Goulburn, I drove up to this house. It was our house. Justin had the fire going. I opened the back door, and I had a sense that although I knew it was my house, I didn't belong there any more. In a way I felt like this wasn't my house. Justin asked how the Academy was, and I said, 'Oh, where do I start?!' I starting racing him through all the ideas I had for property based wealth building and couldn't shut my mind off. I guess he must have thought I was on drugs or something! It was really bizarre. I assured him that they hadn't spiked the water.

Learning to take action

I floated around on a natural high for about a month. I realised there was a whole world of possibilities out there that I'd known nothing about – things that my parents, school or university hadn't taught me. I realised that I was only limited by my imagination ... and my fear. I also realised that my fear was born out of ignorance.

> I have since applied this insight to many areas of my life. I was afraid to start investing because I was afraid I didn't know enough. I also realised that I didn't need to know everything before I made the first act because how do you know when you know enough? You know enough when you act, knowing you don't know enough. This is different to medicine, but then no one is going to die if you buy the wrong property. The more you know the more you realise there is to know. Then you start looking deeper, and you realise you can't know it all.

Most of my knowledge was from books, but the Richmastery Property Academy gave me the confidence that I wasn't missing anything too much, and that I had the knowledge to go out and start doing it.

I was so motivated that when I went on a planned ski trip the following week, every morning, lunchtime and evening I would go on the internet where I was staying and look at property. I must have faxed off about 20 offers during the ski week alone. I was getting up and waking up so excited. It was like Christmas morning, I was jumping out of bed and I'd open the folder from the academy. I went through the entire academy folder all again.

So it was finally time to act. I got our home revalued and the first valuation came in at $360k (in September 2003). This meant our equity was $215k, and I put this straight into a line of credit account to use for deposits on houses.

There had been incredible growth in Goulburn. A lot of people from Sydney were retiring there as it was cheaper to buy a nice home, so they were selling up in Sydney and moving.

Income wise we both were earning good money. I was on $60k per annum gross as I'd just started the practice and Justin was on around $55k a year. Justin was a bit nervous probably because I was so manic about investing. He's only read *Rich Dad, Poor Dad* and *Real Money Real Estate*. Most of what he has learnt is through osmosis from me, but he's been fully supportive and has let me run with it.

As for the 10 Week (2010) Challenge after the Academy, if there was anyone that was going to rise to a challenge, it was me. During the academy I came third in the property game in all three categories. I spent two hours every night going through the figures getting it all exactly right. I said to myself, 'Right, I'm going to win that challenge!' That's why I spent my ski trip sending offers. I knew I needed that extra incentive to have the courage to get started. However, my strategy at the time was wrong, as I focused on areas of high growth and was sending off offers 20% below valuation. Of course, they were all declined.

Sight unseen, and just as well

Less than a month later I bought my first property. This was through the Richmastery Property Deals website. I had become very frustrated that my offers weren't getting me anywhere and I had been looking at the Richmastery Property Deals site every day – in fact it was my home page. I saw one property with a 17% net yield. It was a block of five units in Ayr,

Queensland, which is a cane sugar town about an hour south of Townsville and only a short drive from the coast.

The units were 50 years old. I bought them for $122,500, sight unseen (which was lucky as they were so disgusting that if I'd seen them I wouldn't have bought them). Justin and I flew up after Christmas to have a look at the flats. I almost vomited when I walked into the first flat. There was a cockroach problem, and when I opened the door to the bathroom of the flat where the drug addict lived, I gagged. The floors were black and the shower stank. It was just disgusting – luckily the first unit we entered was the worst of them.

I bought them tenanted, but they had very dodgy tenants. One was an alcoholic who used to threaten the other tenants with a knife. There was a psychotic woman and a heroin addict. I was horrified at the time, but this was really just my fear talking again. Now, I'm glad I bought them.

I got them commercially cleaned and organised renovations, including exterior and interior repaint, new floor coverings, numerous repairs to holes in the wall and other damage; pest removal, and one new kitchen. I did cosmetic things like knocking out some concrete blocks and putting in decorative timber slats. It made them trendy. I changed the front fence by rendering it, installed brass letter boxes and brass numbers on the doors, added timber venetians and painted a feature wall (with suede effect) in each living room and bedroom. Colours are my forté, so this transformed the place. More recently we've installed air conditioners, as the sugar cane company that is tenanting them for nine months wanted these put in.

The renovations cost $69,500. This brought the total cost up to $192k. The mortgage against this property is $176k, so it still holds $16k of equity that we drew against another property. The new valuation is $240k. The rental income is $630 per week (each tenant has a nine month lease). This is a positive cash flow of $190 every week after all expenses and interest. Before the renovation the total rental income was only $385 per week.

I borrowed the maximum allowed (only 80%) from the Adelaide Bank, as it was not strata titled and there were more than four units. This is a higher percentage than most other banks would lend me.

Block of five units in Ayr, Queensland, before renovation: we're glad we bought them sight unseen — they were disgusting.

Buying to hold

The next purchase was in January 2004. This was a four bedroom federation brick house with one bathroom, in Goulburn. We bought it for $210k.

Renovations included making it open plan by knocking out two walls, replacing the louvres and asbestos sheeting with cedar French doors on three sides of the room. We also installed a new kitchen ($5000 from Laws Auctions in Sydney), pulled up the old carpet and polished the boards and put plush carpet in the bedroom, added timber Venetians, repainted the outside, had the roof repainted and restored, and added a wrought iron and rendered brick front fence. We had it all done by tradesmen. We don't do renovations: neither of us can even hammer a nail!

This house was then valued at $380k. It's rented for $220 per week. We could probably get $240 or $250 and even then it would be negatively geared. We did the renovations to value add and sell but unfortunately we did this at the top of the property boom and now houses are slow to sell, so we are going to hold onto it until market picks up.

Bigger development

We also have a 30-lot land subdivision in Goulburn in progress, a joint venture with one other party. We (our trust) own 12 lots, our business partner owns 12 lots, and adjoining landowners own the remaining six lots. Justin, my husband, found out about the land through his work as a surveyor. We bought one lot first and then there was a second lot that came on the market that was adjoining it, so we bought that too.

We purchased the two blocks for $553k with our equity partner. We knew he was interested in investing, he had the cash and we had the deal. We borrowed our half against the land and he went guarantor and put his half in, in cash. So for us it's a no money down deal.

Once the subdivision is completed each 2000 square metre block will sell for between $200k and $250k. They will be marketed as lifestyle blocks as the land is situated in a lovely prestigious area of Goulburn backing onto a native reserve, near a river. All the blocks are north facing with views over to the mountains.

> We put in the Development Application (DA), which in total cost us $70k to get done – in the end we had to go to court! This was approved six months later and as a result the new official valuation on the block is $2 million (DA approval adds value, just like renovating does).

The next step is to begin construction to create each of the new blocks. This involves constructing roads, installing power, stormwater and sewerage, and paying council contribution fees. We estimate that this will cost us $800k.

We will get a construction loan for this secured against the new land valuation and we will 'capitalise the interest' (which means we don't make any repayments, even interest, until the lots settle). To get this type of loan the bank requires some 'pre-sales'. This means we need to sell some lots off the plan. In our case we must pre-sell four or five lots out of the 24 that will be created.

Total costs therefore are $553,000 (land) + $70,000 (DA) + $800,000 (construction) + $30,000 (interest for six months) = $1,453,000. Predicted

The Ayr units scrubbed up well and provide $630 per week rent, up from $385.

Ayr unit front fence: we spent $69,500 on renovations.

valuation once complete is $6 million. We have based this on them selling for $250k each. Even if they only sold for $225,000 the total value would be $5,400,000. Thus our net profit (before tax) will be $4,547,000, of which our share (50%) will be $2,273,500 before tax. We will pay 30% tax on this as we have a corporate beneficiary in our trust.

The construction is on hold as we are trying to negotiate how much the adjoining landowners will pay to get us to do the development and as they are not sure about it they are dragging the negotiation out. This has been going on for two months. After this experience my advice is: don't ever do joint ventures with adjoining landowners.

Once they agree we will pre-sell five lots off the plan in order to obtain the construction loan. We are going to market them ourselves initially, and if this doesn't work we will give a local agent an exclusive opportunity to sell them at a discount. We have the contractors all lined up and ready to go for construction.

During this process the support and advice from my personal property mentor, from Richmastery Australia, has been invaluable.

Our plans after this development are to do more. We firmly believe that, for us, despite difficulties with cash flow during development, this is the best way to add value to property and Richmastery has given us the tools and the know how to be able to do this.

Some of the books that I've read and would recommend include: *Rich Dad, Poor Dad* and *Retire Young, Retire Rich* by Robert Kiyosaki; *More Wealth through Residential Property* and *Building Wealth Story by Story*, Jan Somers;

Real Estate Riches, Dolf de Roos; *Borrowing to Invest* by Noel Whittacker and Paul Resnik; *Seven Steps to Wealth,* John L. Fitzgerald; *Instant Cashflow,* Brad Sugars; and *Real Money Real Estate,* by Phil Jones.

TOP TEN TIPS

1. Be clear about the purpose/type of deal before you make an offer (i.e. 'buy and hold' or 'flip').
2. Buy based on the numbers, not on emotion.
3. Always check the occupancy rates for the town or suburb from a competing agent.
4. Be clear about how to add value for each property: renovate, subdivide, and always buy at a discount.
5. Have an exit strategy, in case something goes belly-up (e.g. interest rates). Try to fix interest rates for as long as you can.
6. Have existing assets/property valued, and arrange a line of credit against the equity in these. Use the credit for instant ability to write out cheques for deposits (you don't want to miss out on those gems). Make sure there is a five day cooling off period in the contract, and use it to do your due diligence.
7. Do a property résumé for each property before you have it valued; this adds enormous value.
8. When renovating, work out your required profit figure, set a budget, make a plan, and stick to it. Prioritise if funds begin to run low.
9. Don't try and do it all. Remember that time is your scarcest resource, so learn to leverage it. Get a great property manager, and always consider tradesmen rather than DIY.
10. Don't do joint ventures with adjoining landowners.

Chapter 5

Freedom fast

'Three and a half years after buying my first rental property I found I didn't need a job to survive.'
— **Dean Jackson,** Wellington, NZ

I'm now 40 years old; when I was 35, I replaced my salary in full time employment with a passive income from my investment properties. I have been retired from full time work ever since and spend much of my time travelling overseas.

I live in Wellington, the capital of New Zealand. I left school at 17 and became a computer operator. The first step towards my financial freedom was when I bought my first home at the age of 21.

Looking at ways of making money

I had a nice Holden Ute and wrote it off. When I got the insurance money I was saving to buy a new version of the same Ute but a guy at work said, 'Don't buy a car, buy a house – you can buy a car later but not a house later.' This was in 1986. The moment he said this it changed my view and I went looking for a house. I looked at 23 in total before I found the one I wanted. I knew I wanted a three bedroom house with a basement and a garage that was near town.

I found a house that fitted my criteria in Kingston and bought it for $83k. Eighteen months later it was worth $130k and, from the beginning, the rent from my flatmate covered the mortgage repayments. After 10 years I had paid it off.

During that time I looked into other ways of making money. I got into network marketing through a guy at work. It did teach me about success principles and the reasons certain people are failures and others are successes. To be a success I do believe you need an X factor – it's not your upbringing or your education, it comes from within.

I found that the networking education system was designed to keep people involved regardless of whether or not they were profiting. The lesson I learned from this was to look closely at people's incentives. If you understand what's in it for them, there's a little less chance of being sold a dummy. This lesson is very handy in many different situations.

Your wealth will grow in proportion to your knowledge. Reading has more impact than you know. If you read a little every day it can act like an affirmation. I have a strong self image, which has been fuelled by small successes in life's journey so far. I was never really concerned with what other people thought. If they are negative it usually points out something that's wrong with them, not me. I do analyse comments from others, though, in case there's something I can learn. There's no point worrying; it's going to happen anyway. Worry wastes time and blocks out productive energy. I can honestly say now I don't worry about anything.

In 1996 when I had paid off the house I was having a good time, spending what I earned. Then one day I met a sports photographer whom I picked him up hitchhiking. I was talking to him about networking and he told me about the property book *Building Wealth through Property Investment* (Dolf de Roos and Jan Somers). I read it and thought to myself, 'Anyone can do this; this is easy!'

First buys

Using the equity in my home, which at that time (1997) was worth $145k, I went out and bought two apartments. At that time I was in a relationship and didn't want to buy a place that required me to spend time doing maintenance and other work on it so I was looking at apartments. They were a relatively new thing in those days in Wellington.

I believed the real estate agent when she said I could get $300 per week in rent for a tiny 30 square metre apartment. She was really persistent about trying to get me to sign up the deal. She wanted me to sign the sale and purchase agreement right there. When I asked for time to think about it over the weekend, she said, 'No, it will only take you a couple of minutes to decide. I'll be waiting for you down the road.' I should have been more assertive but I was a beginner. Now there's no way she'd have any influence over me.

I paid $128k for this one bedroom apartment in Manners Mall, in downtown Wellington. It rents for $260 per week. The vendors were asking $135k, which was top dollar in those days as many people were buying apartments off the plans for about $80k. The government valuation (GV) for more than seven years was only $125k, but it has recently been revalued at $146k.

The second apartment I bought was a one bedroom in Hill Street near Parliament Buildings, with basement carpark. I was told I could get up to $350 per week for it. I bought this in April 1997. They were asking $159k; I got it for $157k.

Both properties were slightly cash positive from day one and made a profit of $20 per week. I sold the Hill Street apartment in 1998, some 10 months later, as I was nervous about being able to get the level of rent I needed and there was a lot of negative media coverage about apartments and their oversupply. I got $175k for it, so I made $11k net of commission.

In early March 1999 I purchased a three bedroom flat with a carport in central Upper Hutt. It was my son's grandmother's flat. I tried to encourage her to keep it but she didn't want the hassle. I bought it for $38k, and rented it for $140 per week, which is an 18% return. It is a company share flat, whereby the building is owned with a company structure, and each flat owner is a director with a proportionate number of shares. This doesn't sit well with the banks, as these properties are more difficult to sell in a foreclosure situation. ANZ and National won't touch it, Westpac will only loan up to 50% of the value and BNZ will loan up to 70%.

Living simply

Depreciation from the apartment buildings and chattels contributed to a $14k tax rebate in the first year and $16k the second year. I used this money along

Island Bay property, with three bedroom home and two bedroom flat, gives a 12.5% gross yield.

with savings from my job to pay for the flat. During this whole period I was earning $75k salary and I always have saved as much as I could by living simply with low expenses.

> I've never spent a lot of money on clothes or cars. If you have a good self image and can delay gratification (i.e. be patient) you don't need to buy things to impress other people. This is very important if you ever intend being financially independent.

In November 1999 I bought a home and income in Island Bay, a suburb of Wellington, for $200k. It is a three bedroom house with a two bedroom flat downstairs. I went for the yield, even though I was a bit concerned about the lack of parking and access. I negotiated a long settlement with access to the flat downstairs and worked on it for three months. I painted it, put in second hand carpet, and fixed up the mould problems that were the reason no one else had wanted to buy it. I rented the two bedroom for $200 per week and the three bedroom for $300 per week, which is a 12.5% gross yield and $80 per week net cash flow.

In April 2000 I bought another flat in Upper Hutt, in the same block as my other one, for $40k. This one was a three bedroom with off street parking. So then I owned Flat 1 and 2 in a four flat building. At a directors' meeting, I had sensed the Blenheim based owners considered it a bit of a burden. I called

The three Oak Street flats provide an after tax cash flow of $190 per week. I will get the fourth one later.

them with an offer of $38k. They asked for $40k, which I gladly accepted. My brother became a tenant there at a discounted rent of $140 per week, but while I was overseas he missed a lot of payments, and each time I asked it was coming 'next week with interest'. I didn't want to evict my own brother so I placed the tenancy under management. He couldn't comprehend the injustice at being the only tenant I handed to a manager but I explained that the other tenants paid their rent. He left with about $2000 in arrears, which I've long since written off. I then did a bit of work to his flat and spent about $2000 and have had an excellent tenant in there since August 2003, paying $170 per week. This is a 20% gross return on $42k.

On 8 April 2000 I also purchased a two bedroom flat in Stephen Street, Trentham, another suburb of Wellington. A valuer I had gotten to know quite well was getting into the rental market and thought of me. He told me this property was coming up for mortgagee auction so I went to the auction on site and bought it for $44k. A friend of the owner kicked the bidding off, and two other investors were competing but stopped short of my purchase price.

I was going to pay for this with the equity against my apartment in Manners Mall and my home in Kingston. I use Public Trust, who are very good lenders. I came up with a 10% deposit of $4400 and then to save hassles I borrowed the rest of the money off my father. I did this rather than getting finance over the other properties as this would have cost me $350 for the valuations. It rents for $150 per week.

Retiring early

In September of 2000 I left my full time job after working there for almost 18 years. I was earning $560 per week off my properties; I was getting $80 per week from my flatmate in my mortgage free home in Winnipeg Way, Kingston. The three Oak Street flats had an after tax cash flow of $190 per week. The flat in Stephen Street bought in $120 per week after tax. The house at Cam Street, Island Bay had an after tax cash flow of $100 and the Manners Mall apartment had an after tax cash flow of $70 per week.

On resigning from my job at EDS my super fund was worth $108k. I paid my father the $40k I owed him for the flat and put $20k into AMP Global Tech Fund in October 2000. By March 2001 I had lost $15k. I was gutted. I felt it was far better to take the remaining money $4300 and use it to buy another property than to hope that the value of these shares would ever recover, in spite of what financial advisors were recommending. Whenever I can I pay lump sums of $10k off my mortgage, the maximum you can pay without being penalised. My retirement is not an extravagant lifestyle but I have $560 after tax each week going into the bank with no mortgage to pay out of this.

Three out of four, and one more later

In July 2001 another Oak Street flat came up for sale. The son-in-law of the old lady living in the flat called me to say she wanted to sell it. He said a real estate agent had valued it at $57k; it was a three bedroom place with a garage. I offered him $50k and they took it and they were saved the hassle and cost of marketing it for sale.

So it was a block of four flats and I had three of them. The flats are between two really nice houses that are now worth at least $250k each and I was aware that if I could secure ownership of all the flats I could change the ownership structure and have each building stand alone, which will increase the value of the whole block. It doesn't sound like anything much but it is exciting as they are four minutes' walk from the city centre of Upper Hutt and are all three bedroom flats with parking.

I talked to the owner of the fourth flat, Betty, and she is the only other owner. We are now the only two remaining directors of the company. I have a three-quarter share and she has a quarter share.

My mortgage free home in Kingston gives good equity.

Betty's carport was about to fall over and she didn't have the money to fix it. I slept on it and went back to her with a deal. I said I will build her a garage along the same design of the other garages; custom built this will cost me $8k. And in return I want the legal option to have her flat. When it becomes no longer appropriate for her to live there I have the first option to purchase her flat at market value less 10% not including the value of the garage. She is happy with this arrangement as it's peace of mind for her and she has a new garage.

My total debt now on the three flats is only $90k. If I spend money on things like the fence and section it improves drive-by appeal.

Reasons for good maintenance

Improvements in the kitchen and bathroom are a must when women are involved in the renting decision.

There are several advantages to keeping up the standard of the property. Firstly, the extra rent that can now be charged will be recovered in a reasonably short period of time. Secondly, the standard of tenant willing to live there will often be better. Thirdly, there will be a sharp reduction in your vacancy rate and the time you waste showing prospects who never call back. Lastly, if you ever refinance, a valuation will come out higher, giving you more leverage for your next investment.

In all these units I have replaced the vinyl flooring and extended it to the front door entrance. This is where carpet seems to get dirtiest. I put proper shower linings around the bath as the showers weren't an original feature and water was causing problems. I have good quality second hand carpet laid, and I give them all a fresh paint and new curtains. I've replaced ancient kitchen bench tops with stainless steel from the recyclers and put some tiling or rimu trim around it.

The idea in general is to get rid of the eyesores by going hard for a couple of weeks during a vacancy. However, if a tenant is fairly flexible, I can make occasional improvements during the tenancy. This improves their standard of living and reduces turnaround time if they leave.

I do all my property management myself; I have used a couple of property managers in the past but they have been useless. I enjoy doing a bit of maintenance and changing a tenancy can be done from the other side of the world. With cheap international phone calls and email, I've replaced an outgoing tenant twice from Europe.

Getting into a business

In May 2002 I started shopping around for business ideas and saw in the paper a taxi for sale with Wellington Combined Taxis with a 14% return if you bought into the company. To do this I had to pass an area knowledge test and get a passenger service licence. I bought a $42k share in the company that is now worth $80k. I also had to buy a new car which cost $35,500 and is now worth $10k. Next time I will just lease the share. I found a driver through the fleet quality manager, and he leases the car off me for $500 per week plus GST.

I had started working full time as a driver/guide for the adventure travel bus company Magicbus in 2001. I did this full time for eight months and had the time of my life travelling around the country. It is the best job I've ever done – I don't call it work. Now, to avoid alcohol poisoning and keep my weight down, I just back them up occasionally as a relief driver.

Trust protection

When it came to setting up a structure I knew it should either be an LAQC or a trust but I wasn't sure and wanted to know more about why I would go with either.

My team has been very important along the way. Ross Holmes, an expert trust solicitor with a passion for the subject, set up my trust. I read his book, *Successful Trust Management.* I felt much better sitting down with an expert only after I had clued myself up a bit. That way not so much goes over my head and I can make better use of his time.

I am glad I have used a trust as I have got this to protect my assets. There are too many stories of guys who have lost half of their possessions with marriage break ups or business failures and I didn't want that. I administer my trust myself, which has been a bit of a learning curve.

The concept of a trust is that you sell assets to the trust at market value and set up an IOU. Gradually you gift the value of the assets to the trust at $27k per year until the debt has disappeared tax free, and you own nothing in your own name.

Quick release

I now have a net cash flow off my properties and business of $825 per week. What's important to me now is a lifestyle where I choose how I spend my time. I'm a busy person by nature but it's what I've been busy at that's made a difference. There are many different strategies, and everyone has different goals. Mine was quick freedom so high cash flow property was a good plan for me.

Three and a half years after buying my first rental property I found I didn't need a job to survive. I had to pinch myself for the first couple of years. It still seems a bit too good to be true. I've spent almost half of the last two years travelling in 15 different countries. It's been four years now since I quit my job and they've been the best four years of my life.

I have read more than 100 books on personal development, making money and property – this really has been the key to expanding my mind. Some that stand out are: *The Millionaire Next Door, The One Minute Millionaire, You Can Negotiate Anything, Rich Dad series, How to Think like a Millionaire, New Zealand Real Estate Investors Secrets, Emotional Intelligence, Why Men Don't Listen and Women Can't Read Maps, The Magic of Thinking Big,* and *Jones on Property.*

TOP TEN TIPS

1. Read books and go to seminars, i.e. invest in an education in personal and financial development.
2. Think long term and delay gratification.
3. Use time productively. Learn from tapes or CDs when you're driving, or look at investments in the business pages instead of watching soap operas.
4. Treat carefully any advice from people when they have no results to show for it, or when they have a financial interest in your decision.
5. Never contract debt unless the return is greater than the cost.
6. Get out in the market. Learn the true value of assets.
7. Develop a cash flow mentality; reduce your weekly expenses so they are less than your income.
8. Keep your properties at a high standard.
9. Treat your tenants well; respond quickly to any concerns or to maintenance they request.
10. Have integrity. Do the right thing and give more than the minimum in your dealings with people. It will come back with interest.

Chapter 6

We know it works

'I set myself goals and every time I achieve these goals I get a buzz and I gain more confidence.'
— **Kelvin Bermingham,**
Melbourne, AUS

I have spent 25 years working in the oil industry, mainly working for BP in the customer services area. I am now with Ready Mix Humes Concrete Pipes. My wife Mary has worked as a primary school teacher. We have two children.

At the age of 50 I realised that if we were to maintain our lifestyle of being able to have trips each year like a world trip, and a comfortable lifestyle, then the pension wouldn't be enough. We decided to invest in property to help fund our retirement. Five years ago we bought a three bedroom managed holiday townhouse in Queensland in a holiday resort, Sails Lifestyle Resort, at Peregian Beach on the Sunshine Coast at Noosa, one of 22 in the complex. The property was rented and we could call up and have our time there when we wanted. It was a positive cash flow property. We purchased it for $135k and it was returning $11,600 gross. It looked after itself, it was ticking along, and we were happy as we could go up there in our holidays and enjoy it.

Getting started

In late 2001 prices were going up in Queensland, and at the same time there were a number of books coming out about positive cash flow properties. I read Margaret Lomas' books on positive cash flow and realised what people had been achieving and I thought, 'I can do this.' I read: *How to Maximise Your Property Portfolio, How to Make Your Money Last as Long as You Do,*

How to Create Income for Life ... I was learning so much reading these books; they gave me directions on what to do and how to do it, it gave me a way to get started.

I also use a software package to help with property analysis, figures and to monitor my portfolio. I like to have everything at my finger tips and looked at different software options before finding the best for my purposes.

My wife Mary says she knew I wouldn't venture into anything new that would put us at risk. She is happy for me to do it all, and sees it as my little hobby. However, Mary and I discuss each deal and talk about things as they arise.

Our family home is in Seddon, 10 km from central Melbourne. We bought it back in 1974 for $28,500. It is mortgage free and when I began investing it was worth $250k. I had put my retirement payout of $65k into the Queensland property, which then made it cash positive. This was my first taste of cash positive property, which made me realise just how much potential there was in it.

Developing strategies and goals

What I didn't understand then was how to utilise the equity in my own home, but I went along to the Property Investment Expo in Melbourne (in October 2001) and listened to a number of different speakers. It struck me that it could be done; the potential was there if you want to go out and do it, and by reading different books and with the right management you can achieve these things. It showed me how I could use the equity in my own home to create wealth through property investment.

After the expo I gathered all the newspapers and decided this is what I was going to do: get more properties on top of two we already had, all cash positive. I wanted to have a mix of types of properties, in different areas, so I didn't have all my eggs in one basket. I wanted to diversify the areas to maximise on the ups and downs of the real estate market.

I have attended this expo ever since and have attended a seminar run by Richmastery Australia there which was excellent. The seminar taught me other investing strategies and different ways to invest that I hadn't known about.

My friends and family thought I was crazy; but my wife let me go as long as she was sure we weren't going to get into bad debt, as long as it was good debt (which I had learnt from the seminars and books), that good debt was where we could claim back expenses and the like and bad debt was personal debt.

> I set myself goals and every time I achieve them I get a buzz and gain more confidence. I love doing research on the different areas, I feel I have a knack for it – I am good at picking great locations close to public transport, rail, schools and the like. I love playing real estate agents at their own game, checking out what properties are worth in rent.

Some of the friends who thought I was mad are now doing it themselves and call me for advice. A friend of mine has bought two properties and he leaves it up to me to find him the deals because he's too busy.

Getting positive cash flows

The next investment property we bought was in Portland, five hours' drive south of Melbourne down the Great Ocean Road. We were going through the paper, the ad said it was a brand new two bedroom unit leased back to a motel; you had the option of leasing it back to the motel for five years or putting it on the rental market yourself. I purchased it for $160k, which is what they were asking. There were two for sale and if I knew what I knew now I would have taken the two. Others were putting offers in and I got it as I met the asking price. The after tax cash flow in year one was $190 per week and after five years will be $312. I purchased it on 21 December 2002. The valuation is now $180k.

I really felt good about this one as it was making me money. We went from there to the next one, which was advertised in the *Melbourne Age*. It was a two bedroom townhouse in Brisbane. The vendors were asking $75k and the rent was $120 per week with low body corporate fees. The person advertising it was a buyer's advocate by the name of Russell Reardon. I saw photos of it and offered $71k and that was accepted. After tax cash flow is $145 per week and I haven't spent a cent on it. I purchased this in May 2003.

After doing that deal with Russell Reardon he offered us another property, a three bedroom house in Woodridge, a suburb of Brisbane. It was a do-up. I did some extra research on the area and decided I liked it. It is a working class area and a number of rental places I spoke to had nil vacancy, so I could see the prices were going to go up and the rents would follow. They were asking $72k; I purchased it for $69k in May 2003 after the building report showed that I would need to do quite a bit of work. I spent $8000 replacing a plaster wall in the bedroom, putting in a new kitchen and new carpet. I arranged for contractors to do this. I initially rented it out for $160, but it is now $180, which makes it positive after tax of $26.50 per week.

Strategies falling into place

Then I ventured into something new and this is where is all started to fall into place. Delfin, a big Australian property developer at Springfield (about 20 km from the heart of Brisbane) had some unregistered land for sale. So I bought a block of land off them. I had to pay cash for it as the banks wouldn't lend money against it because there was no title and it wouldn't be registered for two or three months. So I used existing equity to purchase it for $69k cash.

Once it became registered in December 2003, we selected a builder who specialised in investment houses only. They looked at what tenants would like and how they would like it. So we got them to build a four bedroom house. The cost of the house was $166k, making the total cost for the house and land package $236k. The contract with the construction company was for three months. They had to have it built within that time or pay penalties – this was for the whole package, garden, fencing. That's now rented at $260 per week, and it has been valued at $320k.

I bought my next property on 4 June 2004. It has three bedrooms, two bathrooms and a study, and is located in Kalgoorlie, a mining town in Western Australia. I was looking on the internet, picking out areas. I worked out good areas through talking to people and reading the *Australian Property Investor* magazine (available through www.richmastery.com). I liked this one because it was brand new. I try to stick to new properties as they are low maintenance.

They were asking $229k; I offered them $215k and purchased it for $220k with a two year lease and guaranteed tenancy to an Australian mining

The Carrara Gardens townhouse, bought off the plans. It's close to everything — just what you want.

company, with an option of another two years at $350 per week. It's cash positive with an after tax cash flow of $53 per week.

In July 2003, I bought a property off the plans in Carrara Gardens in the Gold Coast, an hour south of Brisbane. It was a three bedroom townhouse in a gated complex. We paid $205k and put down a $1000 deposit bond then settled on 5 July 2004. It is rented at $255 per week and is now valued at $255k. It is 10 minutes from the beach and five minutes from town at Surfers Paradise. It's also right by the freeway, the railway line – all the things that you look for.

Storage units

Russell Reardon also told me about an investment in storage units in Townsville. A successful businessman had locked in contracts with some major companies from around Australia for storage, which is how he could guarantee returns to investors. I have purchased two shares for $200k along with 30 other investors. In total it was $3 million to buy up front. I get 10% on that until they are completed in August 2005 and then I get a return of $1640 for each unit per month after operating costs – so that's a 14.5% return on your money. The units are selling now for $137,500 including GST, to the average investor. So the banks will lend me 75% of $137k, meaning I only need to use $8000 of my own money for each unit. I have been able to recycle the equity in my earlier properties and use this for the later purchases as their values have climbed.

It works!

I will have achieved a total portfolio value of $2.135 million once the storage units are completed. My total mortgages will be $1.297 million, meaning I have equity of close to $1 million. The total rental income from the properties is $234k per annum. The total expenses are $84k in interest at 6.47% plus other costs which total $30k in management fees and the like, so that's a passive income of more than $100k in after tax cash flow.

At the moment we are only paying 30c in the dollar on our tax as we're on the lowest margin of tax due to all the expenses in the business.

I haven't set up a company because my wife and I are both working. There's no real advantage for us in setting up a company. I can still claim the expenses on the property and our airfares to Queensland to do inspections and that sort of thing. We inspect the properties twice or three times a year and we get three month reports by our managers on all the properties.

I have all my properties managed by property managers and this works extremely well; I have sussed out managers that I can trust.

It's a game, but Mary knows that I enjoy doing it and she is very supportive. It's been a successful game (I have had a write up in the *Australian Property Investor* magazine).

I've spoken to a couple at a Destiny conference about what I've done, and they have done some financial planning for me. I have easily achieved far more than was planned. I've achieved my goal, I enjoy what I do and will keep looking for opportunities. Even if I stop now I will feel quite comfortable. Our policy is to buy and hold, not to buy and sell. We are just normal people doing this and it works – we now know we will be able to keep our lifestyle into our retirement.

TOP TEN TIPS

1. Feel comfortable with what you are doing — set yourself goals within your own comfort zone.
2. Make sure you have the correct financial structure.
3. Stick to a budget and your boundaries; don't overcapitalise.
4. Have a good accountant to make sure you're doing it correctly.
5. Get good property managers.
6. Do a lot of research to get the right information. Know the areas that you're investing in; ring the councils to find out what development is happening.
7. Choose properties near rail, buses, schools, highways. I don't buy any further than 20–30 km outside the main town. Look at the industry in the town, go for vibrant areas.
8. Be willing to walk away based on the figures and a gut feeling.
9. Treat it as a business not as a personal preference. Leave the emotion out of it; it's a business decision. Do the figures and don't fall in love with a property, or try to help someone out.
10. Buy and hold, don't buy and sell.

Chapter 7

Recycling equity

'The realisation that you can recycle your equity and keep doing it, that's one of the best tools we've been able to use.'
— **David and Beryl Colley,**
Wainuiomata, NZ

We had been property investors for about nine years and had bought property solely on the advice of others, not knowing anything about what to look for. We had three properties that we put on the market in Napier in September 2002 and sold at the beginning of the peak. We did not know about borrowing against the equity then.

We came out with $100k surplus and before we did anything with this money we decided to go to a Richmastery Profit from Property seminar in July 2003 to make sure we got it right next time. From that we realised we should not have sold, and so booked to go to the three day Richmastery Property Academy in October 2003.

Just before then I bought two two-bedroom flats in Wanganui for $76k, returning $210 per week.

Gutsy and aggressive

We thoroughly enjoyed the Richmastery Property Academy and signed up to be in the mentoring group to make the most of what we had learnt.

The Richmastery courses have made us much more gutsy and aggressive. We would never have bought at a mortgagee auction or two properties without seeing them if we hadn't had the Richmastery education.

Three of the properties we own we have never seen. They were all bought off the Richmastery website because we just wanted to make a go of it.

> David: 'The most valuable thing I got out of doing the Richmastery Property Academy was the sense that we could actually do it.' Beryl adds: 'For me it was the realisation that you can recycle your equity and keep doing it, that's one of the best tools we've been able to use.'

Before the academy or the Richmastery Profit from Property seminar we knew nothing about analysing deals or figures. We relied totally on the integrity and honesty of the real estate agents and others. When we had purchased the properties in Napier we had relied on a friend and didn't look at any other properties first. Now I read the *Property Press* from cover to cover. When we moved to Lower Hutt a couple of years later we bought two rentals and relied totally on a real estate agent for selecting them. I would never do that now. We were fortunate we were not taken for a ride and this shows how important it is to get some education in this area.

Revaluing for equity

In 2003 we got our own house revalued along with the Naenae ones – we bought our first three houses on the Naenae equity alone. Since then we have bought five properties using our own home as security, and all of these have been off the Richmastery Property Deals website. We did this in four months and because we've bought the whole lot at 20% below valuation we were able to recycle our equity. We have recently got the valuations updated.

As we were both working full time and David was also running two small businesses from home, we used property finders for some of our next purchases. I also bought at a mortgagee auction over the phone. After a tidy up this property gives a 13% return.

We then found two cheaper properties at about $60k and bought and tenanted those, and then the week before Christmas while we were packing to go to China I bought three deals off Richmastery's website. I quickly set about finding property managers to get things started while we were away. We signed the documents at our lawyers two days before Christmas and left him with it.

The good thing about these three deals was that, combined, they totalled 20% below valuation. Just three months after this I refinanced these properties and they now stand self-supported by their own equity, leaving us a nearly freehold house to do it all again on.

At the Richmastery Property Academy there was a challenge for $10k to the person who did the best to increase their equity and cash flow and in February we found out we were the winners.

I then started on my next spending blitz and bought a property in Auckland, newly redecorated, at $45k below valuation. We have substantially increased our passive cash flow to such an extent that I have been able to reduce my workload to a four-day week. Wainuiomata was a great buy; in fact the last five properties we bought combined were 20% below valuation. We had sold three houses and so we wanted to get back better than we were quickly. Therefore, we are happy to pay the Richmastery Property Deals finder's fees, as we could never have found the deals ourselves in that time.

Beryl: 'It would have taken us hours over weekend after weekend to find these deals and then we would have been restricted to buying locally only.'

David says, 'We found the Richmastery Personal Property mentoring brilliant because we've done so much so quickly. It has been very helpful to be able to call our personal property mentor to check figures when we are refinancing or to bounce ideas off her for different ways of looking at things.'

We used a second bank for the homes we purchased in late 2003. We needed to do this after the bank we were with wouldn't lend us any more money. If you buy more than one house in six months the banks shy away from you.

Buying low and adding value

After the last three properties settled we set out to start the process of refinancing. Because the last five property purchases combined were purchased below valuation they could stand on their own equity except the value of their chattels. This has enabled us to keep on purchasing. This is why it is so important that wherever possible you buy below valuation.

We started out with $120k cash. Our home was worth $247k (in 2002). We also had two properties in Naenae. When these were revalued they had gone up $66k in two years. We look at renovations and touch ups to see if we can add value or increase rentals. With the Wanganui mortgagee auction property we did a cosmetic do-up, and a property manager was involved. We use property managers for all our out of town properties and look after the Wainuiomata and Naenae ones ourselves. We find our own tenants and have never had any problems.

Our aim is to replace one of our incomes so that we are freed up to have more time to do what we've always wanted to do. We are already seeing a difference. Beryl is already down to four days a week.

We recently had the three properties we purchased off the Richmastery Property Deals website revalued (only four months after we had purchased them). We then refinanced because we wanted to roll them away from our home so we reassigned the valuations – after that our house became freehold so we can now do it all again.

If we buy again we wouldn't mind buying in more upmarket areas to get some capital growth properties. If you want the returns you have to do that, but if you want to buy a 10% below valuation property that can be hard.

> Our future aims are to totally replace a full time wage in positive cash flow and then to retire early with a passive income so we can enjoy our retirement and go on our overseas holidays each year. We are well on our way to achieving this. We have felt fear along the way – it is scary doing things like mortgagee sales over the phone, but as long as you have a price in mind and you stick to it you should be fine.

Containing the negatives

We don't tell people, family or friends, what we are doing. They just say, 'What if the market crashes? What if it all falls down? What if prices go down?' People say, 'I don't want to use the equity in my own home – what if I lose it?' Even with the first property we bought people said things like 'You're a capitalist so and so, taking money off the poor...'. We talk about it together and make sure that we support each other not to let the negativity stop what we are doing.

A couple of negatives have been, firstly, that maintenance costs have been a lot higher than we would have liked them to be and we underestimated these. It is important to make an effort to maintain your homes. Also, banks have not been the easiest to work, with as we were investing at a rate that took them out of their comfort zone.

We have also bought an apartment in Hobson Street, Auckland, off the plans through the Richmastery Property Deals website using a deposit bond. We signed a Sale and Purchase agreement in December and only paid our deposit bond amount of about $4000 in September 2004. The valuation has gone from $214k to $259k. We wanted to step out and do a capital growth property; there are always different rental markets.

Real value

Since the Richmastery Property Academy we have made it a point to read an inspiring book a month. One that has been helpful has been *Real Money Real Estate* by Phil Jones.

Our portfolio value is currently $2,065,000. Our total mortgages are $1,385,500 and our total equity is $649,500 and this has all been achieved in a period of nine years, but most of it achieved in the last three after doing the Richmastery courses.

On top of this we have put deposit bonds on two apartments, one in Auckland and one in Wellington. One settles in November 2005 and then the other in March 2006. Based on current valuations for those our equity will go up to $838,306 once these deals settle.

The Torbay house gives us a capital growth property.

TOP TEN TIPS

1. Do it now, don't sit and procrastinate — we bought properties when the market was supposedly 'hot' but with Richmastery's help got good prices.
2. When it comes to banks don't take no for an answer; they don't think like investors. Shop around.
3. If you are busy or for those who want a quick start, using property finders is not a bad thing. If you buy a property that is $30k below valuation a finder's fee is well worth it.
4. Build good relationships with the people around you: lawyers, accountants, property managers, handymen.
5. Don't listen to friends and family. They could be a blocking point to your success.
6. Stay focused.
7. Keep company with like-minded people; you will be enriched by them.
8. Always do your own due diligence and research on the house and the area even when you are using a property finder. Only you can take responsibility for the final decision and its outcome.
9. You need to keep life in balance and make sure there's enough money for enjoyment.
10. Continue with your education and personal growth: they are vital to your success.

Chapter 8

Living the good life

"My dream is to write to the Australian government and say I don't need the pension.'
— **Dianne Corfield,**
Middlemount, Queensland, AUS

I am 55 years old and live with my partner Bruce, who is 57. We've been together since 2000. I have two adult daughters and Bruce has two sons and one daughter, both from previous marriages.

I met Bruce after coming to Middlemount in 2000 to visit my daughter who was living there at the time. I had just returned from Canada where I had sustained a failed career and personal relationship. I had also been divorced four years earlier. I was what could only be described as sitting at the bottom of the barrel.

> We have been together ever since and are very happy together. In just five years we have built up a property portfolio of $2.9 million and increased our equity from $200k to $1.4 million, plus had the opportunity to fulfil a dream of owning a yacht. And by becoming property investors, Bruce has been able to reduce his income tax from the top bracket to the lowest bracket.

It all began when I was encouraged by my daughter to begin working as a mortgage broker and to set up my own home based mortgage broking business. Soon afterwards I began my foray into property investing and Lisa introduced me to the Richmastery education. My success is due to my daughter and my association with Richmastery. Without their support and without attending the Richmastery Property Academy I would not have had the confidence or the tools to conduct my business as I am today.

Stuck in a rut

Bruce works in senior management with Anglo Coal Australia, which is based in Middlemount, a coal town with a population of 2500 people. The town was built by Anglo Coal. Bruce earns a salary of more than $150k per year and we only have to pay $144 a month in rent as the mine subsidises our rent. Middlemount is very isolated, we are three hours from any major shops, cafés and anything normal and the coal company owns everything.

For the first two and a half years living in Middlemount I found part time work with small businesses and I worked for the local doctor in the pharmacy section of his surgery. But I found that I was in tears each day when I arrived home from work because I was frustrated with the status quo of my life. I was always a fairly outgoing person and I felt as if I was stuck within the square living there.

My daughter had left Middlemount and was living on the Gold Coast where she had secured herself a fabulous career with a mortgage originator. She knew of my career unhappiness and so she called me and said, 'Mum you have to get on board and start writing finance for people.' This is what she was doing.

In terms of my personal financial position when I met Bruce, I owned my own home in Gladstone, an industrial city four hours' drive from Middlemount on the central Queensland coast, near Rockhampton. This property was being leased out to the National Bank and the bank manager and family live in the house; at that time it was worth $170k (now it's worth $220k). And Bruce had two houses in Ipswich, 20 minutes' drive from the centre of Brisbane. They were worth about $170k jointly and he had them rented out. Property was in a slump back then. All of our joint properties were positive cash flow.

So when we started out five years ago, our joint portfolio was worth $350k and against this we had mortgages of $150k, giving us joint equity of $200k.

I did not take my daughter's advice immediately but we watched how she grew in confidence and we listened to what opportunities were out there for property investors.

Bruce had always had a dream to own a yacht and an opportunity came up for him to buy a Beneteau 411 that was just three years old from a friend. We wanted the yacht for our retirement. The yacht was named *La Belle Vie* and she was already working in the charter industry in the Cumberland Yacht Charter fleet. It was just a matter of us getting the money to buy her for $325k and then she would earn a return and we would leave her where she was. We knew she would be run as a business and at a loss she would also be a wonderful tool to gain some tax relief for Bruce.

A learning curve

Now, this is where our huge learning curve in finance began. In May 2000, we went to the bank for the finance and they would not lend us the money to buy *La Belle Vie*. Bruce was so disappointed. So instead he bought a unit at Airlie Beach, four and a half hours north of Rockhampton, a beautiful spot. The unit was a Sea Star three bedroom with a double lock up garage overlooking the Whitsunday Islands. He paid $325k and put down a deposit of $100k, which he got from his unpreserved superannuation. He rented it out as holiday letting – the property was negatively geared.

Bruce still did not let go of the dream to own *La Belle Vie* and attempted to get finance for the boat again in May 2002 but was turned down again.

The day we were turned down the second time, I was speaking on the phone to my daughter and she became really annoyed with me because I was not listening to her about having a fully optioned line of credit and using our equity to build a passive income. I know now that we had the paradigm that you had to own your own home to be secure and felt it was too risky to take her advice.

I talked Bruce into allowing me to work with my daughter to gain finance for the boat. He agreed but when the refinance documents arrived for finance through the non-banking sector (second tier loans) he was terrified and in a trance about leaving the traditional banks.

So we went away for the weekend to read over the documents. We discovered they were fine and we then established our line of credit against our properties and finally raised the money to buy the boat.

Our capital growth property at Yeppoon, Queensland. Bought for $385k in 2003, it's now valued at $550k.

Out of the fog

All of a sudden I was seeing the light so to speak and I started to get excited for the first time in years. The fog was lifting on my life and I dearly wanted to get back in the fast lane, to follow the narrow path away from the average person. Bruce was still skeptical and he worried about my rash thoughts.

After much discussion I left my job at the doctors' surgery and started a virtual business from home writing finance for property investors' loans working for Mortgage Ezy. I did not own a car so I had to make it work from home. It did not take long before I saw what property investors were doing and I wanted some of the action.

It was Christmas 2003 and we went up to friends in Yeppoon for New Year celebrations. While we were there we saw a house for sale in Golding Street; they were asking $420k. We offered $385k as that was all we could afford because we'd just bought the boat. It was a capital growth property on a hill overlooking the Kepple Islands with massive coastal views. Both Bruce and I liked it and its position. Our offer was accepted. We settled on 12 March 2003; it is now worth over $650k. We rent it out for $295 per week so it is very negatively geared, but we have made huge equity on it in a very short time.

We floated around in shock for a few months. Bruce was going through a lengthy divorce settlement and we found that we had to find cash to complete this part of his life's journey. So we had his unit in Airlie revalued to $480k and the house in Yeppoon revalued at $550k. (The Sea Star unit is now worth $650k). Bruce was then able to use our newly created equity to help complete the settlement. By then he had been separated for six years so it was good to have closure.

On a mission

We still had money left over in our line of credit account. Around this time my brother and I bought our parents' home, an old Queenslander in Gladstone on a large section, so that they could retire to an easy care home in Calliope across the road from my sister. We bought it off them for $170k with the view to building four two-bedroom villa units on the old home site. Recently we sold the house for removal for $15k and now we are moving forward with the development.

> In August 2003 I attended the Richmastery three day Property Academy in Sydney to assist in writing finance with my daughter and Mortgage Ezy. Seeing people coming out of the academy with a light shining in their eyes was fantastic, we loved it and we wanted to do it and wanted to find out more about Richmastery. We were both so stoked about Richmastery: they really had something fantastic to offer. They have a magic tool in their hand.

In early February a client phoned about a loan and asked if I knew of any good deals in Rockhampton. I didn't, but told her to go online and look in www.realestate.com.au and see what she could find. When I hung up the phone I thought, why don't I have a look too, and I found three units for sale.

As we were going on annual leave in two days we didn't need me buying further real estate. But I was on a mission, and yes, you guessed it, we diverted our holiday plans to include a visit to Rockhampton and we bought the units. Thank goodness we were going to Airlie; Bruce had sailing on his mind so he was still coping with my property investing at this point.

Once the units settled (there were the usual hiccoughs) our portfolio included a house in Ipswich, Yeppoon and Gladstone (plus the half share in my parents' Gladstone house with my brother), a unit in Airlie Beach and the three units in Rockhampton.

We added this up and went into immediate shock – we had $1.7 million in property. By then I was taking something for my stomach nerves and Bruce kept going into delayed shock at my pace of doing business. Oh, and we have the boat (valued at $320k)!

By this time my daughter called me to say the Richmastery Property Academy was to be held in New Zealand in May 2003 and I had to attend.

Poor Bruce, he returned to a trancelike state because he was not sure if he could handle me being any more motivated, yet there was something in his eyes that told me he was finally seeing the light. So I put plans into motion to go to Auckland.

Constant learning

What the Richmastery Property Academy did for me was to help me to understand how difficult it was going to be and is still now changing my paradigms.

I discovered it's not what I know or don't know that's my problem, it's what I don't know that I don't know ... and that has been the greatest piece of knowledge that I've ever received. It helps me to keep searching. Every time during the Richmastery Property Academy when I became frustrated and angry I kept asking myself what I could learn. I was trying to learn to read my reactions and learning what I liked and didn't like, and how I reacted. I realised that this was going to happen to me in real life and I would have to deal with it.

Just a few weeks ago a client came to Emerald to inspect property. We invited him to stay with us and I assisted where I could with his search. Well, you guessed it; I found a block of units for sale that I was interested in myself. It was a block of six units in Redbank, Emerald.

They weren't on the market; it is just that the real estate agent knew we had been disappointed about a purchase in Ipswich, which had just failed due to a building inspection report. So he went on the trail and phoned everyone who owned units and he found this fellow who had taken his units off the market because his sale kept falling over due to finance. So we bought

The Yeppon property has given us huge equity.

six units in Emerald in central Queensland, part of a block of 12 two-bedroom units. Emerald is a rural and mining town of 15,000 people, and is very stable. I paid $755k for the block and they return $1260 per week, which means they break even. They are now worth around $800k.

On our dreamboat

I've just had everything revalued and our total portfolio value is now $2.9 million, with total mortgages of $1.5 million. Since we began in 2000 we have created a total of $1.4 million in equity. Our after tax cash flow is over $50k per year and this is achieved because Bruce is in a high tax bracket and we are able to maximise our tax benefit and reduce his income tax considerably.

Most recently we've purchased a unit off the plan in Cairns for $357k. We have secured it with a deposit bond of $5000 and it will settle in late 2005. We will rent this out but see it as a high capital growth property.

The most wonderful thing about all of this is that Bruce has achieved his dream and we now have our dream boat, *La Belle Vie* which means 'The Good Life'.

My dream is to write to the Australian government and say I don't need the pension. Instead I plan to be paying tax for the rest of my life and to be a self funded retiree. It's funny that wanting the boat and having that dream has driven us to achieve what we have. I can't see an end to it.

Helping others

My daughter has now set up her own finance company, Source Finance Group, based in Sydney. I am now working with her. The company is committed to ensuring that borrowers are not restricted by the common 'all monies' clause imposed by banks on all borrowers where they state that all debt is secured by all security held. We aim to source the best finance from carefully chosen lenders to suit our clients' individual needs. The products we choose must satisfy our requirements and need to be 'Investment Grade'. The major financial services that we offer to our clients are Residential Home Loans including First Home Buyers, Lo Doc Loans, Light Doc Loans (PAYG borrowers), Refinancing, Debt Consolidation, Credit Impaired, Deposit Bonds and Mortgage Minimisation Strategies.

Bruce and I discovered that there was another way to buy La Belle Vie, after being turned down twice by the traditional banks, and that is the same kind of service Source Finance aims to offer its clients. We have just got the licence to operate in New Zealand.

My goals within the new company are working with women to help them with their financial future, especially those who are on their own, have been widowed or divorced. I have been working with them as they learn about investment. You can't always have a man in your life but you can always have your money working for you. It's just wonderful, I love it.

TOP TEN TIPS

1. Find a mentor or coach.
2. Understand the power of your equity and that you will not lose your home by borrowing against it; it is safe to reinvest your equity.
3. Don't be afraid to negotiate the price.
4. Don't be afraid to walk away.
5. Never stop educating yourself.
6. If you want a million dollars worth of property talk to someone with $10 million and then copy what they're doing.
7. Remember you're never too old to start a new career.
8. Don't buy anything sight unseen until you've got 200 properties.
9. Understand the power of principal and interest versus interest only loans. In the past, I gave the bank my principal to reinvest. Now I am my own bank manager and I reinvest my principal.
10. Have the confidence to leave the traditional banks and join the non-banking industry; it gives you the leverage you need.

Chapter 9

Positive from the start

'It started out as making money, but it's more than that now. It has given us more choices and freedom.
— **David Gilling,** Dunedin, NZ

I live in Milton, a small town 40 minutes south of Dunedin, a city of 100,000 people in the south of New Zealand's South Island, with my wife and family.

I attended the Richmastery Property Academy in May 2003 and in the 18 months since then we have bought five high to medium cash flow properties. We started with about $40k equity and now have over $300k equity and a cash flow of $24,000 per annum before tax.

I'm a very ordinary bloke with a full time teaching job and four children under 18 years all living at home. Since the Richmastery Property Academy, I have become interested in property and all its ins and outs. It has become a real passion and it has broadened my horizons.

A good beginning

I moved to Milton from Christchurch in 1989 to take up a teaching job at the local high school. Jocelyn, my wife, is a mum and she works as a teacher aide.

About five years ago we bought a student rental. We were thinking about our retirement. It was funny, I didn't know what positive cash flow properties were then but I knew the property must be able to look after itself, as I could not afford to top up the mortgage if it was negatively geared. So we chose a house in a suburb of North Dunedin called Pine Hill, which is quite near to the University of Otago. It was positive cash flow even with a principal and interest loan. It was one of two properties we looked at. The house was a three bedroom place that I converted into four bedrooms. It rented for $240 per week. We owned that place for about four years and learned the trade of being landlords. We made a few mistakes but grew in knowledge from them.

In the end we had to sell the house. Although it was low maintenance it had large grounds that needed constant work, so we sold it in December 2002 for $120k.

Our next purchase was in February 2003. This was a block of two two-bedroom flats in Cityrise, a central suburb of Dunedin. I purchased them for $64k. One of the flats had problem tenants in it and was in a terrible state. There was ash everywhere and multi-coloured glitter on the walls. We spent $3000 doing up the flat inside, scraping the walls, painting and sanding, working nights and weekends; it was finished off with second hand carpet and new vinyl in the kitchen.

We didn't have to do anything to the other flat and since then we have only replaced the carpet in it. This year we spent $10k on a new roof. We now get $270 per week for both flats and soon this will increase to $320 per week. These flats are now valued at $125k and return an annual after tax cash flow of $4500.

A life changing night

Jocelyn read about Richmastery's Profit from Property evening seminar in the local paper, the *Otago Daily Times*. She showed me the advert to see if I was interested. It was $69.95 for the evening seminar. I thought I knew it all, but decided, 'Oh well, why not?' I learned some huge lessons on property that night. It really changed the direction my life would take over the next two years. That evening I purchased the ticket to attend the next three day Richmastery Property Academy that was to be held in Auckland in May 2003.

Going to the Richmastery Property Academy would be the best thing I've done in my life for a long time. I got huge personal growth out of it as well as the property information. It took me right out of my comfort zone and it showed me that I can do what it takes and gave me the confidence to carry on from where I had started.

Lower Wairkari house before $8000 of renovations. It's close to city, schools and shops — ideal.

I found International Peak Performance and Success Coach Kurek Ashley really inspiring. He showed me that we can do whatever we put our mind to.

Creating a team

I came home from the Richmastery Property Academy and got my team together. I found a new lawyer and a good accountant. We set up an LAQC company as a vehicle in which to own the properties. I also stayed in touch with the real estate agent who had sold me the flats in City Rise. He deals a lot with investment property so has been a great help finding property.

Brad Sugars, multi-millionaire, author and businessman, had said at the Richmastery Property Academy that it's better to have a shack that pays you money than a palace that costs you money. I seem to have remembered this and some of the property we have bought could be considered shacks but do provide an income.

Straight after the academy, in late May 2003, we bought a block of four flats in Caversham, a lower socio-economic suburb of Dunedin. They were one two-bedroom flat and three one-bedroom flats. The asking price was $180k; we got them for $165k. The flats are brick so they are low main-tenance. We have done up two of them; renovations included repainting, new vinyl and carpet. In total we spent about $2500 on each place. We rent them out for $480 per week.

We have had a few troubles with tenants in this place and have ended up at the tenancy tribunal as one tenant was behind on rent. She ended up

leaving of her own accord owing $1000 in rent. It was my own fault for letting it get so high. These are property management issues and you learn as you go. We manage all our own properties. The reason for this is that they are all close and we don't want to have to pay a property manager. The thing I enjoy the most is letting out the places. You know you've spent time and energy cleaning the place up and it's your handiwork on display. I really enjoy providing people with a clean and tidy place to live.

Buying criteria

One of my first rules was buying at 15% gross return or more so I was looking around for this. More recently I've had to change this as the market has changed in Dunedin and 10% is more realistic.

We found one deal in Palmerston, a small town 45 minutes north of Dunedin, which did meet these criteria. We bought this in June 2003 for $41k. It was a three bedroom house but has an 18% return. All we did was paint the front of the house. It rents for $142 per week and was valued in March 2004 at $63k. It's only been empty for one week, as McRae Mines is quite a big employer in the area so it is quite a go ahead small town. The after tax cash flow on this property is $2500 per year.

The next property we purchased was in Milton, a cottage for $40k. I got it valued the following week at $49k. We spent $8000 relining walls, putting in a new kitchen, some good second hand carpet and repainted over three long winter months, again working nights and weekends. It was slow to rent possibly, because of its size, so we decided to sell it and did so three months later on a delayed settlement for $67k. In the meantime it did rent for $135 per week.

That same month we also purchased a three bedroom house in Lower Wakari, Dunedin, just 10 minutes' drive from town, close to schools and shops. There was no asking price. But my agent believed it would be worth $135k. I started verbally with a bid of $109 but another buyer came in at $115k; we ended up settling for $117k. I bought this one without looking inside as the market was pretty hot then and the viewing time did not suit us. We were able to drive by and we trusted the real estate agent's judgement and advice as to its future value. Because we were still busy on the Milton cottage we put an ad in the paper for cheap rent short term at $150 per week and said it was an ongoing project. This covered the interest payments in the meantime.

Three months later when the Milton cottage was completed I then got stuck in doing the renovation. Every room was painted and new carpet laid. The kitchen was revamped with new cupboards and vinyl. The front yard was tidied up, and you would hardly recognise it today. We spent about $8000 on it and it now rents for $235 per week, with an after tax cash flow of around $3000. I hardly had a weekend off for the whole year doing renovations but it was worth it to gain cash flow and equity.

Hard work but worth it

Property investment is hard work but the Richmastery Property Academy prepared me for this. We keep working hard as I would like to leave teaching and work full time as a manager of my own properties My goal was to achieve this within five years from when I attended the academy. It may take longer.

We have been basically looking for property that we can add value to, which then increases rents and in turn increases capital value.

Since attending the academy, I have read many books. If I was going to recommend one it would be *Real Money Real Estate* by Phil Jones. I have enjoyed listening to the Richmastery team in their seminars, wondering what their motives are. I've decided that they genuinely enjoy helping people invest in property.

I also recommend *Real Estate Investors' Secrets* by Graeme Fowler, *How to Create Income for Life* by Margaret Lomas, and *The Richest Man in Babylon* by George S. Clasm, which has some simple lessons.

My reason for investing in property started out as being to make money, but it's more that that now. It has given us more choices and freedom. We have had the opportunity to meet different people and discuss different topics. It has been a journey of self discovery and learning which I'm sure will continue as we are still quite new in the business.

TOP TEN TIPS

1. Always buy positive cash flow property.
2. Buy property you can add value to.
3. Don't let your emotions influence your purchase.
4. Always be prepared to learn (attend seminars and read books etc).
5. Use interest only loans.
6. Set up a suitable structure from the beginning, e.g. an LAQC company and/or a trust.
7. Be honest and fair in all your dealings.
8. Be respectful towards your tenants.
9. Be well organised.
10. Use internet banking.

Chapter 10

Buying in bulk

'*From $1000 and a VW to a $750k home in six months...*'
— **Andrew Shanahan,** Sydney, AUS

I have an interesting story of how I came to own a home in Mosman, one of Sydney's nicest suburbs, worth $750k, at the age of 22, six months after having had less than $1000 in my bank account and a 1997 VW Golf. I also ended up with over $350k in ready to use equity in this same property and have now used that equity to purchase other properties and involve myself in other investment classes such as share options and property options.

Putting an option

I was working in project marketing for a real estate company and was interested in property investment myself. My whole family is in property – seven uncles and three or four of my aunties – so it came naturally to me. And because I was working in this role, I was actively driving around and, out of the corner of my eye, looking for opportunities.

I found a property that consisted of three Torrens titled lots, each the same size, on their own block of land with two street frontages. After a quick chat with my dad, I contacted the owners of the property to see if they were thinking of selling. As luck had it, they were. So I said I would get back to them with a proposal. I didn't know at the time but they were visited by two agents to try to sell their property that week and I won their trust by being honest and polite – it goes a long way!

My dad and I decided that it was a development site worth pursuing but in order for me to carry out investigations on the development possibilities I had to have some control of the property. This is where I put an option on the property or properties. After some negotiations, we came to a price for the total three properties of $1.7 million. That was perfect because my car was worth $17k (1% of the price), the standard fee to put an option on a property.

So I asked if I could put an option on the property to have control to investigate the development potential and feasibility. If I decided not to go through with it the vendors would keep the $17,000 option fee.

My dad, being a property genius, wrote up an option agreement and his secretary typed it up in 15 minutes.

I had worked out an exit strategy. I had investigated that each property if sold separately would be worth approx $700k; therefore, $700k x 3 = $2.1 million. So if I couldn't do the development the way I wanted to make it feasible I would sell the three separately within the option period and make a cool $400k. Or I could sell two for $700k each (total $1.4 million) and purchase the remainder for $300k.

There was only one problem. I did not include provisions within the option document that allowed me to market and introduce two other buyers to take place in a simultaneous settlement.

Getting tricky

The vendor didn't like the idea of me showing the property to other people so I was stuck. Why not just sell the option? Things were too tricky by this stage and I wanted to maximise profits.

 Lesson: we wouldn't have ended up in a sticky situation if I had included the provisions in the option document that allowed for me to market and on-sell. Even my father learnt from this experience – that if you are going to have an exit strategy to fall back on you need to state that in your option or contract.

My dad, as smart as he is, possibly rushed the option agreement a little and we both now know to put in an exit strategy in the first deal. If the vendor is not happy with your exit strategy, discuss it with them. If you want to get the deal done, you need to have at least two strategies.

My father in all his years in the business hadn't come across people that were as strict as this before and no matter what path we went down we wanted to come to a successful property sale for everyone. We didn't want to cause problems for the vendor but the vendor's lawyer stopped us being able to come to an agreement.

I had to liaise with the vendor's lawyer and tell him what we were trying to do. He didn't understand it; he had it in his mind that we were trying to sell a property that we didn't own; but in fact we were trying to bring in a third investor as an introduction as another buyer.

I freaked out, and my dad didn't know what to do, I kept trying to explain to the vendor and her lawyer but he was convinced we were out to do something wrong ... we scratched our heads trying to work out how to buy the other two properties without paying stamp duty.

So, with my development potential and feasibility shut down by council, and my exit strategy thwarted by my own ignorance, there was only one thing I could do and I thank my father eternally for this.

Buying all three

The only way I could succeed in this deal to the maximum was to purchase all three properties and then on-sell them ourselves. So Dad stepped in and bought two of the properties for $1.4 million (around $75k stamp duty) and I bought one for $300k (stamp duty of $25k) with the idea that I could do it up and live in it. We successfully sold the other two for $1,450,000 to cover costs in January 2004 and I was set!

To sign up the deal took me about three months; including the first contact with the vendors, doing a project feasibility study and coming back to the vendor with the ideas I had for the development, letting that sink in, then coming back with the idea of the option and getting the option deal signed and putting down the option fee.

Then we got it on option for six months; at the end of the option we had to buy and then market the properties again, that was about two months.

The three units in Mosman have given me equity for later purchases.

I interviewed three agents, told them what I was doing, sussed out how they worked and how seriously they were looking at what I was doing. I wanted someone who was going to see this as an important deal to them. I found a good agent at Century 21 in Mosman.

Since the properties are in Mosman, one of the best areas in Sydney, they sold easily. We found a buyer for the two properties, who wanted a delayed settlement of three months, and then it was done. In total it took 14 months and was quite a lot of work. I learnt about meeting with council, doing development feasibility studies, dealing with architects, talking to local real estate agents and finding the right person to sell the properties – so it was a huge learning curve.

The house that I ended up with was valued at about $650k.

When I first moved in to the property it was 100% run down, totally derelict. I had to rip everything up, the floor and the foundations. The property is 101 years old; it's a shop at the front, a small residence, with a backyard that also opens on to a street so it has two street accesses.

Reno ... with a little help from friends

Now I have done some very substantial renovations to the property all myself (with a little help from my friends who deserve a huge mention) at the cost of around $5000 and added approximately $50k to the value.

I had to dig under the floor two feet, because the soil had risen up and affected the floor, and relay all the foundations, bearers and joists.

I had to replace the part of the roof that was corrugated iron. I found 30 sheets of second hand corrugated iron for a really good price, and only needed 15 and then sold the rest and almost got my money back. The iron was also a heritage colour and because my place is heritage it fitted within the guidelines.

I have rearranged some walls that were non-structural in the bathroom and redid the bathroom; a friend who is a plumber has done all the plumbing for me for free. I have also redone the kitchen using free materials (including a black granite bench top) oven, sink, and cooktop from my auntie who was pulling down her house.

I am putting a bedroom in the roof and looking at another bedroom out the back that I will start on soon; when it's finished it will be two bedrooms and a study. In future I could rent out the property to someone who wanted to have a shop and live out the back as well. This would rent for at least $600 per week.

I've found the project excellent, I'm on to the basics of landscaping my backyard now, still have to finish the kitchen and bathroom. I began the renovations in March 2004 and have been working weekends on and off for the past seven months. Once the renovations are done the place will be worth about $750k.

Subtracting the costs, I am now sitting on over $350k in equity and have used this to invest in positive cash flow properties to pay for my $350k approx loan on the property. The mortgage over the property is $350k plus about $40k in renovation costs. I am servicing this myself by working hard.

Making a job of it

I began working for Richmastery Australia as a property consultant in October 2003. I've been to a number of the Richmastery seminars and I find I just soak up the information working here. I have learnt a huge amount while working with the directors and from doing some of the educational property seminars the company runs.

I have also read some books and learnt a few things from a book called *Real Estate in a Nutshell*, but mostly from working for Richmastery.

To help balance out the negative cash flow (i.e. mortgage interest on my home) I started looking around for some positive cash flow deals and was doing this for my new job anyway.

I found a property in July 2004 after listing a development; I sold 12 of the 13 off the plan and kept one for myself. I bought this off the plan for $167k. It is a three bedroom townhouse in Kalgoorlie in Western Australia. I put down a deposit of $1000, and it will be completed in May 2005, which is when I settle. This will rent for around $400 per week, making it a positive cash flow deal.

The next one I purchased was a three bedroom house in Moree, about 200 km west of Byron Bay in New South Wales. This place is about 15 years old. I paid $75k for it and it rents for $180 per week. Moree is quite a big town, with over 10,000 people. It's a stable place, prices are slowly increasing, it's central to everywhere and the property is in a good central location.

To purchase this I did a line of credit against the equity in my Mosman property. I settled on this on 9 September 2004. I discovered this property through my work as a property consultant.

I also have an option on a property in Coomera on the Gold Coast for $1000, which will settle in August 2005. It has already gone up more than $50k in value in the few months I've owned it.

Mining town buys

I have recently put an offer of $130k on a house in Port Hedland in Western Australia. It is a three bedroom house, renting for $300 per week. Port Hedland is a town of around 8000 people and is a key mining distribution port. The area that surrounds it is massive uninhabited land suitable for mining, so the future should be a long one for its resources. It is also a good port, capable of handling big ships, and there is a large export industry there. So it's a great town, the prices are at a point where it's not profitable for developers to go in to put in new stock, so what's there is highly sought after and never vacant. People are waiting to sign on this property now.

With all these deals I have been using my equity in the Mosman property, gearing it all up for when I go overseas for a year in mid 2005.

The idea is to rent out all the property, which will be self sufficient, and give me between $200 and $300 per week when I am travelling and also to do a few deals in the meantime to build up some capital as well.

TOP TEN TIPS

1. There needs to be some upside to the property, e.g. on its own block of land large enough to do some development, you can make simple improvements or can renovate to add value.
2. The property needs to be in a solid area.
3. Make sure there's some upside for the prospective buyer.
4. If possible, buy more than one property through the same person so you can get a better deal and purchase under valuation. Then sell the other properties for full price and build equity — so buy in bulk if possible.
5. Use options where possible, then get access and provisions to renovate, and once it's finished, market the property, then on-sell.
6. With positive cash flow properties buy in areas with population over 6000 and where it's not profitable for developers to build new housing stock.
7. The towns must have a strong industry.
8. Get a good understanding of the town and the surroundings of the property to assess whether tenants will want to live there.
9. Always get a valuation, a building inspection, a pest inspection and some form of rental proof; put these into options or contracts as conditions.
10. Have a proactive settlement solicitor who specialises in property.

Chapter 11

Believing in property

'To succeed you have to be interested in property. We both have an underlying belief that property will be a winner.'
— **Kay and Dave Harrison,**
Auckland, NZ

I live with my husband Dave and our two daughters who are three and five years old in Silverdale, a suburb on the Hibiscus Coast, north of Auckland. Dave works as a draftsperson and earns a salary of around $50k. I am a full time mum.

Our position when we began our recent foray into property investing was that we had two freehold houses. One was a three bedroom property in Petone, a suburb of Wellington, worth $250k (and which had been Dave's home when he lived in Wellington), and a three bedroom house in Takapu Street in Henderson, West Auckland, which was our family home for many years until we moved recently to Silverdale. This was valued at $320k. Dave had bought both properties before we were married.

Way down south

Dave had been saying for some time that he wanted to buy another rental property. We went to see our accountant and he told us how we could do a positive cash flow investment. He told us Invercargill, at the bottom of the South Island, was a good place to invest. We were going to Dunedin in January 2003 so we looked around there. I couldn't believe how cheap the houses were. We looked at one in particular and Dave suggested we go home and think about it but I said, 'No, I don't want to leave here before we buy one.'

So we purchased a two storey house in Caversham in three flats: two one-bedrooms and one two-bedroom. We got it for $102k and rent it for $295 per week. The two bedroom place is rented for $105 per week, and the one bedrooms are rented for $95. Maintenance is quite a high cost on this property and this could become a problem. We have spent $13k repainting the outside and have purchased a new fridge for $500. Its most recent valuation in September 2004 was $200k.

Getting the right knowledge and tools

Our accountant also told us about Richmastery and the upcoming three day Richmastery Property Academy in May 2003. We thought it was a lot of money but suddenly Dave said, 'Let's just do it.' After attending the Richmastery Profit from Property seminar, we realised how little money it was in relation to how many thousands of dollars we could save investing in property with the right knowledge and tools. After attending the academy we signed up for the 12 month Richmastery Personal Property Mentoring Programme. Although the cost hurt, we felt we wanted to learn as much as we could.

We found the Richmastery Property Academy fabulous. I came home from the three day course and basically hit the ground running. I poured myself into looking at the weekly property newspapers and phoning agents looking at houses, trying to put offers in. Our goal was to buy cash flow positive properties. In our first year after attending the academy we bought a total of four properties (all positive cash flow before tax).

At the academy we had the opportunity to buy a two bedroom, 42 square metre apartment that was at the time advertised on the Richmastery Property Deals website. We purchased this using a deposit bond: we put down a minimal deposit and it settled in late 2004. It is at the Cityzone building in Symonds Street in central Auckland. We purchased it for $186k and it is now worth over $216k. The estimated rental for the fully furnished apartment when we purchased it was $400–500, but rents in Auckland apartments have dropped due to an oversupply and it took us two months to rent it. Now we are getting only $300 per week.

After the academy, I spent three weeks reading the property section of the paper, focusing on West Auckland, the area we were living in. I found it hard

Where we started. Our original home in West Auckland formed part of our investment equity.

work phoning agents and working out the figures. We also purchased the Richmastery analysis software and this made it easier to crunch the numbers.

Dual income properties

The Richmastery team suggested we look at dual income properties, and with this in mind we found a three bedroom house on a great subdividable section with a self contained two bedroom sleep-out unit on it in Nikau Street, New Lynn, a suburb of Auckland 15 minutes from the city. The vendors were asking $215k; we got it for $206k. It was just before the boom and we knew it was a good deal so we bought it.

We got a long settlement (of eight weeks) and it settled in late July 2003. Dave is a draftsperson so he can do the plans and the permitting on any properties we buy. We spent about $10k making the sleep-out a self contained studio flat, which we then made legal with the council permit. We got a builder to do the work who was ideal for what we wanted. We didn't want to get too carried away because if we ever subdivide we don't want to have overcapitalized, as we would bowl the minor dwelling. We didn't do any work to the main house; it was clean and tidy and has loads of potential down the track.

We had no problem renting both the house and the flat for a total of $460 per week. Six months on, in January 2004, the property was revalued at $325k. As you can imagine I was pretty stoked.

After this I started looking on the internet. We were still very green. I would see these places and Dave would be pushing me to get them 20% below.

119

But it seemed impossible to buy under value at that time as the market was booming. Dave wasn't keen to buy for market value but I argued that the properties would go up 20% in two months, such was the extent of the boom – and they did!

There was one in Avondale that we didn't get because Dave was being conservative. He is like this because he experienced the situation in the 1980s when interest rates rocketed up to the 20% range. He kept expecting the market to top out.

Unappealing but lucrative

The next deal I found was through the Richmastery Property Deals website. It was a two bedroom cross lease flat in Hamilton. We bought this sight unseen. We had a hassle with the tenants moving out, but it has proved to be one of our best rentals, which is interesting because when we looked at what we had just bought we thought it wasn't very appealing. It was brick and tile, with no landscaping and just a carport. But, as we've learnt through Richmastery, it's the figures that matter. We paid $84k for it; it valued up to $106k and we get $175 per week for it, with a property manager looking after it.

It was strange buying a place sight unseen. It made Dave a bit nervous but at the end of the day I would do it again.

A hard lesson

Our next purchase was also through the Richmastery Property Deals website. This one was in the town of Bulls, in the lower North Island about an hour and a half north of Wellington. We knew that with the air force moving all their operations down to nearby Ohakea air base in a few years this might be a good place to buy. We purchased the deal 18% below valuation. The purchase price was $64k; it was valued at $76k and we rented it for $150.

We have had a lot of problems with this place. The property had been plonked on the section and there were no paths and no carport of any description. We signed up with a property manager but after two months the place was still empty. We finally found another property manager and after she had been to check it out she said, 'Have you seen this place? There are no paths and the grounds are overgrown.' We wondered what our first property manager was doing. I asked the new one if she could organise the

construction of paths and a carport and to tell prospective tenants that this was happening. This cost us $8000. But it was definitely worth doing so we didn't regret it.

Richmastery now provides a three day due diligence period on their property deals so customers can do all the necessary due diligence on out of town purchases.

We now know the Bulls property will be alright and are glad that we haven't lost a whole heap of money.

Strategies and structure

Dave feels he needs to keep his hands on the hand brake because I want to move at such a fast pace. We make a good team: I work out the numbers and I have to convince him that the numbers are going to stack up. He also has the know how to check out the technical side of a property, including land information memorandum (LIM) reports and the like (which he believes don't tell you anything you can't find out from some phone calls to council).

We find out what services are there, how big the section is, if we can add a sleep-out etc. We just go to the council and get a 'property bag' file on the house. This gives you everything to do with the house.

> We wouldn't go near a place where you couldn't place a second dwelling. If they have a second dwelling but it is illegal we've discovered you can sometimes get the vendor to bring the price down.

Dave also establishes how we could add value: he finds out whether we can do other things such as subdivide. We are interested in subdivisions and commercial ventures but that's the next step.

> We have set up a structure for our investing. We have an LAQC company plus a family trust to protect our assets. We've found it's important to use accountants and lawyers who specialise in property investment. It's nice to have an accountant that can advise us and know what they are doing; that is peace of mind to us.
>
> Once you've decided the route you want to go down next you need a team around you that agrees with that course of action. I believe good property managers are very important. If someone lets us down we ditch them, and when we find someone good we look after them.

We have found many real estate agents are not happy with offers 20% below but the market was on the increase. It's worth shopping around to fine good agents. I found it was sheer hard work making offers. Some agents wouldn't accept faxed offers. That was the time when there were people buying everything and anything as it was a boom. Now you have might have a better response. During the boom real estate agents wouldn't call me back; now they are calling me!

The tables turned

After we bought Nikau Street in New Lynn we stopped telling people about our investments because we got very mixed reactions. A lot of people don't understand what we're doing. We've been selective in the friends we tell and those that we do are very positive and supportive. Now we don't go telling people but if they ask we are happy to share all the information we know.

We've found through property investing and the education we've done that we have had huge personal growth and our general outlook in life is a lot more positive. Dave found the audio tape 'The Power of Positive Thinking' by Norman Vincent Peale has been brilliant.

Dave is still cautious, but less so since doing the Richmastery education. In particular the Richmastery Personal Property Mentoring Programme has given him the confidence to do the figures and rely on those.

Maintenance has had a big effect on the numbers but we have found that our tax refund has helped to balance this out. Our aim is for Dave to get some income tax back as he is in the middle income bracket. The reduction has so far been considerable and next year it's likely he will get it all back. It's been an awesome learning curve, and it was amazing how much our tax bill has reduced. It's stunning really to think how little we knew.

> To succeed you have to be interested in property. We aim for financial freedom. We both have an underlying belief that property will be a winner. We've definitely turned the tables, a couple of years ago we had money to burn but few investments and now we are frugal with money but we know we are creating a future for ourselves.

Some people just blow their money more from their spending habits than anything else. We're happy with the debt we've got as it's good debt. Our total portfolio value is now $1.5 million, with our total mortgages at $480k, which means we have total equity of more than $1 million and three out of four of our properties are cash flow positive.

TOP TEN TIPS

1. Do the Richmastery education; we couldn't fault it.
2. Read books, listen to tapes — you can't put a value on education. If you get only one tip from books or DVDs it's worth the money.
3. We really have seen the value in the Richmastery Personal Property Mentoring Programme; it was hugely valuable having experts around.
4. Find a good mortgage broker who can spread loans around over more than one bank.
5. Don't listen to friends and family unless they're encouraging you.
6. Associate with like minded people.
7. Don't be scared to just go and do it.
8. Take small steps — you know the saying 'one bite of the elephant at a time'.
9. It's safer to have four or five properties than one. If one doesn't rent the others will take the slack.
10. Get a good team of professionals around you; a good accountant and a good lawyer are especially important.

Chapter 12

Subdivide and conquer

'*Virtually every good deal I've done has been through networking through someone like Richmastery...*'
— **Paul Coventry,** Gold Coast, AUS

I'm 50 years old and I live with my 16-year-old son on the Gold Coast at Main Beach about 40 minutes' drive south of Brisbane. I was born in Sydney and have lived on the north coast of New South Wales for 25 years.

Before moving to the Gold Coast I was a cattle farmer in a place called Casino for eight years. I farmed a 700 acre cattle farm, in the middle of nowhere. I had originally bought the farm to subdivide it but the market collapsed and I couldn't do it. My best option was to farm the land, so I became a cattle farmer. I had no knowledge of cattle farming – it was definitely a tough challenge for a city boy. Luckily, I could ride a horse when I arrived on the farm.

After eight years I decided to move to Byron Bay, and went into business there, starting up a New Age bookshop. This was a lot of hard work for little return so I sold the business. In the end the way I made my money in Byron Bay was through real estate. When I first moved there in 1997 I purchased a five acre block of land seven minutes' drive out of Byron for $200k.

I then moved my farm house (an old Queenslander) from Casino north and put it on my land. The house was moved by truck and the drive is about one and a half hours. I later realised it was a big mistake to move the house off the farm as it made the farm more difficult to sell. We sold the farm eventually for $180k but it would have fetched more with the house still on it. To move the house cost me $20k and I was lucky to be able to do it as it

My relocated Queenslander home in Byron Bay during renovations.

was the last block of land in Byron that you could move a relocatable house onto due to council regulations. Once it was there, I did the house up – in total I spent $200k on it, getting contractors in to do the renovations.

Getting into the game

From 1996 to 2000 I wasn't working apart from trading the stock market as I was a single dad and I didn't work in my book business. However, I found I didn't have enough capital to really get ahead trading shares. I decided that the leverage was better in real estate as I had made so much money out of my house, tax free, just sitting there. I thought that's a whole lot easier than sitting at the computer and riding the ups and downs of the stock market. So in 2002 I sold my home in Byron for $830k as I decided I wanted to get my money out and aggressively get into real estate.

> The biggest learning experience that I have had is the realisation that I should have borrowed against my home when I'd first done it up in 1997 and invested in real estate then, before the boom.

I had read numerous books, including *Rich Dad, Poor Dad* and Jan Somers, so I understood the principles of real estate investment. But when I sold my house and I knew I was going to have a large amount of cash to invest in property I felt I needed to improve my knowledge of how to do it.

I saw an ad for the Richmastery courses and attended a four hour Richmastery Profit from Property evening seminar in October 2002. That

Byron Bay home after renovations. Cash from the sale of this home, plus a confidence booster from Richmastery courses gave me what I need to move ahead.

night I signed up to do the three day Richmastery Property Academy in December 2002.

I found the academy tiring because I'm not so young any more and it was long hours (40 hours over three days) but it was great!

 The main things I got out of it were: how to leverage yourself to the max; how to select properties; and how to get added value out of a property quickly – rather than just sitting on a house and waiting for the value to go up.

Since then I've been focusing on deals where you don't rely on the long term capital gain but rather get a big value-add in the short term, which is what they teach at the Richmastery Profit from Property seminar and the Richmastery Property Academy. However, with these courses the focus is mainly on residential property investment.

Going for bigger deals

I've taken it the next step and gone for bigger deals – the likes of land subdivision and development sites. I have gotten a lot of support and knowledge on how to do this by joining the 12 month Richmastery Personal Property Mentoring Programme.

I began the Richmastery Personal Property Mentoring Programme on the Gold Coast straight after I completed the academy and did it for the following 12 months. I found it extremely useful to be around others who were interested in going forward. There are few people that become active with their investing after completing the academy and those who are prepared to go to mentoring generally are investing. So it's a good way to create a network; I've still got some great friends and allies from my mentoring programme who I can ring up for a chat about stuff. I get on with my mentor very well and we stay in touch even though I've finished the mentoring programme. I've learnt a lot from him about development projects and he has put me on to some great deals.

Betting on Casino

I began with $800k in cash from the sale of my house in Byron Bay. I've never used the whole lot. It cost me $450k to swing my first deal in Casino, the same town where I'd been a cattle farmer. I purchased a block of 16 units and strata titled them. Casino is a town that revolves around the cattle industry; it was in a slump when I lived there and when I bought the flats.

But now the town has seen a ripple effect from the coastal property price rises and there has been an influx of people moving there from the city, selling up their homes to buy a cheaper but better home while still having some money for retirement. It's also only about 40 minutes' drive to really nice coastal beaches and there are plenty of jobs to be had there. There's a van park there that has become a favourite stop for the grey nomad phenomenon – retirees who rent their homes and travel around in camper vans – so they are creating it as a centre for these travellers. There's also a large catering group that puts food into retirement homes based there. The population is about 15,000.

I chose Casino because a guy I'd known out there had just become an agent with LJ Hooker. He'd offered me a deal of eight units a year earlier and had told me about how you could strata title units that were under a single title and the opportunity that existed with these deals.

At that time I didn't have the confidence to do it. But then an opportunity to purchase a 1970s' block of 16 two-bedroom units came up. By this time I not only had the money from the sale of my house in Byron but my confidence had also been boosted by doing the Richmastery education and so I went for it.

I purchased them for $900k but my total cost to strata them plus costs and stamp duty meant all up they cost me $950k. I started the strata process as soon as I took possession of them, and it took eight months to complete. They are modest units and, yes, I'm now a slum landlord!

When I took them over they were rented at $95 per week each. I immediately handed them over to a property manager and haven't worried about them since. They were under-rented so without doing any work to them they are now rented for $125 per week and I pay 5% of this to the property manager.

> The rent had been frozen at the flats for 10 years so all the tenants stayed even with the rent increase. There's a lack of rentable properties in Casino, which is another reason why I chose it. Once I had strata titled each of the units they valued up to $95k each (I had paid $60k for each of them). If I sold the best ones now they'd go for $110k. My latest valuation is that they are worth between $95k and $110k.

Some hard lessons

I then created a line of credit against the new equity that had been created from the revaluation of the Casino flats – and I was ready to move on to my next deal. What I didn't realise was that I was about to learn some hard lessons.

Next I put down an expression of interest on four units off the plan at Tweed Heads, on the southern Gold Coast, an hour's drive south of Brisbane. I paid $210k for each for them but soon after their market valuation came up to $280k. Then, when the developer realised how much they were worth, he rescinded all the contracts. I thought this must be illegal. I had put down an expression of interest, signed contracts and paid a deposit bond.

I looked into litigation against the developer but this would have cost me $100k. He did the same thing to everyone who had signed up to buy them. I realised I had to walk away.

Next I put five expressions of interest on five 800 square metre blocks of land in Coomera, a big development area between Brisbane and the Gold

Coast. I put down $2500 in a deposit bond on each one. They were $177k each. My plan was to on-sell them for over $200k and walk away with a profit of $200k. But this didn't happen. Once again the developer rescinded on three of the five contracts. I was lucky that a friend of mine who is a developer stepped in and I was able to keep two of the blocks. I had put down $2500 on each one and was able to on-sell these, making a clear $10k over and above the cost of all the deposits, which was lucky as I could have lost money. The turn around time to on-sell the two blocks and thus get my money back was six months. I decided once again that litigation was not worth it.

> So I found out the hard way that with expressions of interest, they are just that. I think you are better off with a put and call option, and as a purchaser you can get out of them; you just lose your deposit.

These two experiences were a real knock but I had to pick myself up and keep going.

Green acres

My next purchase was a five acre subdividable block of land with a three bedroom house on in. It was situated in Oxenford, which is near Coomera, 30 minutes south of Brisbane just off the main arterial route. It's a rural property with high density residential pushing out into it. I purchased it for $650k including stamp duty.

I found this deal through a mate who is a big developer. The owner was asking $625k and was living in the house on the property. I put down a $10k deposit and negotiated a delayed settlement of four months with the owner on the understanding that he could stay in the house until settlement.

During this time I started the development application (DA) process for the subdivision. This process has had many problems attached to it and has definitely required persistence.

Initially my town planner had thought we could build nine duplexes on the property and we had a pre-lodgment meeting with the council and they approved this plan in theory. But six months later the council people had turned over and this plan got completely knocked back on issues such as the steepness of the land, the bushfire plan and the density plan. So we lost six months. My town planner called me and said that the council had refused the DA; I thought they weren't going to let me do anything at all.

However, I persevered and now have approval in principle on our tenth lot plan, which is for eight blocks with two potential duplexes. So far it has cost us $77k just for the DA to date. It cost me less to get a DA for an 84 block subdivision on flat land. I am happy with this plan because two of the smaller blocks at the front are perfect for building duplexes on and I hope to do these developments myself and hold onto them as rentals.

So after all this time, money and trouble it's worked out well and I will soon have approval to subdivide this land into eight blocks. The property will be worth $2 million once it is subdivided.

I plan to sell six of the blocks (which are 700 to 900 square metres) for about $200k each, plus the existing house on a 3000 square metre site for $400k. The 8000 square metre block at the back should go for around $400k too.

Total costs for the subdivision and DA including interest should run to about $400k and that plus $650k I paid for the land means my total costs will be close to $1.1 million and the total value of the land is $2.1 million. I should have the DA out within two months and then the land construction should be finished three months after that.

I will then sell some of the blocks and, because the blocks are owned by a development company in a trust, I can build the two duplex houses with the profit from the sale of these and won't need to pay tax because, theoretically, I won't have made a capital gain.

The duplexes will cost about $90k per side to build and they will rent for about $250 per week. This is net, so I could end up with $1000 per week net across the four places with no debt against them. Thus my profit will stay there as a cash flow and I will have the ability to borrow against it.

In total the deal has cost me $300k out of my pocket to do it and I borrowed $400k, so the return on my investment will be almost 300% in two years.

On the waterfront

My latest deal was done through Richmastery Australia's Property Deals website. I purchased three expressions of interest in 800 square metre blocks on the waterfront in Cairns. I got these for slightly different prices, one for $210k, one for $230k and another for $270k.

They are currently valued in the high $300k to low $400k. I had to pay a finder's fee to Richmastery and I put down $1500 per block. I found out about them when I was doing the Richmastery Personal Property Mentoring Programme and I was offered them by my Richmastery mentor.

> I plan to sell one block to cover the cost of the land on the other two and then raise finance to build two up-market houses on the other blocks. For each of the buildings I expect to spend $400k and believe I will end up with $500k equity in each of the two blocks I hold on to.

Others in my mentoring programme bought them as well.

I really recommend the Richmastery Personal Property Mentoring Programme. It keeps your energy going through the tough times and helps you keep coming up with great ideas. Virtually every good deal I've done has been by networking through Richmastery or local real estate agents.

Jump up the food chain

You need a really good team around you. Your lawyer must be willing to aggressively look after your position. I use a female legal team: Sandra Bostock and Helen Frazer of Bostock and Frazer Law based in Marine Parade in Southport on the Gold Coast. I went through a few lawyers before I found them and I am very impressed with the job they do for me. My accountant, Stewart Webley's firm UPA, is located on the same floor as my lawyers, which is fantastic as it's very easy for them to communicate with each other. They cost an arm and a leg but you can't do without expertise in this area. You also need good finance people behind you.

I am continuing to look for land subdivision potentials in south-east Queensland. I believe there are still a lot of opportunities to be had from the Sunshine Coast to the Gold Coast as this region has an almost guaranteed steady growth. Prices have dropped back a little since the boom but due to the demographic forces they will keep driving forward for the next 20 years.

> My advice is jump up the food chain – don't get stuck on the ground with everyone else. The best way to do this and to get the good investments is to network so you find out about the best deals before they hit the market.

After my current deals are completed I will have increased my original $800k into a projected equity of $3 million in just two years.

TOP TEN TIPS

1. Develop your networking skills.
2. Learn how to negotiate.
3. Learn how to write contracts (I believe this is the key to doing development deals safely and minimising risk). Find an experienced mentor to teach you how to write really favourable terms such as delayed settlement, non-refundable deposits to hold properties until DA is approved, and extended due diligence periods.
4. Choose a good lawyer. Don't be afraid to fire one that's not performing or is not willing to aggressively defend your position.
5. Don't do anything major without consulting your lawyer but, finally, make your own decision. To be successful your risk profile must be higher than your lawyer's.
6. Get educated.
7. Read books — Robert Kiyosaki is great.
8. Realise that there are very few people you can genuinely trust.
9. Be discriminating about who you choose as business partners.
10. Be persistent — you have to keep going, the next deal is there, you just keep going until you get it.

Chapter 13

Realising visions

'Without action all visions are only a dream.'
— **Richard Potter,** Auckland, NZ

The seed of property investment was first planted in my head after I had returned from travelling for four years overseas in 1988. During that time I met a motor mechanic in Mission Bay who had 65 houses. He was only 35 years old, and he had recycled his equity by buying smart and at the time still hadn't paid any debt off.

I ended up travelling back overseas because of the share crash in 1987. Jobs were hard to come by. Rather than stay in New Zealand and learn from this guru I took off overseas to the Caribbean where I stayed for the next 12 years. Hindsight is a wonderful thing!

Negatively geared start

I bought my first home in Nelson in 1992. It was a five bedroom house that I purchased for $125k. At the time it stretched me financially, and I returned to the Caribbean to reduce the debt. I finally returned to New Zealand on my yacht at the end of 1999, in time for the America's Cup and the new millennium.

It wasn't until the end of 2000 that I started investing in more property, using the equity out of my Nelson home. By this time the house was worth $150k and I had $125k worth of equity in it. Now I have a property portfolio worth $2.5 million, with a net worth of $1 million. I achieved all of this in four years.

Briefly, I had six properties before attending the three day Richmastery Property Academy in October 2003. I had made a few mistakes. For example, I had bought all negatively geared property, four of which were bought off the plans and then built, of which two were apartments that were under 50 square metres – another mistake. Most banks at the time wouldn't lend over 50% for these 'shoe boxes'. Times are changing rapidly and you are able to get up to 75% lending on them now with some banks, such as Westpac.

Through doing the academy I soon realised that I needed some positively geared properties to balance my portfolio and to enable myself to be able to afford to keep investing. The way my portfolio was, if I lost my job my properties were like a pack of cards.

On the positive trail

I have recently purchased nine positive cash flow properties. I have also taken up the Richmastery Personal Property Mentoring group so that I can learn how to structure my portfolio properly and maximise my deposit recycle time.

I believe that you shouldn't sell a house during the 'boom' of the housing cycle; just buy another one. The increase in house prices will allow you to recycle your equity a lot quicker. Investors will have to buy smart or create the extra equity to stay in the game once the boom is over.

> When I was growing up my parents had many houses, which they renovated and sold on for a profit. Today they only have one property. Yes, it is a five bedroom house, but if they had been able to keep each of those houses, their portfolio would today be worth many millions.

After sailing back from the Caribbean in 1999, I was living on my boat in the Gulf Harbour, Auckland marina until I got a job as a yacht broker. After four months, I moved into the city and got a job with a publishing company selling advertising. Three months later, in September 2000, I bought my next investment property on Waiheke Island in Auckland's Hauraki Gulf with the deposit from the equity from my property in Nelson. To me it seemed a little island close to a big metropolis, like Martha's Vineyard or the Channel Islands, so I could see its potential. I bought a three bedroom, one bathroom home,

One of my Tokoroa properties. I bought nine positive cash flow properties there in five months in 2005.

on the northern side of the island, which was only 10 years old. I bought the place for $282k; now in 2004 it is worth $585k. I rented it out for $285 per week as I couldn't afford to live over there myself.

Queensland gateway

I bought a Japanese import car with no band expander on the radio, so was listening to Leighton Smith on Newstalk ZB talking to property developers: Gateway to Queensland. I went and saw them in their Quay Street office. At the time there were a lot of people rubbishing what was happening over in Queensland, mainly due to the agents who were selling through seminars. Gateway to Queensland had been operating in Auckland for the previous six years, so I had faith in them. They held my hand through the construction of a 220 square metre, four bedroom, two bathroom brick and tile home on a 780 square metre section in Mooloolabar, on the Sunshine Coast. It is next to the Sunshine Coast University and is only one hour's drive north of Brisbane. I purchased it in August/September 2001 for $NZ300k and paid a deposit of $80k from the equity in the Waiheke house. This Mooloolabar property is now valued at $500k and has a five year rental guarantee of $250 per week.

Gateway to Queensland was also doing a development at Gulf Harbour, on Auckland's Whangaparaoa Peninsula. I signed up to purchase, off the plans, a three bedroom, three bathroom townhouse with a single garage for $285k. It was completed in July 2003. They paid all the interest while it was being built, on the draw down loan. It is now valued at $340 and has a $385 per week guaranteed rental for five years. I have had a good experience with Gateway to Queensland.

In October 2003 I bought a one bedroom apartment in Auckland's CBD for $275k. The real estate agent told me I'd get $400 per week for it; I ended up getting only $290 a week. Lesson learnt – real estate agents exaggerate. Because it was only 44 square metres the bank lent me only 50% finance. That was before I had done the Richmastery education and now I know that if I'd done my research I wouldn't have gone ahead with the purchase.

I bought a second apartment through listening to Newstalk ZB again: a two bedroom, 40 square metre apartment for $190k, now valued at $240k and not completed until 2006.

Balancing portfolio with cash flow properties

I learnt a lot through taking action. Through every action is a reaction, and without action all visions are only a dream. I did learn, though, that action without planning can become rather hectic to say the least.

Now it's become a game. It's just money and assets. As long as you have your health, family and friends that's all that matters. For me if all fails I have my yacht paid for, so I could always take off for another shore if need be.

I decided to attend the three day Richmastery Property Academy and the main thing I learnt was about balancing my portfolio. Mine was a deck of cards. If I lost my job, I'd lose everything. I only had had one rule when I started and that was you only need 20% deposit. I then had just been going again and again. One word that stood out during the academy was ACTION. Doing the academy in October 2003 made me realise I needed cash flow properties. In January 2004 I became a Club Richmastery member and bought my first cash flow property through their website, www.richmastery.com.

Structure and team

After the academy I went to Gilligan Rowe and Associates and was advised on a correct structure. I then set up LAQCs. I kept my own accountant because he is great: humble, efficient and not exorbitant. The firm he is with, Davidson and Associates, also deals with overseas property deals, so it is convenient when owning property in Australia.

I am still getting the rest of my team together. One of the hardest people to find has been a good mortgage broker. I have had some fun with one broker who lent me twice the amount I needed. To fix that problem I just bought another house!

I had one tenant leave, owing me $6000. I soon realised I needed to start monitoring the rents. I was naive, and I thought if people owed you money they would pay it. I was wrong! Now I use property mangers to leverage my time, so that I can look for the next deal. I have had some trouble with property managers. It took three months to rent out one of my apartments. Some property management companies are useless at finding you tenants, but are great at managing.

I use one insurance broker for all my properties. He's one of the best in my team. I make sure that all my properties have the same renewal date, hence bringing a bit of leverage to the negotiating table.

Nine in Tokoroa

In the first five months of 2004 I bought nine positive cash flow properties in Tokoroa, a small forestry town in the central North Island. They were all around $75k and all positively geared, bringing in rents of between $160 and $180 per week. I haven't had to do any work on them. I have had to go to the Tenancy Tribunal over a few problems in a block of four flats purchased there. One of my tenants took all the door knobs, curtains and even the fuses out of the electrical box.

It has been a good lesson. Finding a good property manger is a must. A good lesson learnt is to always buy in a good part of town, and don't buy houses where tenants are beneficiaries. Another lesson is: don't buy a block of flats in a street with other flats in it. Buy where there's only one block of flats in the whole street.

Today, I am still in a negatively geared situation so still need an income. Last year I left my job as they increased my targets by 40%, decreased my commission by 25% and took 45 clients off me with forward bookings. Hence if I sold the same as the year before I would have earnt less than half as much as the year before. This seems to be the case for a lot of big corporations.

A passion for property

I then went to work selling advertising for the Auckland branch of *Homesell*, a national newspaper specialising in private sales of residential housing. Their packages included newspaper advertising for eight weeks, eight weeks on the website, a for sale sign for the street, an open home sign, a guest registry and coloured, brochures – all for the small sum of $700. I had the central and west areas of Auckland. It was great as I was out and about seeing properties every day. The website is www.homesell.co.nz (available through www.richmastery.com).

After four months I was asked to work for *Kiwi Property Investor* magazine where I am now working full time. Being the largest business selling magazine in the country I jumped at the chance. Not only does the magazine have such great information on house sales and rental figures, but also has a wealth of informative articles on asset planning, accounting, insurance, valuations, property management and feature interviews with the likes of Bob Jones and Tony Alexander. Since I have been there we have started a new section on investment properties for sale, which include all properties that are: subdividable, have minor dwelling unit potential, off the plan developments, B&Bs and other accommodation properties, high rental yields, retail, commercial, marinas, areas of high capital growth and the like. I have a passion for property and what better place to be working, where every day I am learning.

My partner and I have now moved into my home on Waiheke Island, a 35 minute ferry ride from downtown Auckland. Every night we go home to the beach. We both commute daily from the island to work but if we need to stay in the city overnight we use my yacht as our inner city apartment.

I have read many books; some I would recommend are: *0 to 130 properties in 3.5 years, $1,000,000 in Property in One Year* by Steve McKnight, *Life Deals the Cards, You Play the Hand* by Boyd Gunn, *Think Rich Grow Rich* by Napoleon Hill, *The Cash Flow Quadrant* by Robert Kiyosaki, *The One Minute Millionaire* by Mark Victor Hansen, and *Real Estate Riches* by Dolf De Roos.

TOP TEN TIPS

1. Take action.
2. Balance your portfolio.
3. Get the right structure legally.
4. Get your filing system right from the beginning.
5. Get leverage, e.g. with my insurance broker I get a better deal as he handles the insurances on all my properties, which all have the same renewal date.
6. Make sure you don't have more than 20% equity in a property. If you do it is only rotting.
7. Never take 'no' for an answer; ask another person. There are many different ways to finance a deal.
8. Ask questions, even dumb questions. It may be a dumb question to them but the professionals won't tell you unless you ask.
9. Always buy in a good area even if it's in a small town.
10. Go to as many seminars and read as many books as you can, and work on improving your weak points (mine is filing).

Chapter 14

Freedom in three years

"I left the Academy with a confidence and a self belief that this was doable..."
— **Kim Metcalf,** Perth, AUS

I am 39 years old and I live in Perth with my wife and our three children who are all under five years old.

I went along to a Richmastery Profit from Property seminar in Perth in October 2002. I had already been studying property for more than five years and owned an investment property in addition to my family home. I had read a couple of Jan Somers books, had bought and used her software and been to several seminars, and generally thought I knew what I was doing. However, the Richmastery Profit from Property seminar immediately showed me that my strategies were not going to make me financially independent in the next 20 years.

The seminar presenters were impressive; they came across as down to earth, average believable guys like myself who had done it. They weren't trying to sell me something.

They had a number of new ideas that I hadn't come across before, like positive cash flow and the importance of using the market value of a property and previously I had only known about negative gearing so these new ideas just gelled with me.

Making my investments work

I earn a six-figure income working in telecommunications and I am a qualified engineer. I had over $200k equity in my family home but this was locked up with the investment property I already had. To access the equity I had to sell the investment property; without selling it I had only about $50k equity. I believed that, with a bit of help from people who knew how, I could make these work for me. I had decided to take action and made the big decision to attend the three-day Richmastery Property Academy in December 2002 on the Gold Coast at the Royal Pines in Surfers Paradise.

During the academy I came to understand in detail about positive cash flow and recycling equity and left the course feeling I had the confidence to go and apply these strategies in the market.

In the first three months following the Richmastery Property Academy I set myself some investing rules. My objective in starting to invest is basically to make myself financially independent and get myself into a position where I can retire from being an employee within three years.

> I'm a person who's fairly motivated and disciplined anyway, but I left the Richmastery Property Academy with a confidence and a self belief that this was doable, and a determination to use the resources available to me to address all the obstacles that I would come up against.

I felt that people who were less bright than me could do it. Even though I didn't know everything, if I was prepared to take action and learn from people who had done it then I could achieve my goals.

I bought the Richmastery Property Analysis software and joined a special 12 month Richmastery Personal Property Mentoring Programme in Sydney and Melbourne, as I go there frequently for work and so was able to attend every couple of months.

In the first three months I called my mentor three or four times a week. These days I might call him every two or three months as I know more and only need to get advice when I do new things, like commercial deals or when I was looking at buying a friend's property.

I was particularly impressed by the 'Cash Flow' game that we played at the Richmastery Property Academy, and in the months after I left the academy I sold my second car, paid off and cancelled several store and credit cards and sold my negatively geared off-the-plan 'investment' apartment for $15k less than what I paid for it 18 months earlier. These actions were painful but necessary to restructure my financial position to the point where I could borrow for new properties.

At the same time I sought advice on the most appropriate legal/tax structure for my new endeavours and put it in place. I learnt that it's not how much you earn but how you manage your income minus expenses that is important. So I basically took my financial position and went to my mortgage broker and he agreed I needed to take the above action.

Fourteen income streams

During the second half of 2003 and first half of 2004 I purchased 14 income streams at a cost of $1.2 million, all with borrowed funds. They are all in regional areas, positive cash flow before tax and bought under market value. Purchasing in this manner were the rules I had set for myself after the Richmastery Property Academy.

My first purchase settled in 18 August 2003. It is a block of four three-bedroom houses in north-west Western Australia in a town called South Hedland. This is the major port for all the mining in the north-west of Australia, and has a population of 13,000. I found the houses for sale in the Perth newspaper. They were on strata titles on a 2000 square metre block. This arrangement is called group housing or villa houses. They were built in 1999; they are new, transportable houses and the builder has built a concrete plinth in there and then put everything in.

I found it very difficult to buy property at 20% below valuation as suggested at the Richmastery Property Academy because the market was quite hot. They were asking $399k. I had the whole property valued at $455k and negotiated a sale price of $388k. The vendor, a builder who wanted to sell up and leave town, was motivated. So I knew it was a good deal.

I had the property revalued at $515k eight months after settlement, so I was able to recycle my deposit. I have been able to increase the rents from $200 per unit per week to between $250 and $270 per week (i.e. $1000 plus per week for the block) and have no vacancy problems. The block is now worth $575k. I have refinanced it for more than what I originally bought it for and used that for deposits for later purchases.

This property is the jewel in my crown because it's a high cash flow property but has also given me high capital growth as well.

In February 2004 I bought two two-bedroom home units in another north-west Western Australia town called Derby. It is a fishing centre and a service town for the surrounding areas. They were both on the market at the same time for $115k from the same agent but from different vendors. I found them on the website realestate.com.au.

I put offers in for $99k for both at the same time so played each vendor off with the other. One vendor negotiated down to $102k. I advised the real estate agent if I could get the other one for the same price I would purchase both. I purchased these units for $102k each. I have had one repainted and now believe I can refinance them to $120k each. This is because they are two of eight in the same complex and recently another one in the same complex sold for $120k. When I do this I will have recycled my equity within six months of settlement.

One was vacant and one was rented for $250 per week when I purchased them. I now have them both rented for $280 per week with new tenants, one of whom works for the power utility company that has signed up for a long lease. These are good cash flow properties and the possible announcement of a major offshore gas project off the coast of Derby this year will be great news for real estate values in the area.

Multiple income properties

I then purchased two more positive cash flow houses through the Richmastery Property Deals website.

One was in regional Queensland for $56k, which settled in March 2004, and one in Northern Territory, at Katherine (which is the third largest town in the NT with a population of 5000) for $84,250.

I bought these properties sight unseen. I looked at the information provided in the Richmastery Property Deals due diligence kit, sourced building and pest reports and decided that the deals were good enough in terms of cash flow to go ahead.

I have taken the opportunity of the tenant leaving the Queensland property to do a cosmetic renovation (painting inside and out, putting in new

House in Katherine, NT, bought sight unseen from the Richmastery website. The figures stacked up.

vinyl floor coverings, new aluminium windows and some minor repairs) at a cost of $8000 and I will refinance it to around $80k within six months of settlement. The new tenants are lined up for 12 months at $180 per week (the previous tenant was paying $140).

The one in Katherine rents for $200 per week. I have only needed to do minor maintenance on this property.

I have found that managing a block of units is no more time consuming than managing a single house and decided that I would focus on multiple income properties. I am happy to take longer to find a block of four or six units that I can do something with so it is more efficient for me than trying to buy four or five properties in that same time.

In June 2004 I settled on a block of six two-bedroom units on a single title in Gladstone in North Queensland, which I bought through the Richmastery Property Deals website for $430k.

I am renovating these units and have converted them to strata title to significantly increase the rents and the market value. The renovation and strata titling will cost me $100k and they will be worth between $700k and $800k conservatively once they are finished.

This deal was important for my portfolio because my first batch of properties had effectively consumed the equity I started with in my family home and to keep the momentum going it's important to create equity faster

Block of six two bedroom units in Gladstone, North Queensland, before renovation. I find multiple income properties are no more time consuming than single houses.

than normal market movement by purchasing under market value or by adding value through renovation, subdivision and the like. This project should take less than six months to generate significant equity, which will allow me to refinance and start the process again.

Sticking to simple strategies

I am deliberately sticking to these simple strategies that I have built up good experience with (positive cash flow, recycle deposit within 12 months). I believe the anticipated success of this current project will launch me into a position where the critical mass of my portfolio will start to make it easier to accelerate the growth of my properties towards my goal of $5 million market value in three to five years from the date I attended the Richmastery Property Academy.

Stop Press! I next secured a block of eight units in Darwin for $700k in February 2005. I stumbled on these units on www.realestate.com.au in October 2004 and realised I had seen them six months earlier. My investigations uncovered that they had been on the market all year, and two previous offers had fallen through. The vendor wanted to move them to free up capital for another project. I took my time and got pre-approval for 70% finance of my offer price. My offer was $95k under the original asking price and only marginally higher than the July 2003 price paid by the vendor. After 10 days pondering my offer the vendor accepted. These units will return just under 10% rental yield and I believe Darwin is on the verge of a strong period of capital growth.

The current market value of my property portfolio including my family home (and Darwin) is just over $3.5 million at a Loan to Valuation Ratio of 80%.

My overall LVR will hover around or just under 80% for the next few years as I will use any growth in values to fund new acquisitions, but in time it will trend down.

> I approach my property investing activities as a second job and I am determined to reach a position where it can replace my full time job within five years.
>
> My reason for doing this is so I can have more time to spend with family, to volunteer for church activities and to eventually get my golf handicap in shape. I have observed a number of peers studying for MBAs and second degrees and I believe I invest less time in my property activities for greater direct benefit.

I have found the Richmastery tools, education and mentoring have given me the vision of how I can achieve my financial goals through property and the practical know-how to navigate the minefield of obstacles you face when starting out, any one of which could stop you in your tracks. I have found the people to be honest and reliable; if they make a mistake they fix it. Since completing the Richmastery education I have assisted on the Richmastery Property Academy in Auckland to continue learning and to meet other investors.

TOP TEN TIPS

1. Get a good team of experts to help you.

2. Don't skimp on gaining skills or education. Everything I've spent on seminars, software, mentoring and books is dwarfed by the profit I've made on just one of my deals.

3. Be prepared to make sacrifices, to cut out your credit card and your second car, in the interests of improving your lending capacity and achieving your long term goals.

4. Think for yourself; don't believe everything you are told by others (even your mentor, real estate agents, or what you read in books). Do the research yourself and make decisions based on the figures.

5. Get all your properties managed by professional property managers.

6. Only buy when you have a way of recycling your deposit within 12 months, i.e. by buying under market value, renovating or the like.

7. You can't afford to break your rules.

8. Don't be afraid to make mistakes or to admit you've made them.

9. You must believe that you have the ability to be successful.

10. Make sure you are diligent about pest inspections and treatments. Property managers should be able to advise the correct frequency for each location, and organise the whole thing. I have been 'bitten' by this a couple of times.

Chapter 15

From cattle to cash cows

'It was the outline of how to go about property investment that I found fantastic. I saw there was a simple step by step way of doing it...'
— **Shane and Ali Allen,** Waipukurau, NZ

I live in Waipukurau, a small farming settlement in the lower North Island of New Zealand, with my wife Ali and our three sons.

I was working in the goldmines in Kalgoorlie in Western Australia between 1987 and 1992 earning good money. I was cash rich and equity poor. During this time I bought my first two investment properties. Both were sections of bare land; one was a section in Perth that I purchased for $21k in 1988; the other was a five acre block in Margaret River, an exclusive tourist town near Perth, which I bought in 1991.

In 1992 I left the mines and went travelling through Africa and that's where I met Ali in 1993 – she is from Cape Town.

Becoming cash poor, equity rich

My mother's family had a family farm in Waipukurau and my grandmother was still on the farm, which was run by managers. My mother contacted me and said it's time for your grandmother to move into a rest home and there's an opportunity for you to run the farm. For us the timing was perfect. It was a foot in the door to New Zealand, a job, a place to live and a familiar and wonderful place to raise a family. We arrived back in New Zealand at the end of 1995 and managed the farm for a year for not much money.

I decided to sell my blocks of land in Perth and Margaret River. I discovered that the Perth section was backfill and that to build a house on it you would have to refill it. So all I could get for it was what I'd paid for it years earlier, just $21k. This was a good example of how if you are uneducated it's easy to make bad decisions with property investment.

Luckily the Margaret River section had appreciated and we sold that for $AUS183k ($NZ200k) and I'd bought it for $71k.

The family farm is 700 acres, with a four bedroom main homestead that is our family home (which my grandmother didn't leave until 1999 when she finally went to the rest home) and a three bedroom cottage, which we now rent out for $100 per week.

In 1995 when we first moved to the farm the government valuation (GV) on it was $610k, but it was probably worth about $800k in 1995. Between 1995 and 2003 we bought 100% of the farm by buying out other family members. Over a period of eight years we have paid a total of $780k for the farm in different instalments to family members for their shares.

The GV is now $1.2 million and the market value is now $2.1 million. There is also $250k worth of livestock on it, predominantly sheep and beef cattle. We breed sheep and sell lambs and I trade cattle. Farming is such a fickle thing – it's so weather dependent; in 1998 we went through a really bad drought.

However, through thick and thin we've done quite well with our business and now all we owe on the farm is a mortgage of $160k ($100k on a fixed term and $60k on rapid repay).

I run the farm full time and Ali is a full time mum and part time on the farm. The farm has been a doer upper; we've put in new cattle yards, renewed pasture, done lots of fencing and renovated the two houses both inside and out.

We went from being cash rich, equity poor to cash poor, equity rich.

Understanding the figures

Alison read Robert Kiyosaki's book, *Rich Dad, Poor Dad*, and said to me, 'You better read this book; it's very interesting.' Soon after, in September 2002, I attended Richmastery's Profit from Property seminar in Napier, presented by Phil Jones. At the course I made the decision to attend the three-day Richmastery Property Academy in May 2003.

I have always been interested in property. I knew there was an easier way to make money and just reading the little blurb for the advert and going along to the seminar, I realised that it was just about facts and figures. There was no hype; it all made so much sense to me and I got quite excited. I was ready to start putting into practice all the principles I had learnt.

I could see it was basically learnt systems; there were the seven points and then the structures that they put in place – I knew I could do it. I remember being told we would cover a week's worth of information in just three days but that it would be 40 hours long. It was the outline of how to go about property investment that I found fantastic. I was buzzing afterwards and was very excited. I saw that there was a method to it, a way of doing it, a simple step by step way of doing it ... it was the way they showed us how to do it at the academy that was fantastic.

To help with my investing at the academy I signed up to attend the 12 month Richmastery Personal Property Mentoring Programme. I got assistance from my mentor and really got to understand how the figures worked, and once I got that, it was great – I had really learnt how it worked.

The first property I purchased was a city zone apartment in Liverpool Street in central Auckland while I was at the academy. They handed out the form to us at the course and then ran through the figures and sold them all. I thought, 'If I'm going to get into this let's just do it.' I bought another one of these apartments through Richmastery Property Deals website a month later.

After this things were slow. It was the worst time to try to buy. It was a sellers' market and the real estate agents were arrogant, not bothering to return calls. This kept happening from May right through to November and in that time I didn't find anything. I put in some offers but nothing stacked up. Overnight the Hawke's Bay turned into a capital growth place. I made a dozen offers in total during that time.

Taking the plunge

One day, I was speaking to a mentor from Richmastery and I asked him if there were any positive cash flow deals that he knew of. He said a deal had fallen over on some flats in Rotorua that I should check out. So I drove for four hours, looked and them and drove back four hours, knowing that I would buy them.

It was a block of 10 one-bedroom flats in Malfroy Road, which is walking distance (1 km) from the centre of Rotorua. I signed them up and then had three days to carry out due diligence on the deal before it went unconditional.

Luckily a building inspection and a valuation had already been done by a Richmastery Personal Property Mentoring Programme student, who had lost the finance on the deal. Anything like this with such a great positive cash flow and 15% below value was almost impossible to find at the time.

I learnt that the flats had a bad history; they had been run down and the police had often visited, but the vendors had tidied them up and lifted the standard and the location was good as it was close to town. We were also getting quite desperate to purchase some property as we had been looking so long and the numbers stacked up, it was a positive cash flow deal and 15% below valuation. So we bought them in December 2003 through the Richmastery Property Deals service for $395k plus the standard finder's fee, and they valued up to $480k. We borrowed only 50% from the BNZ and the rest came from equity off the farm. When we bought them seven out of the 10 were rented at $110 per week each.

Three of the flats were empty and in a bad state. I lived in one of the units and went hard out, painting and cleaning, replacing toilets seats, carpets and vinyl and adding new vanities. I really took the flats to a complete new level.

In total I spent about $15k renovating seven of them and I now rent all of them for $115 each. With me doing all the work we saved about $15k. It was worth doing and on average they have been rented at 90% of the time since then. The property managers get 7.5% plus GST but the cash flow is $20k per annum and after tax it is still around $6k or $7k.

I analysed the figures differently with the block of flats. To be safe I factored in eight weeks' annual vacancy. I am now finding the flats have an average of two to three weeks' vacancy a year. With the single bedrooms

The Malfroy Road, Rotorua flats: Shane lived in one unit while renovating them, saving about $15k.

many of the tenants are first time renters and are quite transient. Since we've done them up we're getting better tenants and we are being quite fussy about who we let to. Our property manager has been instructed to take only good people. It's a simple equation: if you have dog boxes you get dogs.

We refinanced the flats with Southland Building Society at a fixed rate for two years at 7.5%, interest only. We have a 70% lending based on the new $480k valuation, giving a mortgage of $336k. To get 100% finance they will need to be valued at $565k, which we will try to do at the end of the two year fixed mortgage period.

Once they were refinanced we freed up equity that we had with the BNZ. We were able to keep the revolving credit account of the $395k that we had set up for the purchase of the flats.

The cash cow

The farm is in a trust and the BNZ has security over the farm. We keep our property side of things totally separate. For this we set up an LAQC company – called Equalizer (after the TV show starring Edward Woodward). After refinancing the flats we had a whole lot of extra equity for the deposit on our next purchase.

This was another flats property: a block of 12 in total (four one-bedroom and eight two-bedroom) in Faraday Street in the heart of Napier, just 1 km from the city. It's surrounded by shops, near the bus route and all services. We settled in June 2004.

The rents for all the flats are different: from $180 to $210 per week. The caretaker, who looks after rubbish, pays $145 per week for a two bedroom flat. The rent is around $100k per annum and we get close to $3000 positive cash flow off them a month. The property brings in, conservatively, about $10k before tax annually.

The flats had come up for tender in February 2004, with a listed price of $1 million. The vendor had had a tender of $970k, which the vendor had declined, but finally decided to drop the price. The agent said she was willing to take $950k. I came back at $900k; she counter-signed at $930k. I played the waiting game and stuck with my price. The vendor got desperate and the agent finally called to say, 'I can't believe it – she's signed it.'

The agreement was conditional on due diligence. We then had a building inspection done and the balconies needed repairs. We got a quote for $5k to fix them and the valuation only came in at $950k, so at $900k the deal would only be 5% below valuation. I spoke to Richmastery's Wellington director. He said, 'It's really high cash flow, which you guys need, and you have a ton of equity anyway. You can't let these ones pass you by – go for it.' I said we'd go unconditional if they would pay for the balconies to be fixed. In the end it worked and we got them for $895k.

We got finance with SBS again and financed it to 70% with them for $630k, and used $265k from the BNZ revolving credit.

The Malfroy Road flats provide cash flow of $20k per annum.

Our cash cow: block of 12 flats in Faraday Street, Napier. Rent is around $100k per annum with $3000 positive cash flow a month.

The upside was they were all tenanted and they have six and 12 month tenancies in place and nine of them are fully furnished. It has a massive positive pre-tax cash flow and all the flats were in great order from day one and they came fully furnished, with sheets, blankets, towels, beds, chairs, dining room suites and washing machines. The location is excellent and although we only managed to purchase it at 5% below, it's a cash cow.

When we took over there was a bit of strife with three or four problem tenants in there. When you buy a block of flats, beware that the vendor might have filled them with any old tenant just to fill them up. There was fighting and the cops were around, and in the first six weeks these problems had us concerned. We were worried; I felt like I got more grey hairs and there were definitely sleepless nights getting it sorted out. But we got in a new property manager (through a tip from someone in our Richmastery Personal Property Mentoring group) and she sorted things out.

Forget the bad press

Buying the flats deal blew our available equity. However, we settled on the two city zone apartments we purchased in Auckland when they were completed at the end of November 2004. They are now rented for $300 each per week but it did take us a while to rent them as the Auckland rental market is flooded with apartments.

The first one, which we purchased for $174k at the 2003 Richmastery Property Academy, is a two bedroom, 38.5 square metre apartment. The second one I bought for $160k a month after the academy from Richmastery

Personal Property Deals via a property finder. It's two bedroom and 42.5 square metres. The guy who had bought it couldn't get finance so the deal fell over. We paid a finder's fee of $2999 per unit.

> Both apartments were 15% below registered valuation at the time we purchased them. They have just been revalued: the first one for $221k (up $61k) and the second one for $216k (up $56k). These settled at 80% finance with Westpac at the end of November 2004. The BNZ equity over the farm paid for the rest. However, Westpac say we can refinance and get 100% as they have gone up in value so much. If we do this we will still get an extra $18k equity out of them due to the new valuations.

I was amazed at how much they had gone up as we were nervous with bad media reports about apartments. However, our Richmastery Personal Property Mentor says, 'Don't listen to the bad media – it's all hot air.'

The plan is to refinance and we will have $100k more equity to work with. Then we will revalue the farm, the Faraday Street flats and we will be able to recycle our deposits and starting searching for the next deal.

Forward with confidence

I am quite excited now. I am interested in getting Martin Ayles' DVD set and to look at subdividing and doing renovations so we can diversify and move away from blocks of flats and instead try some three bedroom houses.

The Richmastery Personal Property Mentoring Programme has been the best thing and such great value, because there's so much to learn. And every time you are looking at something new, you can call them and they set your mind at ease. We thought the Faraday flats were way out of our league but now I feel completely at ease because I've been educated by Richmastery and we are using their strategies and going through it step by step and it's working for us.

We still stay in touch with everyone in our mentoring group even through our 12 month programme has finished – 80% of our group still meet once a month (a group of 10 of us).

We have a great team; our lawyer is fantastic, David Dicks in Waipukurau, as is our accountant, Nick Grant at Atrium, also in Waipukurau, who specialises in farming but they also have a property whiz in the company too.

It's good to have our lawyer and accountant right there so we can visit them any time. We have a good rapport with all those in our team and we've had great tax deductions already.

I went and saw Mathew Gilligan from Gilligan Rowe and Associates to get some expert advice on how to set up the correct structure for our investing after seeing his presentation about asset planning at the Richmastery Property Academy. I took GRA's advice to my own accountant and he put the suggested structures in place. Attending the mentoring programme also helped me with setting up the correct structure.

Thanks to Richmastery and the Napier Richmastery Personal Mentoring Programme we are well on the road to successful property investing.

We've learnt so much – with every deal we've become more confident. The plan is that the farm will be leased or managed in two years' time and we will move to Napier so the kids can go to school there and I will do properties full time.

So we have everything working for us. It's not as if it's been easy; we've slogged our guts out and we pay ourselves only $780 a fortnight over and above the farm expenses. We don't have any luxuries – we are waiting for all that – everything has gone back into the mortgages.

> We have friends who have bought boats and all that and they are all struggling with their farms and their debt. We want to be debt free in terms of our personal debt. With our property debt we don't mind because we know it is good debt that looks after itself.

I love property, I love watching the TV programme *Location, Location, Location* and seeing the real estate agents work. We have read *Real Money Real Estate* by Phil Jones and found it a brilliant book. We subscribe to *Kiwi Property Investor* magazine (available through www.richmastery.com) and we use the Richmastery Property Analysis software and find it totally invaluable.

In two and a half years we have built up a total portfolio value of $4.1 million, our total mortgages are $1.75 million, meaning our total equity is $2.125 million. Along with this we have an annual after tax cash flow per annum of $134,710.

TOP TEN TIPS

1. Location is fundamental, even if it is an average suburb be sure it is in a good part of it.
2. Make sure there is an angle: scope for improvement, adding another room etc.
3. Be organised with banks, finance, valuers and lawyers before the deal comes along.
4. Don't dwell on dropping a good deal; there are plenty more around the corner.
5. Put the hard yards in; the quicker you do them up the quicker they are rented at a good rate.
6. Have a good registered property manager, one you can relate to.
7. Get the right tenants. Don't rush, as wrong ones are hard to get rid of.
8. Spread your investments around the suburbs and the provinces and different types of properties.
9. Don't expect big returns immediately. Be patient; they will come.
10. Enjoy yourself. Actually, this will happen automatically with good deals.

Chapter 16

Do up and do well

'My goal is to rebuild and to add equity by buying properties I can renovate or subdivide.'

— Andrew Brenchley, Gold Coast, AUS

I bought 14 properties in four years worth about $3.4 million. I have been featured in *Australian Property Investor* magazine and *Acreage Living* magazine. I gave up my day job and have been investing full time since January 2003.

I started investing in property in January 2000. I was based in Sydney, and was the GM of a small landscaping company and had been building the business for five years. The strategy I had was to build up the business, to generate more income and to invest in property.

I had always been interested in property. In 1994 I had tried to get a loan for a unit in 1994 but my income wasn't large enough to get it. I had then put my money into a worm farm business but it hadn't worked. I had a contract with a company to produce the worms, but their company went broke.

Key books' simple formula

In 1998, when I was 24 years old, I read Jan Somers and Dolf de Roos' book, *Building Wealth through Property Investing* and saw John Fitzgerald flogging his book on TV and I read that too. These were two key books for me. They gave me a simple formula on buying investment properties. Jan Somers has a really good way of making it simple. Her philosophy is to buy a house anywhere and keep it, which is the same as Fitzgerald.

But I still found I couldn't buy any property as I wasn't earning enough, so I looked for a job that would earn me more money. This happened at the end of 1998 when I started as head of a maintenance division for a garden management company. The company managed the maintenance of gardens for the likes of the Sydney Olympics.

I went to Adelaide in December 1999. My girlfriend at the time was from the city and her father lived right on the water there.

This was where I bought my first house in January 2000. It was a two bedroom brick house on a corner block, 100 metres from the Murray River. I purchased it for $78k and put down a deposit of 10% cash, which I had saved. I borrowed 90% on a principal and interest loan and rented it for $125 per week. When I got more educated I changed everything to interest only.

Buying off plan

John Fitzgerald was doing a seminar in Sydney in May 2000 so I went along to this. He ended up being a developer. He had one of those seminars where they say, 'Come up to Brisbane and look at my houses and I will pay for your airfare.' I went in July 2000 to see some land and building deals that he was developing in Wynnum West, a bayside suburb of Brisbane, 20 minutes from the city centre. We purchased one for $200k through his development company, the Custodian Group. Then I was shocked to discover that I could have bought this same type of house for $160k. So the next day I cancelled the Custodian Group contract the day after signing it – luckily in Queensland you can do this as there's a compulsory five day cooling off period in contracts. My solicitor sent a letter and I got out of the deal.

I then bought another off the plan, a land and build deal, also in Wynnum West for $166k instead, just 50 metres away from where the Custodian Group house would have been built. It was a four bedroom brick and tile. I paid a deposit of $16k from my savings and the house was finished four weeks later. I then rented it for $250 per week and got a P and I loan.

For the next 12 months I dabbled in the share market and did day trading with about $4000. I put all the profits I made back into Newscorp shares and when I had $15k I sold them just before the Newscorp shares fells through the floor. I was lucky that I had a good stockbroker but I felt it was a very risky game.

Four bedroom brick and tile in Wynnum West, Brisbane, bought off the plan.

I used this $15k to put down a deposit and pay for costs like stamp duty on my next property deal. I came up to Brisbane again in June 2001 for my cousin's 18th birthday. While I was there I checked on my other house and saw a house I liked for $190k.

> It was a four bedroom home in a suburb next to Wynnum West called Hemmant (also about 20 minutes from Brisbane city). So I called the agent and asked why they were selling; he said the vendors were going through a divorce. I asked how much they owed on it, and he said $138k. I said, 'That's my offer.' They accepted an hour later. I rented this for $250.

Then I advertised for a mentor on a website discussion forum on the internet because I wanted to do different types of property deals. I thought perhaps it could be something different to buy and hold, but I didn't know what. Eight people came forward and offered to help me. I interviewed them all and chose the one who was the most passionate and was doing it full time and who had achieved the best results.

Wrapping

He convinced me to start wrapping – which I totally hate now. The first property I bought to wrap was an arrangement where I was the money partner. My business partner would find the property, buy it under my name, say for $60k, for someone who couldn't get finance and then sell it on to them for $80k and we would also mark up the interest rate by 3% more than we were paying. The purchaser would then give me a $2000 deposit for which they would use the government first home buyer's grant. My partner

Four bedroom home in Hemmant, Brisbane. The agent said the vendors were getting divorced. I asked how much they owed on it, and he said $138k. I said, 'That's my offer.' They accepted an hour later.

would then on-sell it to a third party under an instalment contract and then it's a 25 year loan to me and they can buy me out at any time.

The buyer's risk is that if I go broke the buyer loses the house so they lose everything, and because of this I no longer think this is right. But at that time I didn't really know that. Now I just don't think it's safe for the buyer or for the wrapper (because if the house goes up in value you lose the capital growth).

I got married in March 2002. At that stage the properties my partner and I had bought were mixed; the first property was in my name, the second in hers and then we started a company, of which we had equal shares, called Goalforce, attached to a trust (Goalforce Property Trust). We set this up with the intention of buying and holding. My mentor helped me to work out the right entity for holding assets in and then I went to a property accountant.

I bought my first wrap for $60k in Hunter Valley, Cessnock, which is two hours' drive north of Sydney, in January 2002. I marked it up to $100k. So I was making $60 per week positive cash flow. The vendor sold us out for $100k in early 2004, which means he took over the mortgage with the bank.

The next deal I did with my business partner was in Cessnock, a country town of about 25,000 with strong wine and mining industries. We bought this house for $82k with the intention of subdividing the section and moving a second house on to the new site. I bought the house in my name and put up the money. My partner did project management to subdivide the section and bring in the house in on a truck. We spent $70k on renovations, moving and subdivision. We sold the whole lot for $300k and made $150k in about eight months. I learnt lots doing this. We had some problems with the house mover, who wouldn't put the roof back on, but apart from that it was pretty easy.

Then we bought three more wraps in October 2002. I was still thinking it was a good idea then. They were all in a place called Casino, three hours south of the Gold Coast in northern New South Wales. It's a quiet country town with good industry, mainly mining. The deals were $48k wrapped for $60k; $88k wrapped for $110k; and $74k wrapped for $90k.

It was the same arrangement: I put up the money and my mentor found the houses and did the deal. He would advertise in the paper 'Rent to Buy – Vendor will Finance'. He asked people heaps of questions, arranged for income verification. One of the purchasers was a prostitute who couldn't get bank loans. We made $60 per week positive cash flow off each property.

Then I bought a three bedroom unit in a block of 24 on the beach in Sydney off the plan in September 2002. This was in Collaroy, one of the stunning Northern Beaches. I used a deposit bond of $3994 to secure it. I paid $615k for it and had to settle on completion in December 2004. It would now be worth about $650k.

In January 2003 our company bought another place in Cessnock, a three bedroom house with a big backyard and a carport, for $150k. We subdivided it. To finance this deal I set up two lines of credit: one off my first investment house in Adelaide and the second off the house in Hemmant, Brisbane. I pulled $127k equity off these two properties into a revolving credit account and used this to fund the subdivision, which cost $124k. I then sold the front house for $175k and got the back block and section revalued at $190k.

The house we moved onto the site was in good condition. We joined it back together, put a deck on it, painted it inside and outside. It had Weathertex plastic weatherboards, which we replaced with new ones. We did much of the work ourselves. I have kept this one and rented it because I had worked on it myself and felt emotionally attached. It's now rented at $190 per week against a loan of $127k. This project took a year and a half in total and during the process we were able to rent the front house out for $170 per week. The loan was 95% of the purchase price of $150k.

Joint ventures

I then moved to the Gold Coast in February 2003. My marriage ended and my wife stayed in Sydney. I used to come to the Coast on holidays and I loved it, I wanted a slower pace, a lifestyle change; I was working 60 hours per week and getting stuck in traffic and I just wanted to get away from all that.

I thought, 'What am I going to do now?' The answer was: do what I know best, buy a house, renovate it and sell it. I had a few months off, then I bought a four bedroom brick and tile house, 200 metres from the shopping centre, with a park in between, in Wynnum West.

It was on the market for $300k; I got it for $280k and spent $9000 renovating it in the first five days after I settled. I had 42 days from signing to settlement. We settled on Friday, the renovations started on Saturday and we finished on Thursday. I had a valuer there on Friday and he valued it at $330k. I took the cash and rented it for six months for $250 per week. Six months later I sold it for $350k – after costs I ended up with $48k.

The renovation included rendering, which is when you put a thin layer of plaster over the brick, I had 18 Italians there rendering on the Sunday. I then converted the single garage that was attached to the house into a fifth bedroom or study. It still had a double garage out the back. We put some feature walls in and re-landscaped the whole place (I did this part myself). We put in new lights and painted the render a cream colour. We put in timber Venetian blinds. It looked a lot newer; the difference was amazing. I had had 42 days to prepare the work to be done in time.

Australian Property Investor magazine contacted me wanting to do a story; there was a survey they had run which I filled out and they contacted me in September 2003. I discussed everything I'd done and talked about joint ventures and then after the story was published it opened up a whole heap of new doors. I had mentioned joint ventures and got some calls from mums and dads who wanted to start investing and didn't know how. About 50 people called, some people wanted advice and some wanted to be equity (money) partners. So I met all of them and helped how I could.

There were two ladies who wanted to give me money to invest in joint ventures; they wanted me to buy the house and do it up and split profits, but I didn't warm to them or feel comfortable. These are big projects and I didn't

One of the Hendra renovations before and after. One of my joint venture deals.

feel we would be able to get on. They were nit-picky so I told them I didn't want to work with them.

I met another gentleman with a big security business on the Gold Coast who I felt I could work with. I found him a house in Brisbane at Hendra, just 6 km from the city centre, in a trendy area. It was a two bedroom Queenslander (a timber weatherboard 1930s style house – they are gorgeous homes). I purchased this for $371k plus stamp duty of $20k and closing costs (in total $400k purchase).

Then I began the renovations: we lifted it up, it was already 2 metres off the ground, so we jacked the whole house up a further metre and then put stiles (like pallets) under it and concreted new posts in. We then put two bedrooms and a garage downstairs and a deck on the top and a patio off the back at the bottom, with nice bi-folds upstairs onto the new deck. In total we spent $80k on renovations and put it on the market in December 2004 for $635k as a private sale. We will split profit and pay 30% tax on this. It was about a year's work.

On joint venture deals my partners pay the deposits and the costs of renovation. I provide the time.

The next joint venture has just started with a different person. It's also in Hendra and we are doing the same thing, lifting the house and putting three bedrooms downstairs. We paid $365k for this particular house, and it settled in October 2004. It's also a Queenslander with two bedrooms, polished floor, sleep-out and separate dining areas. It will be the same deal with this money partner.

> On these joint deals I don't have to come up with any money, it's just my time. The partners pay the deposits and the costs of renovation, they get the house in their own name and pay the mortgage during the renovation. I can get my tax right down through my business expenses.

I like going to seminars but the best way I like teaching people is one on one, which is why I like the joint ventures.

I have read many books, and some that come to mind are those by Brad Sugars, John Burley, Jan Somers, Robert Kiyosaki and *The Magic of Thinking Big* by Dr David Schwartz.

I have also done a few seminars, including the Reno Kings.

Over the two years since my wife and I separated we have had to sell all the houses we owned together. I didn't want to sell them and it was certainly a hard process, but I now have some cash to reinvest and so I am looking for the next deal for myself now although I will also continue to do joint ventures.

> I've got three joint ventures on the table at this time plus my own plans. I really enjoy this kind of work and want to do it and my goal is to build my own portfolio back up. My goal is to rebuild and buy some more cash flow positive houses and to add equity by buying houses I can renovate or subdivide.

Home delivery

After the API article and hearing people's feedback and questions I realised there was nothing published about the process of relocating a house on a truck to a new site. So I wrote down the process we had gone through and created a work book.

I am really passionate about what I do. I now keep property journals each day of any project I am working on. It's a day by day run-down of how it's all done and the process I go through.

TOP TEN TIPS

1. Protect your credit rating. If you get a bad credit rating the cost of your finance goes through the roof.
2. Buying under market value or buying equity is buying well.
3. If renovating, run the numbers realistically.
4. Never take advice off people who don't have the results you want.
5. A building and pest report is useful for negotiating the price down.
6. When looking for financiers with a buy and hold the only thing that's important is the interest rate and getting benefits like no establishment costs.
7. Buy land with a house, not air in a building, i.e. a unit.
8. Buy your investment properties that are cash flow neutral or positive, then buy your own house. Rent until you've got your investment properties.
9. Its not timing but time with an investment property. Houses generally don't go backwards in value. The right time to buy a house is now and the right time to sell it is never.
10. Always buy under the right entity (under a trust structure). Australia is one of the most litigious countries, but if your properties are under a trust you're protected.

Chapter 17

Accelerated success

'We set down our goals and worked out strategies to achieve those goals.'
— **Gary McMahon**, Hamilton, NZ

I n 2001, when I was in my early forties, I started thinking about my financial future. I was married with three daughters and had been working in the dairy industry for eight years. During those years my wife Pam and I had built up a strong share milking business and wanted to invest some of the equity we'd made. Now three years later my family and I are living in Hamilton on a 10 acre block upon which we run a strawberry farm. We are in a much better financial situation and property investment has made this our reality.

Building equity

After I left school I went to university but didn't finish. I then went back when I was 30, after we had had two of our children, and completed a Bachelor of Management Studies majoring in Accounting and Marketing at Waikato University. I then worked for 18 months in an accountant's office, which has proved invaluable, as it gave me the financial and tax experience to get into property investments. I did a lot of accounts for dairy farmers, and could see how dairy farmers were building equity and buying farms.

I really had a dream of owning my own farm so I decided to go share milking to build equity. People always told me the best way to buy your own farm was to go share milking. We worked hard and built this up to the stage where we had two share milking jobs totalling 650 cows; we owned the cows and the machinery but not the land and we get half the income off the milk and the farm (land) owner gets the other half.

Investing the equity

I knew I needed to invest some of the equity we had built up. We invested in a dairy farm in the South Island in 1999 in Invercargill along with equity partners we had found by advertising through the National Bank. We put money in and also helped to set up the business. We then ran it along with an equity manager who managed the property.

In 2002 we sold one of our share milking jobs and bought another big farm in the lower South Island and converted it to dairying.

I had always been interested in residential property investment. I'd read some books quite a long time ago about how to invest in houses, including Dolf de Roos and Jan Somers, *Making Money in Residential Real Estate*.

I was interested in inflation and the financial side of things; how things went up in value over time. While I always believed that houses doubled in value over time, I never actually tried residential investments. I think I was probably too cautious to invest, and all our money was invested in share milking anyway because that was what we were focused on at that stage.

Could've done better

We finally purchased my brother's property in 2000. It was a four bedroom house on a double section. He wanted to sell it as he was going to Australia. We paid $165k for it, which was about market value.

We were always keen to add value to things and we did the kitchen up and in total spent $20k on it. There were two titles, one being an empty section valued at $53k and the house title valued at $165k after renovating the kitchen. We then rented the house for $180 per week. It just broke even but was almost negative gearing. We thought we'd done okay but once I'd been to the Richmastery seminars I realised we hadn't done very well at all. With more education I saw that it wasn't a great investment property at all and there were many other things I could have done with this same money that I only found out about later.

Maximum motivation

We had good cash flow from our share milking business and I was looking at off farm investments but knew I needed to learn more. I always believed that spending money on education was a great thing to do and the Richmastery Profit from Property seminar advert just popped up in the property investors' magazine I subscribed to. So I went first to the four hour evening seminar and then enrolled to do the three day Richmastery Property Academy in May 2002.

I had been to various other seminars but did not get motivated enough to purchase, including one run by Olly Newland a year earlier, which while it was good didn't motivate me; I came away hyped up but didn't do anything with the knowledge.

Because we had invested all our equity into the dairy farms in the South Island, we had no spare equity and an overdraft of over $90k, but we did have very strong cash flow. After attending the Richmastery Property Academy I came away extremely motivated to purchase property and I learned some very useful techniques that suited my personal financial position.

One of the biggest learning curves for me at the academy came from playing the Property Game. The way they simulated the auction during the Property Game really got me excited. On the first day I bought whatever property I could, and the simulated market went against me and I lost all my equity by the end of the day. I was extremely disappointed and wondered how I was going to play the property game now. So I sat down with the numbers and worked myself a little strategy on how to get back into the game. By the end of the game on day three I was in the top eight for equity increase – that's what motivated me.

> I'd played the Property Game and worked out a winning strategy, after losing everything on day one, which enabled me to be in the top 10% of the 200 attendees. I thought if I can do that in a game there was no reason why I couldn't do that in reality.

The main lessons I learnt during the course were to watch the numbers, to buy below market/fair value, how to use the banks to your advantage, how to add value and create equity, and how to find good deals. All these strategies have worked for me.

Twenty-one in six months

I couldn't wait to get out there and do it. The main problem I faced was that I had no spare equity to purchase investment properties with. I am a person who loves a challenge so I had to start thinking outside the square and come up with some innovative ideas.

Anyway to cut a long story short, I thought of some creative ways to finance property and in the six months after attending the Richmastery Property Academy I purchased 21 properties at a value in excess of $2 million.

I used the Richmastery model and set myself some rules. I also went along to the Richmastery Property Finder's course with Joanne Waters. They were looking for property finders at that stage and I was keen to train for this.

I paid the $1500 and trained with them. Then I went out and started looking. After a short period of time, I could see all these fantastic deals happening and I could see an opportunity to purchase these deals for myself rather than on-sell them. So, I set up an LAQC company having realised the importance of structuring things right from the start after listening to Mathew Gilligan from Gilligan Rowe and Associates (GRA) at the Richmastery Property Academy. He was very good and helped me with that. My plan was to buy and hold.

The first property I bought following the academy was in Invercargill, New Zealand's southernmost city. I found a mortgagee auction of three one-bedroom flats in a block of five. They were going for $19k each and were returning 21% at a rental of $70 per week each flat. At this price I would be getting them for 20% below their market value.

As I had set my criteria, 20% below market value and at least 10% or better yield, this deal was perfect for me. You could find deals like that more easily then; now they are harder to come by.

I needed a deposit of $8500 so I pushed my overdraft a little further and also put some on my credit card and I scraped enough together to buy the flats.

I purchased another house in Invercargill for $40k soon afterwards and rented this at $120 per week or 15% yield. This valued up to $50k and the Southland Building Society allowed me to refinance the block of three flats

Our business provides good cash flow for investment.

after two months. They revalued at $24k each and doing this gave me an extra $25k in equity.

I then got the agent to knock on the door of the other flats in the block of five and soon after another flat in the same block came on the market. I used the revaluation funds to purchase this two bedroom flat for $28k; and rented it for $100 per week. I eventually got flat number 4 and secured the whole block of five flats. The main techniques I used to purchase these was by being able to buy well below market value and then revaluing the original three flats so I then had more funds to purchase flats 4 and 5. From my initial deposit of $8000, I had purchased the whole block of flats for $116k. The total rental income was $440 per week, or an impressive 18.9%. After another six months I was able to revalue the properties at $175k and then pull more equity out.

Joint venture deals

In the meantime I decided to look at joint venture deals with people who had spare funds available. My theory was that we would set up an LAQC, owned 50% by each of us, and the silent investor would loan that company $100k, which would be structured as a loan to that person and interest being paid quarterly. Due to my experience with the joint venture equity share farms, I made sure that things were structured properly to protect each shareholder's interests. The main aim of this structure was to achieve a win-win situation for both parties: the investor would gain from investing passively in an aggressive property company, and I would gain from having other people's equity to build a successful property company.

I formed two of these companies, one with a private individual, and one with our existing partners in a beach house we owned at Whangamata. With the latter, we refinanced the beach house and raised $100k to start up the company. With the former, once my silent partner and I had the structure and finance in place, we set very stringent purchasing criteria and I went about looking for those properties. The criteria we set are: any properties I purchased had to be 15% below registered valuation, 10% return or better, and we had to be able to refinance within three months on the increased equity to enable us to purchase more property.

I purchased 21 properties following these rules between June 2002 and February 2003. I bought a number of properties in Hamilton. The first was a three bedroom do-up that I bought for a $101k. We spent $8000 on renovations and had it revalued at $128k. We did the work, painting, polishing floors and generally tidying it up, nothing structural. We then rented it for $240 per week.

After that I kept on doing the same thing; I bought five properties for the first equity partnership company with our $100k: three in Hamilton, one in nearby Te Awamutu and one in Tokoroa south of Hamilton; I then waited three months and refinanced; we were very aggressive. This was with Southland Building Society again and also with the BNZ.

I then purchased another three properties for this equity partnership company in Hamilton. By this time we had eight properties with a value of $750k, and we were finding that the banks would require us to wait six months before we could refinance.

 One very important thing that I learned was that we needed to buy properties with strong cash flows to fund the extra borrowing that we made from refinancing.

The funding for the second equity partnership company came from our partnership with our friends in a property at Whangamata, a popular holiday spot on the Coromandel Peninsula east of Auckland.

And yet again

We had bought a beach house for $465k in February 2001 and by June 2002 it had gone up to $600k. So we borrowed another $100k against the property and we set up a third LAQC, Waterfront Investments Ltd, and proceeded to do the same thing again. Under this company I purchased seven properties, six in Hamilton and one in Tokoroa. All were positive cash flow and bought at a discount.

We bought four and then we had to wait three months before we could refinance; we did this with Sovereign. I actively sought out banks that would let us do this after three months.

I used the mortgage broker that Richmastery promoted; she was very helpful in assisting us achieve our goals of recycling our equity in the time that we did.

> After a while the agents got to know the type of properties I was looking for and the better agents would find the deals and bring them to me. I learnt that the deals are always there – if you start looking for opportunities it is amazing what you find.

Waterfront Investments Ltd bought another property in the exclusive Auckland suburb of Remuera. We decided we wanted to invest in the Auckland market to expose us to a higher capital growth area. This was a house on a subdividable 1482 square metre section that can be subdivided into three sites. It is negatively geared but the intention is to subdivide and build three new upmarket townhouses.

> Another important thing I have learnt is to be prepared to pay for good advice. On the face of it, this Remuera deal looks like a development which could put us at risk of being called developers and affect our investor status. However, after consulting at length with my accountant and also getting a firm IRD ruling, we are not viewed as developers due to the fact that we are subdividing with the intention to build rental dwellings for long term hold.

This property cost $851k and I didn't worry about valuation as I knew the value was in the land; each section once subdivided will be worth $400k. We're now subdividing, which has been a slow process and costly. I don't recommend it. Developing is a specialist area and I think there's more money to be made out of investing and holding.

A cash flow business

Pam and I bought the block we live on in June 2003. It had a three bedroom family home on it and had been run as a strawberry business that was run by the former owner for the past 20 years. He had decided to sell it when he turned 65 and wanted to retire. He had stopped growing strawberries some time earlier. However, when we bought the property he kindly taught me how to go about growing strawberries and we now run our own strawberry business on the property. We have built a shop and expanded the business. Our plan is to develop it into a consistent cash flow business that will help fund our future property investments.

A month after we bought this property the area became subdividable. This was good fortune as it is a top location for lifestyle blocks just on the outskirts of Hamilton. We've now gone through the process of getting a resource consent and have the option to subdivide it into three blocks. Our intention is to build rental properties on two of these sites also, once again avoiding the developer title. With rezoning, the value of this property has increase twofold.

Win-win beach house solution

The last property we bought was at Whangamata. Our beach house that we own with our friends is a three storey property on a cross lease. We own one half (two lower stories), which are two separate units on the same title and the top storey is owned by someone else on a separate title. It is situated in a prime waterfront location right on Whangamata beach.

We bought the downstairs for $465k in February 2001 just before values increased rapidly with the property boom and our ultimate goal was to buy the top storey, which had a superior view. This was the driving force behind us setting up another investment company, so we could use property investment as a tool to position ourselves to be able to purchase the top storey when and if it became available.

We were fortunate enough to purchase the top in May 2004. I approached the owner and have arranged a deal whereby we agreed to purchase the property at a fair price to both of us. We gave him a deposit and he has left the rest of the money on vendor finance for seven years. He has the right to rent it from us for those seven years at which time we will settle the loan and we will then have access rights. This deal was negotiated to achieve a win-win solution for both parties. We are happy that we have secured ownership of this prime property, and the vendors have made a sale with the right to occupy the property for seven years and also now receive an annual cash flow from the repayment of the loan.

Another thing that I have learnt is that beach property tends to be low cash flow, high capital gain type property. You need to have cash flows elsewhere to be able to fund them. It was always our goal to achieve ownership of this magnificent property, and by setting a strategy we were able to achieve our goal.

Part of our strategy here has been to buy high cash flow properties to help fund the high capital gains properties. We purchased a property in Tokoroa in November 2002 at a mortgagee sale. This cost us $32k and was valued at $43k; it is rented for $120 per week, being close to a 20% return, and is in a good area. We have had the same tenant since we bought it.

Goals set and achieved

Our original bottom half of the Whangamata building has now been revalued at $1.04 million, a huge increase in value from the $465k we paid for it four years earlier. Waterfront Investments Ltd now own assets worth $4.7 million, with total equity of $1.6 million. The amazing thing for me is that we (our partnership with our friends) have only actually invested $285k of equity in the four years since we started. Some of this equity has come from refinancing our residential property investments.

I believe that the safest way to build equity and cash flow in the property game is to take a 'buy-and-hold' strategy, or a 'buy, do-up and hold' strategy. They are not get rich overnight strategies, but over time the investor will achieve success with minimal risk. We are constantly reviewing our portfolio for poor performing assets and we are not scared to sell some if they are not performing.

We have achieved enormous success in the last three years with our property investments, as the timing has been superb. For me the most important thing has been the fact that we set down our goals and worked out strategies to achieve those goals. Richmastery have helped enormously by educating me in areas in which I did not have experience, and giving me the tools to accelerate our success.

TOP TEN TIPS

1. Learn how to be good with numbers.
2. Don't be scared to invest in knowledge; investing in yourself is the best investment in the long run.
3. The land appreciates and the house depreciates, so buy the biggest piece of land in the best location that you can afford. The house generates a cash flow that allows you to be able to hold the land. A house can easily be moved but a piece of land can't.
4. Be focused and goal oriented. Set realistic goals and have strategies to achieve them, constantly monitoring the process.
5. Get your structure right at the start.
6. Get alongside successful people or get advice from people who have done it before not just people who talk about it. Attend Richmastery Personal Property Mentoring.
7. You accelerate your progress in property investment if you buy right, try to make money when you buy, or else look at ways of adding value to create equity.
8. You must be passionate about what you are doing.
9. Do shares and joint ventures if that's what you like.
10. Get out there and do it and have fun.

A numbers game

I migrated from Cyprus to Melbourne, Australia in 1978 when I was 12 years old. My father spoke English as he was working for the UN in the English bases. He had an application to come to Australia, prior to the Turkish invasion of Cyprus in 1974, from his sisters who lived in Melbourne and had migrated in the 1960s.

I moved to Australia with my family and finished my secondary education in Melbourne and then went to Melbourne University in 1983.

I started investing in real estate in 1989 when I got my first job with the Department of the Treasury in Canberra working as an economist. I was 22 years of age then and my aim was to get an education before focusing on investments. I graduated in Economics and Commerce with Honours in 1989 and in January of that year I was posted with the Department of the Treasury to Canberra. My first job was in industrial relations and involved the accord the government struck with unions to ensure that wages grew in line with the consumer price index.

A family affair

Six months into my first full time job, I joined forces with my brother who was at the time studying for his trade certificate, and we bought our first house. I was looking for a place to stay to save on rent. I had a small amount saved, about $5000, and my brother had double that. My mother was generous and she gave us the same amount we had. We purchased a five bedroom house in Woden, in South Canberra, about 13 km from the city. The purchase price was $115k.

I moved in there, while my brother was still in Melbourne. I rented a room to a flatmate. It was great for me, the best thing I've done. It helped me to meet people in a new city, and the board covered some of my expenses. At the time I wasn't very aware of financial issues. I went for a very conserva-tive approach of principal and interest mortgage.

This is how we started and in my view a very good way to start, as I had a place to live plus it was also partly an investment. I did some work to it and my brother contributed to the maintenance. I had to strip wallpaper and paint the house inside and its exterior timber eaves and windows. It's amazing how fast I learnt, I'd never used a roller before, but got into it and did a reasonable job. I did the tiling in the bathroom. My uncle from Melbourne helped me to complete the job. I did a lot of landscaping, built stone retaining walls, learn-ing all the way, which I now see was a valuable experience.

Not much happened then until about 1992 when I got married and went with my wife back to Cyprus. It was the first time I had been there since we had left for Australia in 1978. When we left it had been war, with refugees, and planes flying over and dropping bombs on nearby villages. We instead found it quite a rapidly developed country with a relatively good standard of living.

Learning to make money

My wife and I came back to Canberra and bought our second house. Our intention was to move into this house and sell the one I bought with my brother, but eventually we decided to hold on to it. In 1992 it was worth about $200k; we continued to live in the house, and we bought a second house in Tuggaranong, 21 km from the centre of Canberra. This was to be a rental investment. It was a three bedroom home with an en suite, garage, and good size block and we bought it for $150k. We rented it for $200 per week and I managed it myself. It was a newish property, built in 1985, brick and tile and so low maintenance.

I began gradually to show a greater interest in real estate and by 1997 we bought our third property. I read lots of books. Despite the fact that I am an economist by profession, my knowledge was academic and I didn't know much about how to make money. Our institutions don't teach us how to build wealth; they teach us how to build a career. I believe we should be taught financing and investment in schools from an early age.

Our family was very supportive as they funded our education and encouraged us to save.

The next house we purchased was again in the Woden area. We got it for $150k. It is a three bedroom house with an en suite, a double brick garage and with a very good size block. I used the proceeds from a block of land that I had sold in Melbourne, which was passed on to me from my parents, as the deposit to buy the house. The land had sold for about $66k; I got half this amount as my share. I mortgaged the rest and rented it out for $200 per week; on a P & I mortgage, it was close to positive.

By 1997 interest rates were considerably lower than they were when I first started out in 1989 and the combination of lower interest rates and higher yields, and with the benefit of negative gearing (especially as my salary income was rising), encouraged me to buy our fourth property in 1999.

This was a renovated three bedroom house on a good sized chunk of land (700 square metres), which was a subdividable site in North Canberra, about 4 km from the CBD. It had no garage but did have a carport and off street parking. We got this for $167k. It was initially rented for $190 per week, but now we get $340. I borrowed against my equity for the deposit and paid cash for stamp duty.

Income and equity rising

Our income from rent was increasing so was our equity and when the market started moving up we bought our fifth property, again in the Woden area. This

This three bedroom house in Woden was our third buy — almost positive cash flow.

was a house in original condition, needing renovation, but was in a good location and was on a big block.

We bought this in 2001 for $185k. I did extensive renovations, painting it, polishing the floors and I took an owners' builders licence to build the garage. The new bathroom and kitchen were done by tradespeople. I project managed everything and this sparked a great deal of interest in this sort of thing for me. All of this time I was still working full time but working on the house late, hammering away into the night. I spent $70k on renovations, and the house is now valued at around $450k.

To reduce my debt level, we sold two of our houses that we bought when we first started out. I sold the original house I bought with my brother in 1989 (for $115k); we got $275k for it (half of that was mine). The second house bought in 1992 (for $150k) realised $207k.

In hindsight I shouldn't have sold those houses as at that point the market was moving up. That's one of the lessons! You can never really pick the market. I lost $200k by selling them too early.

Looking for properties with a future

With the $138k proceeds from the sale of the first house I paid a considerable amount off our own home and borrowed more to buy another place in North Canberra in a central location. It was an old cottage house that needed extensive renovations, which I undertook to do myself. The cottage was three bedrooms on a good size block (800 square metres), which is a subdividable area. We bought this for $230k in early 2002. We were beginning to target properties that had a future and had value built into them, not just close to the city but also subdividable.

I spent $30k on renovations, but I hired a retiree who charged lower hourly rates to help me. I got tenants in and did the renovations while it was tenanted. It was repainted and had a new bathroom, new curtains, carpets, landscaping, and trees felled to let sun in. The valuation is now $360k.

As you can't claim depreciation, interest and expenses on your own home, we had learnt it was better to pay off our own mortgage first.

Fourth house, in North Canberra. Lower interest rates and higher yields made buying it more attractive.

I had learnt this from reading a lot of books; I had been scouring the internet and finding sites that had courses or information on property investment. I haven't done the Richmastery courses. I did go to some other seminars, but as a trained economist I felt I already had covered a lot of the ground.

One of the most influential books that I read was *Think and Grow Rich* by Napoleon Hill. It's purely theoretical but inspires you to start thinking about wealth accumulation and taking action. Others include Steve McKnight and also Jan Somers: the most recent one I read of hers is *More Wealth in Residential Property*. She is one of the most detailed and highly analytical residential analysts; in her latest book she compares buying a house in different economic cycles and she still comes up with the view that investing in real estate is good.

For example, in the 1970s we had high inflation, high interest rates, now it's low inflation and low interest, but in both situations the value of houses remained above inflation at about the same rate (2% per annum).

Focusing on positive cash flow

By 2004 all of our properties have more than doubled in value over a relatively short period of time from the time of purchase due to a strong real estate market in Canberra. Our overall debt is 35% of our assets in real estate holdings and we have approval from the bank to borrow more than $1 million to acquire more property. Net income from our properties after expenses is $15,000 to $20,000 per annum. We are now focusing on properties with positive cash flow.

Lessons learnt

During this period of investing in real estate I have learned some valuable lessons.

> Real estate provides terrific returns over the long run but there are occasions where things may stay stagnant for a very long time and then all of a sudden it booms. Therefore if you can hold on to your properties (and have the capacity to acquire more though borrowing) do not sell because you are likely to miss the cycle and forgo future capital gains.

Most of the investments are in my name as I am the highest income earner and if we have a family my wife will take time off. I don't have it in a company; I'm not convinced that having it in a company is in my best interests, as in a company you don't get any negative gearing. You can't offset any losses against other sources of income; you can only offset your losses against future company income.

But if I make $100 loss from my investments I can offset that from my salary income in my current situation, which reduces my income tax. If I have a company I can't do that. It would be best to have a company if I was working for myself.

Real estate is a numbers game. The more you look for properties the more you are likely to find what you are after. It is important, though, to stay focused and allocate some of your time in searching for properties on a regular basis.

Currently I think the best way to be active is to identify positive cash flow properties to ensure that you are protected from any sudden rises in interest rates and a change in the economic mode. Positive cash flow properties are a lot harder to find in most capital cities but the market is beginning to turn and they will become more likely to find if you know how to turn them into positive cash flow.

For example, I am currently working at converting one of our inner city properties near the university to student accommodation by building an additional three bedrooms and charging by the room. I have also bought a another property near my home for $273k, less than $42k below its asking price because it has an unapproved bathroom which I am getting it approved for less than $1000 in lodgment fees for a new revised plan. I had it rented out for $310 per a week before we settled.

Because the market has been so hot, I am focusing primarily on positive cash flow properties, to avoid going into the red. If I have cash flow I can keep buying properties. I just have to become smarter in finding them, such as rundown properties or in suburbs that have not yet moved up. This has led me to decide to take up a builder's licence through TAFE (equivalent of a polytechnic in New Zealand). I see this as a nice way of keeping my options open, if I want to move in this direction by reducing my full time employment hours. I also save money by managing my properties myself, learning valuable skills and saving 10% on agent commissions. I reduce my repair and maintenance costs by hiring retirees and mature age workers.

(Note: Chris' family name was withheld by request.)

TOP TEN TIPS

1. Get into the right frame of mind when investing by reading extensively.
2. Associate with positive people.
3. Make investing a part of your life; enjoy the game, like a hobby.
4. Location and timing are important.
5. Stay in good sized cities, close to major facilities and services.
6. Look at rezoning, redevelopment, sites that have potential.
7. Buy and hold is a good strategy because you can never really predict the right time to sell.
8. Treat your tenants well.
9. Reduce costs by working smartly, refinancing to get a better deal from the banks, using leverage to get deductions on interest.
10. Don't invest in real estate in boom times unless you buy a bargain.

Chapter 19

Riding a rocket

'When do we stop? Don't know if we ever will — we love it too much!'

— **Lynnette and Eddie Butler,**
Nelson, NZ

My husband Eddie and I live in Nelson, at the top of the South Island, with our two children, aged six and four. We met in the air force on our recruit course and then got together in Woodbourne, Blenheim, a city not far from Nelson. We both trained for four years, Eddie as an aircraft technician and me in avionics. When we finished our training we lived in Blenheim because I was posted there, and so Eddie changed his posting to join me.

The air force was our leg up as we lived cheaply in married quarters, which allowed us to buy a section in Renwick, Blenheim for $20k. We used Eddie's hotrod money as a deposit and had a vendor finance mortgage. After all our weekly expenses we only had $10 left over each week. Two years later we sold the section to buy our own home.

Painful buying

I found shopping for a house with Eddie tough because he was very scared of debt. His family hadn't had debt for 10 years, so to him borrowing $100k was scary, and yet the houses we could afford weren't perfect enough for him! Our first home in Blenheim was bought for $105k; its market valuation was $115k. It was a three bedroom villa, with a lovely big sleep-out. We did a small amount of decorating and put on a new garage.

Eddie left the air force after nearly eight years and got a job for Air Nelson. I stayed in Blenheim while he commuted, staying in Nelson four nights a week and then coming home to Blenheim for the weekend. Eddie was studying during that period to become a licensed aircraft maintenance engineer. Eventually this commuting got just too hard, and I put in my notice and put the house on the market. We'd been there five years. It took 11 months to sell and we got $134k for it.

Buying in Nelson was, like it had been in Blenheim, painful. Eddie wanted the perfect house and we'd been looking for ages. During this time we discovered we could build a new house for not much more than an existing one, then sell it quickly for a good margin.

We bought a section in Lusty Place, Stoke for $70k, which we paid cash for, and then built a house on it for $101k. Once the house was completed the property was worth $196k. We had expected to have two wages when we built it but then I became pregnant. We were there for five years and had our two children. However, we were still struggling to pay the mortgage and in fact we were going backwards.

Looking for a better way and a good buy

We'd been reading books, such as *Rich Dad, Poor Dad*. It's funny that they're not 'how to' books but they get into your head. They gave us a mindset, a can do attitude. We could see that, like our parents, we could work hard all our lives for someone else, and at the end have a mortgage free home and a small nest egg which then could erode away to nothing through ill health. Our parents hadn't even got to retirement before this happened to them! We didn't want to find ourselves in that situation but felt we were heading the same way, never able to get ahead.

> The options we had were to invest in shares, or a business, or property. We chose property because we didn't have any cash, only equity.

We made the tough decision to sell our home and free up some of that equity by buying a cheaper house. We sold Lusty Place for $231k in February 2002 and walked away with equity of $80k.

We then bought a four bedroom home in Washington Road in Nelson for $147,500. At the time all our friends were upgrading and doubling their mortgages and they thought we were a bit nutty as Washington Road was a bit of a downgrade. During our first week there Eddie helped catch some amateur car thieves, so we wondered what we'd let ourselves in for. But that was the only trouble of that sort we had, and it really was a good move for us. When we bought it we knew we would be there for about 18 months, and then rent it our.

The plan was then to use the equity we had in our new home and buy a rental property. But the market had taken off and it was hard to find properties where the numbers worked. We shopped hard; we often went to 14 open homes in one day with two little kids in tow. Sometimes the girls refused to get out of the car.

We looked at about 60 properties a month for nine or 10 months. Eddie didn't like shared driveways or cross leases so it took me a while to work him around these obstacles! Finally we saw a property that we liked but someone had beaten us to it and had an offer in. I put in a back up offer of $130k, which was the asking price. In the end I negotiated the vendor down because the property failed the building inspection; it was valued at $125k.

Major do-ups

I attended a property seminar run by Daryl Fisher that suggested I set up an LAQC, so we did this and put our first rental straight into it. This first one, Washington Terrace, was a two bedroom pole house in central Nelson with a one bedroom flat underneath that was not built to building standards. We had to completely rebuild the external walls on the flat. We were told it was two weeks' work, but four months and $60k later we finished the renovations. We redecorated the flat and added a second bedroom downstairs by putting in a new wall. We brought the flat up to legal standard and put in a new bathroom upstairs.

We kept the tenants upstairs during the renovations, paying rent of $200, and once we'd finished, we rented the bottom flat for $200 also. At the end of the project, the house was valued at $200k. It's now valued at $305k and the total rent is $440 per week.

Before we had taken possession of Washington Terrace, Eddie had purchased another property just before Christmas while I was away in

The pole house in Washington Terrace, Nelson required substantial renovations. At the end of the project, it was valued at $200k. It's now valued at $305k.

Christchurch. The real estate agent knew what we were looking for, as we had put some offers in through her before, and called Eddie to say she had a place we should see. It was a two bedroom house upstairs with a pottery shed on the patio, and a bedsit downstairs. The vendors were asking $149k. We offered them $144k on Christmas Eve. They accepted it immediately as they had already bought another place. And so we bought another property in Jenner Road, Victory, Nelson.

To purchase this property we had to refinance from ASB to ANZ, as ASB wouldn't go to 95%, interest only. In the end we only needed to go for 80%, as we had enough of the major work done on Washington Terrace for the valuation to have improved sufficiently.

The new house was a do-up. Our renovations included lining the potter's shed as a sleep-out and fixing up the flat below so that it was a nice little home. We finished the upstairs first, and let it out. The tenants said they wanted it furnished for three years, so we spent $4000 and furnished it. (They paid an extra $40 per week for that, but then only stayed until November! However, the new tenants rented it furnished too.)

Meanwhile, we redecorated the bedsit below, repainted, put in new vinyl, new bench top, and then rented it for $150 per week. We spent $20k all up but added huge value. The property was revalued at $215k based on the rental. It's now valued at $285k.

When we began the work at Jenner, we decided to move in for a few weeks and ended up staying seven weeks! We were living on mattresses, our youngest in a port-a-cot which she was too big for, and we were all stressing out a bit as we were, at the same time, looking for a new house for ourselves. But the market was on fire; we were putting in lots of offers but were missing out.

Our own home, finally

Our next purchase was another do-up, with a six month settlement. It needed a new kitchen, new garage and new ranch slider. They were asking $219k and, as the market was so hot, we offered $223k. There were lots of offers and we made our offer more attractive to her with a long settlement date, which suited us just fine too. It was only on the market for a week. The house is in Richmond near a good school, which our girls can walk to. We felt that we had found our home and were relieved to know that this is the house we want.

We didn't do the ranch slider, kitchen and garage – we did the whole house! The house is now completely insulated, rewired and replumbed, so it's good as new. The renovations are still in progress.

But at that stage we were still living in our four bedroom house in Washington Road. Before the move we got the old home revalued at $250k and sold it into our LAQC. We've rented it out for $350 per week. We then transferred our personal mortgage over to the new house.

A quick land deal

During the settlement period for the new home, we ended up buying a section off a builder through the *Buy, Sell, Swap* paper. He had bought it from

We spent $20k on the Jenner Road house but added huge value. Post-renovation it was revalued at $215k and is now valued at $285k.

the guy who'd done the original development (for about $60k), but had a new opportunity present itself before he got round to building on it, so we bought it off him for $85k. In the end we decided it was uneconomical to build a new rental for ourselves, after having house plans drawn up, valued, and had rent appraisals done. So at the last minute we put it in our family trust and then spent $150 getting rid of the rubbish and mowing the lawn and we sold it two weeks later for $130k. We ended up making $40k (after costs). You just have to love a deal (and a market) like this! The profit on this deal paid for most of the renovations on our new house.

West Coast buys

In January 2004 we looked at some properties that we had seen on the internet in Hokitika, a town on the West Coast of the South Island about four hours south of Nelson. We didn't buy any of the houses we saw there, but on our way home we stopped in Greymouth, a bigger town 20 minutes north of Hokitika. We saw one in a good part of town, and got it for $80k, the government valuation (GV). In the Nelson market you had to sign on the bonnet of the car or you would miss out, but down there it took six weeks just to get the deal signed!

The house was a three bedroom with two lounges in Shakespeare Street. The rates are $1800. It was tenanted at $160, but we had had it assessed by a property manager at $180. It had looked good with furniture in it but when that was removed it was a different story. When we took it over we found the place wasn't in nearly as good condition as we thought. A whole sash window and most of the wall below it needed replacing, and this had been missed on the building inspection.

We spent approximately $15k renovating it. There was a huge laundry room, so we moved the laundry into the enclosed porch and created a new room, plus turned the second lounge into another bedroom. We repainted the bits of interior that hadn't been done in a while, and recarpeted throughout. We also put in an off street carpark and tidied the yard. We had tradespeople do all the work, and I project managed it over the phone. It is now valued at $140k and rented at $250 to a family who love it.

We brought two more properties in Greymouth while we were negotiating this deal, through the same real estate agent. The first one was at Packers

Quay, Blaketown, and backs onto a lagoon. It was a four bedroom house with a double garage (single door though!) on two sections. Some 202 square metres of it was leasehold and 202 square metres freehold. We bought this for $63k. The rates are high at $1200, but we knew it would rent at $150. After renovations of $15k we rented it for $190. We have been able to freehold the leasehold section for $4000. It was revalued at $78k.

The third place we brought was at Runanga, a small settlement 7 km north of Greymouth. The lady who owned it was moving to a pensioner flat. She had lived in the house for over 50 years, the house was in mint condition and funnily enough it had no stove, only a coal range. We paid $55k. The rent appraisal was $120 but we rented it for $160. This was a good buy as it has a lovely outlook. We used a property manager to find a tenant for that one, but we have had no problems renting out any of our houses in Greymouth. In fact there seems to be a shortage of rentals down there.

The reason we started looking down the West Coast was for cash flow and now we found we had the cash flow but we were fast running out of equity to fund deposits on new houses.

Investing in education

Around this time we were also shown the Richmastery website by a friend who we'd played the Robert Kiyosaki 'Cash Flow' game with. Then one day I was reading *Kiwi Property Investor* (KPI) magazine (which we get as part of our membership to the Nelson Property Investors Association but which is also available through www.richmastery.com) and I read about the three day Richmastery Property Academy.

Eddie knew I really wanted to do the academy and although it was $3995 plus travelling and accommodation and other expenses, we knew we were going to get a decent chunk of this back in tax, so we decided to invest in our education. We had the philosophy that if I learnt one new thing it'd be worthwhile: mistakes can be very expensive when your business is property. So I enrolled to attend the Richmastery Property Academy in May 2004.

Equity property

Meanwhile, we found an equity property in Nelson through a private sale in the paper. This was a duplex of two townhouses in Murphy Street, Victory area. The buildings were six years old. They were asking $360k for the two; we paid $318k. Each has two bedrooms and they are 63 square metres houses, back to back, fully furnished, and came with good tenants. They now rent at $505 per week and are valued at $350k.

> We had become complacent and didn't get a building inspection done this time, largely due to the houses being of permanent material, and only six years old. This was a mistake which we didn't pick up until later when we discovered the house had a broken laundry waste pipe in the wall. Just to add insult to injury, our insurance company wouldn't come to the party, as they said the damage had been there before we bought the house, and the previous owner's insurance company weren't accepting liability either.

However, after we had fixed the leak, the problem was remedied quite easily, so this was quite a relief. But the place was empty for seven weeks because of this problem and it took us two weeks to find a tenant.

Changing habits

I attended the May 2004 Richmastery Property Academy in Auckland, soon after buying Murphy Street, but before the leak raised its ugly head. The academy totally motivated me; I came back home from Auckland after the three day course riding a rocket.

I had been chatting with Martin Ayles (an Australian renovations expert who presents at the academy). We discussed some things, and he issued me a

We bought two townhouses in Murphy Street, Nelson at a discount for $318k; they are now valued at $350k.

personal challenge. You see, my office is disorganized with paperwork everywhere, and no systems or cash books. The challenge for me was to tidy my office, clear the bench and change the habits that created the mess. I reported to Martin every four days. It terrified me when he issued that challenge. The penalty if I missed reporting in with him every four days was a $2000 fine. But the fine wasn't the scary part of the challenge – the scary part was changing me!

I knew I needed to change. It's one of those things that if your husband tells you a million times you ignore him, but if a perfect stranger tells you then you do it. I felt a real transformation. I've slipped back a little since but things are heaps better.

When I got back to Nelson, I went really full on for six weeks, and cleaned out boxes of paper work, and I also did three years of taxes for our previous business, as well as our new one, and implemented some systems. Eventually I suffered a bit of a burnout. It's quite scary to put in 150% for weeks on end and I overdid it. It took quite a while to recover from that.

No stopping now

Our latest purchase was a property in Russell Street, Nelson which settled in February 2005. It is two stand alone little 55 square metre Hardiplank 'box' townhouses, on separate titles. We purchased them for $245k and they were valued at $300k. The rental return is $470 per week. Even after redoing the driveway, which was rough and had a nasty hump at the top, we are achieving over 9% net return. In Nelson, a high capital growth area, that is fantastic.

We have gone full on for just on two years now, but for what we have achieved, it has all been worth it. It's hard finding a balance between our family and friends, and our property, but if you put first things first, you can do it. Our kids are growing up with lots of family moments, yet are becoming quite wise in what we are up to as well. It is one of our goals to educate the girls enough that they'll own a place of their own right from leaving school, and let their flatmates help pay for it! And when do we stop? Don't know if we ever will – we love it too much!

Currently our total portfolio value is $2.156 million, and total mortgages $1.574 million, giving us total equity of $582k. Our total after tax cash flow is $32k approximately, from rentals of $146,380 per annum.

TOP TEN TIPS

1. If it was easy everyone would do it.
2. Entities: sort them out before you start.
3. Spend your money ten times over (in your head) before you draw it out of the bank.
4. You need to assemble a good team (broker, accountant, valuer, conveyancing, builder, electrician, plumber, rental manager, etc). If you're not happy with the service you receive, replace them!
5. Don't begrudge paying the valuer.
6. We have accounts all over town asking for trade price. Get a discount; buy your own materials rather than having the contractor supply things.
7. Don't be afraid to go to different valuers, you need to have a good relationship with the one you choose.
8. Be fair and value your tenants. A-grade properties attract A-grade tenants.
9. Make sure you have your chattel apportionments done on your properties. It will save you a fortune in tax. Valuit (0508 4 VALUE) are the experts in this field.
10. Don't be afraid of being a tall poppy. Stop and have a cup of coffee — you've got to value yourself and your family life more than anything.

Chapter 20

Changing attitudes

'The biggest thing we learnt was to take action ... the information is useless if you don't use it.'
— **Jennifer Lim and Jared Hoy Fong,** Auckland, NZ

My partner Jared Hoy Fong (28) and I, Jennifer Lim (24), have 10 investment properties that we have purchased over the last 18 months and this is the story of how we did it.

Jared had been working in IT for five years for a small company. He had risen to the role of GM and he felt there was not much more he could achieve there. He felt that for his own personal growth he needed a change.

Jared bought his first house in January 2000 after seeing Robert Kiyosaki speak. He had had his car stolen and decided to buy a property with the insurance payout. 'Looking back I can see that I went in blindfolded. I paid the top price,' he says. It is a two bedroom terraced house in Balmoral, a suburb in central Auckland. It had a registered valuation of $195k. It is rented at $330 per week and although it is now worth $240k, it has a bad return.

Jared says, 'I bought it for all the wrong reasons: because it was a brand new terraced house and I thought it looked trendy. I didn't get a building inspection (although this was before the leaky building saga broke in New Zealand). I paid a 10% deposit and got a principal and interest mortgage for the rest. I wouldn't do any of these things now and only learnt to do the numbers after this experience.'

I met Jared in October 2000 when I was studying Marketing, IT and Business at Auckland University of Technology. Jared would leave me studying in the evenings and head along to seminars about property with his father,

Grange Road flats, Mt Eden: the 'worst house in the best street'. The kitchen before renovations.

Ron (who features in chapter 1). His father regretted selling properties so I was able to avoid the mistakes he has made and learn from his experiences.

Changing our views on money

Jared says he had a completely different attitude towards money before the Robert Kiyosaki seminar. Before that evening he was earning money and spending it on partying and on cars. Kiyosaki was a great motivator in changing the way he thought about money. Basically it meant making use of your money and rather than spending it on 'looking' rich (which a lot of people do) using it to 'become' rich instead. We now spend money only on things that appreciate rather than depreciate.

I learnt to save and, unlike other students, I don't have a big student loan. During the entire time I was studying I always tried to save from my part-time job. I worked for an IT company 20 hours a week so lived on this income and managed to save too.

I graduated in March 2002 and started full time work for the IT company. I had about $10k in the bank and we were planning to go on our OE or 'overseas experience' (as it's called in New Zealand). Jared had been waiting for me to graduate but, when I finally did, at the same time he got a promotion at work so we didn't go. I thought I could spend the money upgrading my car and perhaps go on a trip overseas.

But Jared said that if I buy a house and do it right, I could probably buy a car and go overseas as well. So I read up. I only read one chapter of *Rich Dad, Poor Dad* and I had a goal. I had enough money for a 10% deposit on

Grange Road kitchen after tidy up. 'You soon learn how to speed things up.'

a very cheap house.' That was in April 2002. By the end of the year we owned another five houses.

I realise now it's all about educating yourself. A lot of people don't know how to do that. Now it seems logical. I don't understand why people are not taught this stuff in school.

Buying five houses

In June 2002, Jared bought a two bedroom unit in Onehunga, a do up. To buy this one he got his first house in Balmoral (the terraced house) revalued and used the extra equity to buy the Onehunga house. We repainted it and did cosmetic work. Jared bought it for $156k. It's now worth $260k and is rented at $260 per week. We spent $2000 on renovations. It was simple stuff – paint, new curtains, new door handles and light shades. We managed to do it up before settlement and had it rented by settlement.

Then I bought my own place in Onehunga in the same month, June 2002. Boy was it a mess! The vendors were asking $120k and we got it for $115k. We put on an extra room by adding two walls and a door in the large lounge. This cost us $5k, including the cost of other renovations. It took us three weeks to do it up. Jared and I did all the work ourselves, tidied it up, painted, carpeted and so on. The valuation immediately after the work was completed was $160k; the property is now worth $255k. We found it very exciting; we weren't nervous at all.

Straight after that, because the value of the Onehunga property had risen to $160k we refinanced and upgraded my new car, paid off half my student loan (about $10k) and still had enough equity to buy the next place. We realised we needed to set up correct entities before we carried on, and so set up an LAQC each.

In February 2003, Jared purchased a flat in Grange Road, Mt Eden, a nice suburb in central Auckland. He saw an ad for a tender for a deceased estate in the paper. We had been looking for the previous couple of months around the areas so we had a rough idea of what it was worth. We put in a tender for $128k and got it. It was in a block of 10. If you drive past the block it doesn't look like it belongs in Mt Eden. But as they say: buy the worst house in the best street. The flat is quite large, 50 square metres, so we added a wall to make another small bedroom because it had worked so well in Onehunga. In total we spent $5k on renovations. It rents for $260 per week. Just one month later it was valued at $160k.

In Auckland it's hard to find good cash flow positive properties so you have to be creative and be able to add value. We have focused on Auckland because we know the city much better than anywhere else in the country and because Auckland is a desirable place and the country's largest city it will continue to grow.

In February 2003 we purchased a 33 square metre studio unit in Remuera, a well to do suburb of Auckland. We got it for $109,500, which was below the asking price. We rent it out at $200 per week. The vendor was selling two units in the same block so we negotiated them down quite a bit. We ripped out a wall in the bathroom and joined it with the toilet and put in a new shower. It made a massive difference; it was much lighter. It's now valued at $150k.

We got really excited about each of our new properties and what we could do with them. We try to do as much as possible ourselves before getting a tradesperson in. During this whole period we pretty much didn't have a social life. It was straight after work, weekends and taking the odd day off work to get it done but we were doing it together, which made it quite fun. We would work on each other's properties; we enjoyed it. The first couple of renos took ages – we sanded everything back to perfection. You soon learn how to speed things up and we got faster on each property.

Learning to take action

In May 2003 we attended the three-day Richmastery Property Academy. A month or so earlier we had gone along to a Richmastery Profit from Property evening seminar at the Sheraton Hotel in Auckland and had signed up that night. We found the academy was very good. It confirmed that what we were doing was right and a few more things. Jennifer says the best part for me was the presentation by International Peak Performance and Success Coach, Kurek Ashley. He made it all come together about your mindset. From that stemmed a lot of personal development.

> Since the academy we have both done a lot of personal development work; I listen to all the Tony Robbins DVDs and tapes. Jared really likes Brad Sugars' DVD – he's so laid back but switched on. The biggest thing we learnt was to take action, as all of the information and education is useless if you don't use it.

As a result of attending the first one, we crewed on the Richmastery Property Academy in May 2004.

After completing the academy in May 2003 we formed a joint LAQC. We thought we should do this as it made sense and we are more powerful financially with our combined incomes plus the amount of equity we could cross over and use.

The first property we bought in our new entity was in June 2003 in Otara. We found this quite scary as it has a reputation for being Auckland's worst suburb. But we had learnt from the academy that we were too tied up in some areas and only wanting to invest in good places.

So we took the plunge and went outside our comfort zone. We purchased a three bedroom house with a double carport in Otara for $121k. It was valued at $152k at the time and will most likely be a lot higher now. It's rented at $275 per week. We spent $4k on cosmetic renovations including painting, new curtains, door handles, light shades and a new fence. It has turned out to be one of our best properties.

> We were still a bit nervous when we signed up as cash unconditional, but we have discovered that clean offers are more powerful and you can make them as long as you have done your due diligence. You can often get the property if you are competing against another buyer with a higher price but who has attached conditions.

The next property we purchased in November 2003 was another unit in the Onehunga block where we already owned one. We found out about this because one of the neighbours in the same block, whom we had become good friends with, called to say that the unit was selling. We checked out what the owner had paid for it by searching QV (Quotable Value) on line. He had paid $122k so we offered low for a private sale. He counter-offered for not that much more so we got the place for $125k. Again, we put in another wall, which cost more this time as we had to get a market rate builder in. We spent a total of $6k on the renovations, adding the extra bedroom, new carpet, painting new curtains, new door handles and light shades. A month later it revalued up to $245k. It rents at $255 per week.

Our next purchase was in January 2004 in Manurewa; like Otara this is a low socio-economic suburb in South Auckland. It was a huge place: a four bedroom, two level house. It had a kitchen and a kitchenette, two lounges, a closed internal access garage, which we converted into a playroom come bedroom with tiles and by gibbing the walls. We bought it through a friend, a property trader who found properties. It was valued at $230k; we bought it for $210k. We spent $15k doing renovations. We put down new carpet, painted, put in new light shades, switches and power point fittings, new door and cupboard handles, new curtains and terylene. Its current valuation is $257k and we rent it for $400 per week.

We found another place in Mangere, another low socio-economic suburb in South Auckland. It is a four bedroom house on a huge 1200 square metre section. The real estate agent who sold it to us did not know that we were investors; we generally don't tell them we are unless they ask. We put in an offer that finally got accepted. The agent also added in the contract without our consent that we would have to pay the deposit on the agreement being agreed upon – not on it going unconditional – much to our lawyer's disgust.

We purchased this house in January 2004 for $181k; its valuation was $195k. It is rented for $340 per week. With its huge section the property will be worth a lot more now.

Next we bought another place in Mangere in February 2004. It is a three bedroom house with a huge 1200 square metre subdividable section. We got this for $189k; its valuation a month later was $230k. We spent $6k on renovations including the usual: new carpet, repainting, new door handles and light shades. We bought this property because it is subdividable and already well below valuation. We plan to subdivide and build on it in the near future.

Getting the figures to work

In South Auckland we use property managers as it is a hassle for us to have to show people through and advertise for tenants because it is quite some distance from where we live in central Auckland. We have had problems with slack property managers but finally found one who does a great job.

> We do our figures with a calculator on all properties. We use the 2 to 1 Rule where possible: if the house costs $100k, you need to roughly expect a rent of $200 per week for it to be 'good' positive cash flow. All our properties are positive cash flow. One of the things that we've learnt is that even though you can do all these things to a property to up the value and up the rent, the figures have to work from day one when you buy. We have walked away from deals that don't stack up. If the figures don't work don't do it.

We both quit our jobs in March and April this year to work full time in property and our home based business. Our total portfolio is worth $2.5 million, and of this we have $1 million in equity. This earns us a passive income of $55,241 in annual after tax cash flow.

TOP TEN TIPS

1. Make sure the property you purchase works for you after you settle (i.e. positive cash flow without having done anything to the property).

2. Take action. Even if you don't know absolutely everything yet you'll learn along the way!

3. Concentrate on cash flow first, then equity.

4. Don't overcapitalise when renovating (in terms of both time and money).

5. Always ask for a counter-offer. That is, don't ever make two offers (or more) in a row on the same property.

6. Don't get emotional.

7. Don't buy in small towns that have little growth.

8. Have a good team of experts and tradespeople.

9. You don't find the deals — you create them!

10. Most importantly, have fun!

Chapter 21

No money down

'Since 2000 I have purchased over 18 positive cash flow properties ... I have never spent one cent of my own money.'
— **Stuart Pope**, Nelson, NZ

I moved to Nelson, at the top of the South Island, from Invercargill in 1998 following my marriage break-up. I was at an all time low. Over the previous 14 years I had set up and run a successful engineering company, Southland Hydraulics, but this had to be sold as part of my marriage settlement and I came away with almost nothing.

I decided I wanted to learn more about investing in property. I started going to seminars on the subject, including ones by Dolf de Roos, John Burley, Brad Sugars and Richmastery. I also read as many books on the subject as I could find.

Since 2000 I have purchased over 18 positive cash flow properties in Nelson and Invercargill with a total value of $2.55 million, increasing my net equity to $1.091 million and returning me passive income of $60,494 after interest, rates and insurance before tax. I have never put one cent of my own money into any of my property deals.

Learning on the job

In Nelson I eventually worked in a mortgage brokering franchise, Equity, which taught me all about money, banking facilities and how to deal with personal bank officers. Part of my job was to interview clients and to determine their financial position. This was responsible for me cleaning up my own financial position as well as learning the pros and cons of credit cards. When I was with Equity they trained me how to sell investment properties in Australia, and through this I learned all about negative gearing, appreciation, depreciation, retirement investment.

I moved into selling investment properties on the Gold Coast; in hindsight not such a great thing but it introduced me to the various advantages available.

We were having difficulties running the Equity business from a distance so we decided to resign the franchise. My partner and I then formed a company and we continued introducing solutions where we controlled the back up service to clients. Some of our clients at this stage were able to invest in property. So I assisted them in the property selection process. I helped them to set up their bank accounts and get the whole process working for them.

Learning more

It was around this time I decided I wanted to learn more about investing in property. I started going to seminars, with the first one Dolf de Roos' seminar in Wellington in 1998. I also went to John Burley's, Brad Sugars' and a Richmastery Profit from Property seminar in Christchurch. I found them all extremely inspiring. I even had a one on one with Graham Fowler in Wellington.

I bought as many books as I could find and had an insatiable appetite for reading them to the point of absolute frustration for my partner. I have read *Real Money Real Estate* by Phil Jones, and more than 100 other books on property, personal development, business, legal, accounting, tax, trusts and personal biographies. *The Four Laws of Debt Free Prosperity* by Blaine Harris and Charles Coonradt is the best, along with John Burley's *Money Secrets of the Rich*.

I have subscribed to *Kiwi Property Investor* (KPI) magazine (available from www.richmastery.com) since it started; I now read it religiously. I am very interested in seeing people realising that property investment is real, that they can do it and it is not rocket science.

I learned a lot at these seminars and purchased all the books and software on offer. I now focus on passive income and positive cash flow properties.

'What are you waiting for?'

After one of the seminars they encouraged you to go out and do it – 'What are you waiting for? Next week go out and put 10 offers on properties!' But I had no equity and no money saved.

I looked at properties, put some figures into a spreadsheet that I developed, and when they came out with positive cash flow I put in unconditional offers. Dolf de Roos says, 'See 100, offer 10 and buy 1.' So I saw approximately 20 properties, put offers on six and was successful with five. All of a sudden I had five unconditional deals and I felt as if I'd done something wrong because I was only supposed to get one out of the six. So I redid all the figures and convinced myself that they were all good deals. At that stage I was way out of my comfort zone and my partner was freaking out.

I contacted several clients who were in very good financial positions and gave them the opportunity to purchase these investment properties. I on-sold four of these to clients as I had purchased them 'as agent' so could transfer to their names. I kept one and that's what started me off.

Starting with a wrap

From Richmastery's seminar I had learnt about setting up LAQC companies. So I set up my first LAQC company, 2SP Freedom Property Ltd. Now we were investors.

The first property I purchased was a four bedroom weatherboard house on a large back section off a joint driveway in Kowhai Street in central Nelson. The list price was $125k; I purchased it for $100k. I was able to do that as the vendors were separating and were thus very motivated vendors.

I knew I needed a 20% deposit following the formulas I'd learnt from the seminars and books. I had no money. So I advertised for an investor for the $20k. This worked surprisingly well, and I found an investor to lend me $15k, for which I paid 10% interest and I was still $5000 short. Then I decided to wrap the property (a technique outlined by John Burley) where a 'tenant' enters a long term sale and purchase agreement, with me being the bank. They paid $5000 deposit to buy the property over 25 years for $125k. I then borrowed the rest from the bank.

The wrap programme worked exactly as John Burley had said it would. I had absolutely no issue with the tenants; they spent money on the house because they viewed it as their property.

Within a short time I revalued the property at $125k and recycled my equity.

The couple that I 'wrapped' onto only had the $5000 deposit and couldn't get a normal bank loan. They recently sold the house for $250k; I got my $125k back, they made $100k – a win-win situation for everyone.

Looking for motivated vendors

I continued looking for more investment properties for myself and clients. I started collecting properties by buying them when vendors were extremely motivated for whatever reason, such as with deceased estates, divorce, people moving out of an area resulting in a vacant house, bad tenants. This meant I was able to buy them at least 20% under valuation and offered unconditional agreements.

I think being aggressive with real estate agents also helped because they could try and find more offers so I would put time limits on a lot of my offers, so if they hadn't signed it by such and such a time I would withdraw it. Legally they had to present every offer to a vendor no matter how silly it was. On more than one occasion, once the vendors had signed it, the real estate agent expressed to me that they never thought the vendor would accept the offer. So that's why you have to insist they present every offer.

Focus on passive income

We ended up winding up the financial services company we started and I secured a job as an engineer for a local marine based engineering company, earning $55,000 per annum. At roughly the same time my partner decided that after two years in Nelson away from close family and friends she wanted to return to Invercargill. So she did and we broke up. I bought her out of the house owned by 2SP Freedom Property Ltd. To top it all off, the house I was renting was sold.

My ex-wife had since moved to Nelson and I shared a room with my son at her place and paid rent. We later agreed on a shared arrangement for custody of my son.

I became focused on creating my own passive income. I looked at all sorts of multi-level marketing ideas but it just didn't fit right. So I developed a little spreadsheet which recorded properties as I bought them and clearly showed me the passive income I was getting out of the properties after insurance, rates and general expenses. It also records property values, net equities and the like; it is tailored to my passive income focus. So every time I bought a property I added it to the spreadsheet.

For me personally the no responsibility as far as family was concerned aided my aggression. I only had my son to worry about so financial uncertainty wasn't such an issue, and I therefore took bigger risks.

Creating additional companies

From the Richmastery Profit from Property seminar I learnt the need to do chattel valuations on all my properties to maximise depreciation. The after tax position can only be assessed at the end of each year due to improvements and expenses.

I had 2SP Freedom Property, which I put the first few properties in. But I then found growing resistance from the bank to increase lending. So I decided to form another LAQC company and accumulated four properties in that, then started another LAQC and took this to a new lender. This allowed me to use different lenders so as to avoid cross guarantees with the existing properties.

Best Nelson deals

My first investments were solely in Nelson. Looking back some of the best deals are as follows:

The deceased estate I bought in Kawai Street in 2001 was a great deal. It had a tenant who had been there for three years, but the house had been on the market for six months and the family was desperate to sell. It had a government valuation (GV) of $90k, with a list price of $84k. My unconditional offer for $69k was accepted.

Definitely my best Nelson buy: two titles with two two-bedroom flats (at left) and two one-bedroom places with a three bedroom house behind (right). I didn't put in a cent; they're now worth $700–800k.

It was a small two bedroom back section Hardiplank house with a small garage and fenced section, and was rented for $160 per week. The valuation dated March 2004 was $190k and it is now rented at $185. The deposit was from recycled equity.

I met a good real estate agent socially through my golf club. She started off as a PA for a real estate agent so she started feeding me through what she thought were good investments, but I've found the agents don't really know what good investments are and they sucked in a heap of people through the boom.

She put me onto a two bedroom flat that was one of four in a block in Stoke. It was very run down and untidy and the vendors were motivated to sell because of a problem tenant. I purchased it for $62k; it was listed at $85k. I did some superficial tidying, spending $500–600. The first tenants into the property wanted to decorate the flat. I said I would pay for the materials and they paid cheaper rent and completely renovated it inside. That property was valued in March 2004 at $185k and it rents for $195 per week.

The winner

Here's the mind blowing one. In April 2002, my same real estate agent said she had an elderly gentleman interested in selling his property in Washington Drive; he wanted $380k. I took a quick gulp as it was a lot of money. The government valuation (GV) at the time was $339k, so he was asking way above GV in a depressed market. So I went with the agent and the vendor to inspect the property, which had five rental units (five income streams).

There were two titles: two one-bedroom places with a three bedroom house behind on one property, and two two-bedroom flats on the adjacent one. All are roughcast with an iron roof and very well kept. They were all fully tenanted with one tenant having been there for 20 years. Total rents were $695 per week.

So I did all the sums on 100% financing while I was at the agent's office – it was something like $15k positively geared per annum. I needed $70k for the deposit so I asked the agent for a private meeting with just the vendor and me, which they reluctantly agreed to. I asked the vendor what he was going to do with the money when he sold the property. He said he was going to play the stock market and put most of it in the bank. I said to him that I would pay his price, which was well above GV, if he would lend me the deposit at 10% interest per annum and I would get the rest from the bank. He agreed to this, after considering it overnight. Because he hadn't listed it he managed to negotiate the agency fee right down. I have never had to spend any money on maintenance. Rents are now about $750. But the value of these properties has skyrocketed. The latest valuation in September 2003 was for $600k but now it is probably worth $700–800k, all without me putting in one cent. I still owe him about $25k, which I'm still paying 10% on.

> I was testing different ways of doing deals where you got your money out or putting no money down – if I had never asked him what he was going to do with his money I would never have been able to do the deal.

Refocus on Invercargill

When the Nelson market got too hot real estate agents resisted presenting my offers to vendors. So I moved my focus away from Nelson. Having come from Invercargill (at the bottom of the South Island) I knew the city well, and when a new policy of zero student fees was brought in at the Southland Polytechnic there was a huge influx of people moving to Invercargill and, consequently, good demand for rental property there.

So I made a few trips down south to visit family, enjoy the fishing and diving and check out the property market. These trips were tax deductible, of

When the Nelson market got too hot I refocused on sound properties in Invercargill, like this one.

course! The property market in Invercargill had definitely hotted up since I had left in 1998 but was still returning well above 10% gross.

It was September 2003. I found vendors weren't as keen to accept my lower offers and I had to do more negotiating, while still maintaining at least 10% gross return. On several occasions I walked away from deals because vendors' expectations were too high. But I ended up purchasing eight positive cash flow properties with above 10% returns.

Favourite buy

My favourite deal is the last one I found when I was down in Invercargill for family reasons. I was checking out the local property magazine and I came across a large property split into two three-bedroom rentals in central Invercargill, with a total asking price of $140k and returning $300 per week. I called the agent and agreed to meet him at the property, and met three other agents there with their respective purchasers. So I put an offer in at the asking price. To the agent's surprise and mine the out of town vendor accepted. I didn't have to spend a cent on the property as it was already tenanted and they have stayed.

Management

I have all my Invercargill properties managed but I look after my Nelson ones. I find I have to stay in touch with property managers to keep them on the ball. I have bought 'Mr and Mrs Jones New Zealander' properties, not student flats, in Invercargill.

Managing my own Nelson properties has been okay; I've been to the Tenancy Tribunal once but nothing dramatic. I monitor my own rents and I've set up my own systems. I have a team of plumber, joiner and electrician that I call on when anything is needed.

Equity managed businesses

I continued reading and learning. I went to another Brad Sugars seminar in Wellington in mid 2003, which inspired me to start my own business.

With Southland Hydraulics, most people who bought my goods and services did so on credit, so we were always struggling with cash flow. So I decided the sort of business I wanted was where clients paid in cash or by Eftpos. Through Brad Sugar's seminars and books I realised this could be all sorts of retail type businesses. I also knew I didn't want to work in the businesses but have them provide me with an income.

The first opportunity to arise was with Margaret, my ex-wife, who told me her boss had been trying to sell her beauty therapy business. She wanted $60k and I offered $20k. She didn't immediately accept but did so after a couple of weeks. So I installed Margaret as manager and she was rapt! I had acquired my first business, Elegance Beauty Ltd; it was March 2003.

I had 100% shares. My aim is to have equity managers (a manager with a shareholding) so I'm not involved in the day to day running of the business. I sold Margaret 30% shares for $7000 and it's going very well.

Through scanning the newspapers I found a woman wanting to sell a very small hairdressing salon, right in the CBD, that was very badly run; she wanted $8000 and I negotiated to pay her $2500. I immediately advertised for a manager. I invested about $15k in the salon and completely renovated it. My manager recruited good staff and the business has blossomed.

I repeated the process in February 2004, buying a beauty and tanning salon and installing a manager.

I've found with businesses that now they are finding me, and this was the case with the next business too, a barber shop in Halifax Street in the CBD. The vendors wanted $40k for the business and lease; I negotiated $12k financed by the vendors as I knew they were going to walk out of the business and they didn't have any other offers.

so I have all these businesses being managed by FBD Ltd which is starting to tax my time and my relationships so I have decided that I need to change what I do in my general 8–5pm job primarily because my businesses demand 500% more time than the properties do to manage and run.

Keeping score

All this time I've been working full time five to six days, up to 50 hours a week in my engineering job and about 20 hours a week on property and business management. So the idea is to retire from my full time salaried job.

The market is settling down now. Real estate agents are coming to me with deals, there are a lot fewer 'to let' columns in the paper, and I am biding my time and learning about businesses until property comes back.

The property market is very cyclic; if you don't catch this cycle wait for the next one and be able to read it.

I recommend you keep a score card of net equity, assets and liability so you know where you are all the time.

TOP TEN TIPS

1. Education; go to seminars and read books.
2. Goal setting — my aim was passive income.
3. You have to have mentors: align yourself with people who've done it.
4. Get the right professional team; I've been through three lawyers and four accountants before finding the right ones.
5. Believe in yourself. I have always been very positive in the face of adversity.
6. Be assertive with bankers and real estate agents.
7. It's a numbers game; focus on the numbers not the emotion.
8. Get a formula and stick to it.
9. Good deals come around every day. Don't be hung up on ones that you miss out on or that don't meet your criteria.
10. Have fun!

Chapter 22

Give me passive income

'I focused on positive thinking and in six months it all exploded.'
— **Adam Laurie**, Melbourne, Aus

I attended the Richmastery Property Academy in August 2003. Before this I had been a little lost in my life. I had been a good employee, had built a successful business up and sold it and I was back to being a good employee again. But I knew there had to be another way.

> I attended the Richmastery Profit from Property seminar in Melbourne. I was so impressed that I paid my deposit that night to attend Richmastery's three day Property Academy in Sydney. Since then my outlook on life has changed.

I no longer work for a boss and have bought a mortgage broking franchise and this business is starting to prosper. I have since subdivided my owner occupied property and realised an extra $200k just by paying about $5000 in surveys fees and council fees. I have helped friends buy run down properties to renovate and rent out.

It looks like for taxation reasons I will have to buy an investment property in the very near future. I have great confidence in doing this after what I have learnt from my experience with the people from Richmastery.

The seed sown

I had been a retail butcher since 1981 before setting up my own business cleaning rental properties with a business partner. Running this business we found ourselves surrounded by investors. We would clean many different houses and then invoice the owners and realise that many of these people owned as many as 10, 11, or even 15 investment properties.

In the first year in the business we turned over $140k, but we got sick of cleaning and sold the business for a profit. I went back to being a good employee, working for a wine company. But the seed of my interest in property investment had been sown.

At that time I sold my owner occupier property in Blackburn, Melbourne. I had bought it brand new for $138k. It was a villa unit, two bedrooms, with a semi en suite, a separate toilet, lounge, dining, kitchen and laundry, double garage and a private lawn. It was one of three on an acre block. Just 16 months later I sold it for $198k in 1999 at auction. The market wasn't hot and the agents had said I would probably only get $155k for it. But I felt it was worth more, that it was worth about $185k. So I negotiated that the agent would get 1% commission if it sold between $155k and $165k, 2% if between $165k and $175k, and their normal 3% if it sold over $185k – so I did well to get $198k. I realised I'd just earned $60k in 16 months for doing nothing.

I decided to move to Yarra Glen, 40 km out of Melbourne. It was then classed as rural but now it's more of an extension of the city. I bought an old weatherboard home on half an acre for $115k. They were asking $138k. I offered them $110k, they said no as they had already turned down an offer of $110k. In the end I purchased it for $115k plus costs of $7500 and stamp duty of $3000, with a four month delayed settlement with option to reduce time.

I moved the settlement forward on my home and swapped securities. I ended up with an $80k mortgage at Yarra Glen plus a racing car and a new fridge and a few other doodads.

I went all hell for leather to pay off my new house at Yarra Glen and paid off the mortgage of $80k in three years. I had had it drummed into my head by my parents that you had to pay your mortgage off and that you weren't allowed to owe money to anyone. I worked more overtime than probably the average person was working in a week, I was working a good 85 to 90 hours a week for the wine company and had a weekend cleaning job.

I had a friend who was interested in investment books. I kept saying it doesn't work, but I did notice how he is a very positive thinker and a lot of other people I spent time with were very negative. They would say, 'Don't invest in property; just pay your house off and then buy a newer bigger house.'

Then my friend bought two investment properties in early 2002 and my interest was piqued. I had no idea how he had done it and I wanted to know more. I was reminded of the owners of the investment homes we had cleaned who had multiple properties (I used to think that this was just luck).

Learning multiple investment strategies

Soon afterwards I hit a brick wall in the vineyard job so I left and worked for myself subcontracting as a viticulturist but I didn't enjoy it. It was also hard to find work where I lived so I decided to sell house and move somewhere I could find a job. I thought if I could get $180k for my house, I could buy another house in the suburbs, find another job and get another loan.

But my friend the investor tried to talk me out of it. He was reading *Australian Property Investor* magazine (API available through www.richmastery.com) and found an advertisement for Richmastery's courses, he tore it out and gave it to me.

Around this same time he pulled me along to Henry Kaye's free seminar. I'd been to about 10–15 free seminars; they gave nothing and it was $14k to do Henry Kaye's weekend programme. We thought he must be joking.

Then we went along to the Richmastery Profit from Property evening seminar. It was $69.95, at the Novotel in Glen Waverly, Melbourne. My friend said if you don't like it I'll give you the money back. I went along and I just thought, wow, it made the most sense of all the seminars I'd been to. The Henry Kaye one was all about buying off the plans, deposit bonds, and was just too out of reach for someone like me.

After attending the Richmastery Profit from Property seminar I told my friend it was so fantastic that I had booked to do the three day Richmastery Property Academy. He thought this was great. As I had paid off my house and had $25k in the bank I was able to book early and get $500 off the Richmastery Property Academy so I got a $1000 discount straight away. So all up including my flights it cost me about $2700.

From what I had learnt at the Richmastery Profit from Property seminar I knew doing their three day course was the right course for me to do. I knew it would give me information on a range of investing choices: to be a buy and hold investor, to buy, renovate and sell, or to become a developer; whereas with the likes of the Henry Kaye type seminars they would say we have got an apartment block, do you want an apartment? With Richmastery's courses you learn multiple investing strategies.

My friend went to other seminars and we swapped notes. I started reading books then too, including A *Millionaire Mind, Streets Ahead*, and *Real Money Real Estate* by Phil Jones.

Focusing on the positive

Before I went to the academy I was ready to sell my house, I was going to cash everything in and look for an afternoon job earning me $400 so I could do as little as possible. But during the academy the Richmastery team asked us to say what we wanted and what we had. They asked: 'What's your situation?' I said I own my own home and they asked if the section was subdividable, and I realised the next door houses and mine might be subdividable.

After the academy I felt very positive, there were so many people from different backgrounds investing, whereas I had always thought success was

After completing the Richmastery Property Academy I had the confidence to help a friend buy and renovate this investment property.

My friend's renter after $15k of renovations immediately became cash flow positive.

what sort of job you had. We had doctors and lawyers on our table in their mid to late 50s and they had nothing but their good incomes, they'd spent everything.

I also really got the point about positive cash flow and not falling into the trap of not buying a house because I wouldn't live in it. I learnt that as long as the house has sexy figures it doesn't matter what colour the curtains. Because I'd read a lot most of the information was familiar but when I saw it explained on the screen or by the speakers it became much clearer.

Peak Performance and Success Coach Kurek Ashley says if you think negative, everything negative happens, and then it was like a revelation. So from then on I focused on positive thinking and in six months it all exploded. The Richmastery presenters also said it's hard to get off the wage, but try to think outside the square – so I thought, 'I'm sick of being a good employee.' I looked into something that would bring me in a passive income without me working.

Since the academy I have watched both business expert Brad Sugars' and Kurek Ashley's DVDs (I was inspired by them both when I heard them speak at the Richmastery Property Academy). These help keep me focused and positive.

Subdivision and a franchise business

I looked at cell phone franchises, spray painting detailing – all businesses that would give me an income. At this same time I looked into subdividing, and the council said no. So I took it to the tribunal, who said the council cannot say no. So after a year and much work with the Friends of the Environment and also dealing with submissions from local people, I am about to get a Permit for subdivision to divide my section into two lots of 1000 square metres.

I went along to the franchise show. I was always into mortgages after seeing Guardian Mortgages, who had come down from Queensland, and I thought it sounded good, so I had a good look at that. I spoke to Money Depot about becoming a franchisee. I met an honest person and they had one store going. I was the second or third to come in, that was a year ago.

I paid my deposit and then I started school for 10 days and then did the lender accreditation to learn about the business. I spent February and March setting up an office. So far I've invested $60k of the equity in my own home into this business and it's starting to take off now.

There can be a delay in being paid with mortgage broking but I love the fact that I help people. It also helps that I have a keen interest in property investing so I can answer their questions. They always have to check with their accountant, often they get told by their accountants that property is a bad investment and so on, so now we have sourced some good property lawyers, accountants and conveyancers that I can refer my clients to.

I am in the process of completing the subdivision, putting my house up for sale and the section without actually creating the new titles. The whole lot is now worth about $380k.

I have a passive income through mortgage broking that if I continue to sell at the rate I am now will be $70k a year at the end of three years.

 Once I sell my home and the section, I plan to buy a negatively geared capital growth property and a couple of positive cash flow properties to balance it out and complete the triangle – this is a tip I learnt from Richmastery.

I'm not looking to retire in the next 10 years as I enjoy what I'm doing with mortgage broking, and I will earn more out of this than property and I'm learning a lot about people investing.

I have many 50-year-old clients saying that playing the share market is not working for them and they wish they had invested in property five years ago. I also have many clients who are pensioners who can't pay their rates as their homes have gone up in value. We are now starting doing reverse mortgages, which they do in the United States, where if people are over 60 they can access equity in their homes without paying interest and interest is calculated and paid out of their estate. I have clients who are thinking of borrowing against their home, buying an investment property and living off the income from the investment property.

Doing a deal for a friend

Since completing the Richmastery Property Academy I helped a friend buy an investment property. We spent $15k renovating it (mostly exterior), and it became positive cash flow. I did the deal for him; he bought it for $225k and they said he'd get $215 for rent. Now he gets $275 a week.

I had been looking seriously at doing what Martin Ayles, the renovation expert, had done, but that worked when the market was hot. You could buy, renovate and sell a property and make an easy dollar, but this income is now in jeopardy as the market has softened.

The banks are making it much harder to invest and are not lending in certain areas of Melbourne, like high-rises and duplexes.

Looking ahead

A lot of people are saying I shouldn't sell my home but I can't earn enough rent off the new section as it is bare land. So I will sell both my home and the new section and buy two rental properties. My accountant has told me to start looking at investment properties.

You don't pay lenders mortgage insurance if you pay a deposit of at least 20%, so I will plan to only get loans to 80% of the value and because I am a mortgage broker, I can get a 0.3 to 0.5% discount on interest rates on loans.

I plan to source properties with land value, as they are not making any more land, so will try to buy an average house on a good block of land. That's the thing that Richmastery taught me.

I have my eye on some 1000 square metre blocks with three bedroom homes on them, all in a preferred subdivision area, that are going for $250k and can be rented for $275 per week.

In just 18 months since attending the Richmastery Property Academy I have achieved a total portfolio value $410k, a total business value (my business was purchased with my home equity) of approx $140k, while my total mortgages are just $65k. My total equity has increased from $115k to $485k.

I am receiving no income from rental properties as yet because I am about to sell off the subdivision and buy at least three positive cash flow properties. However, I am earning a passive income from my mortgage broking business that will be as high as $70k in three years' time.

TOP TEN TIPS

1. Buy on sexy figures, not sexy paintwork.
2. Shop around for the best finance (five hours can save you hundreds or thousands of dollars).
3. Buy properties with land content (they are not making any more of it).
4. Buy positive cash flow properties (an investment must make money, not cost you money).
5. Buy in suburbs next to suburbs that are increasing in value (they will increase next).
6. If buying rentals, choose properties that are low maintenance and close to services that tenants need (transport, shops, supermarkets etc).
7. Don't overcommit. Make sure you are comfortable with your situation.
8. Research, research and do more research — make sure you know the area you are going to buy in.
9. Build a great team around yourself; employ professionals (lawyers, accountants, quantity surveyors).
10. Education, education, education. Read books, go to properly run workshops, ask lots of questions and, of course, listen. Successful people will tell you all the secrets if you let them talk and just listen.

Chapter 23

No sitting still

'I have re-set my target to make $1 million passive income after costs from property over the next five years.'
— **Lindsay Topp**, Christchurch, NZ

I am 34 years old and live with my wife and family in Christchurch, the largest city in the South Island of New Zealand.

I started building my portfolio a little over two and a half years ago. I guess I introduced around $50k of my own money and now I own a little over $5 million in real estate (with shares in another $4.5 million odd that is development stuff).

Getting systems and structures sorted

I have always had an interest in property. I started out in business 10 years ago, and I always set up my businesses so they can run themselves; five years ago I focused on putting systems in place so I could move aside.

I did the Richmastery Property Academy in May 2003 after going to the Richmastery Profit from Property seminar in Christchurch a couple of months earlier. The main thing I got out of the three day course was what Matthew Gilligan, the Asset and Structures Planning expert from Gilligan Rowe and Associates (GRA) in Auckland, said about getting your structures sorted. I called GRA on the Monday following the Richmastery Property Academy and flew up to Auckland for an appointment with them a week later.

Christchurch renters

At that stage I had two businesses. I also was involved in a syndicate (with three other colleagues) that was in the process of building four apartments in Queenstown, of which we would keep one each. I also had a property in central Christchurch, which was a house in four flats: one three-bedroom, one two-bedroom and two studios.

I had bought this property for $187k in September 2002. It is situated in Churchill Street right in the inner city of Christchurch. It's an old house on a site zoned to fit 10 apartments. Two of the back flats (one of the studio flats and the two bedroom flat) were in very bad condition and were condemned. When I purchased it there were street kids living in it. Initially, my dad and others helped me renovate it. We repainted the whole place, inside and out. We put in new carpet and floor coverings, a wardrobe and new doors into the smaller flats, but I didn't need to do anything to the three bedroom flat. I spent $20k in total and got it revalued at $300k.

When the tenants moved out I spent another $15k on the two flats that hadn't been condemned, while the three bedroom and the other bedsit remained rented. I then got the place revalued for $385k in January 2004. It is now rented for $600 per week; the three bedroom gets $220 per week, the two bedroom $150 per week, the studio $120 per week, the second studio, which is a garage turned into a bedsit, is rented for $110 per week. This gives a before tax cash flow of $13,700 per year.

Apartment developments

With the Queenstown apartment development, Vailmont Apartments, the syndicate bought the section and built apartments for $495k each. We all put in $30k deposit and borrowed the remainder. My apartment was valued at $875k on completion in November 2003. The development took 16 months to build. One of the syndicate members, Chris, found the land and put the project together as well as managing it.

While the apartments were in the final stages Chris put another deal together and came to the syndicate members and offered each of us a fifth share in a development to build three luxury homes in Queenstown. (We each had one fifth shares to avoid the 25% threshold of being tainted as a

Two one-bedroom flats in Wellington Street, Christchurch. I turned the lounge of one flat into an extra room. The flats give a 13% return.

developer.) The four parties would put up $60k each and Chris would put in nothing (as with the apartments); this was his finder's fee and he would also be paid to manage this development.

I have since started another development with Chris called Arrowfield Mews (www.arrowfieldmews.co.nz). I am having a lot more to do with this project. Martin Lawn of Concept Builders Queenstown is building and project managing this development on a fixed price basis, while I am looking after all the admin side of the project (budgets, accounts and cash flow etc).

Arrowfield Mews is now under construction and once completed will total 22 three-bedroom luxury homes near Lake Hayes, and opposite Millbrook Resort, a stunning part of Queenstown, in the South Island.

The homes have started selling at $650k each and are valued at $745k. We've sold 11 and have taken the rest to the open market and will sell them once they are completed. The latest sale off the plan was for $700k. We are doing a show home launch in March 2005 and after that we expect to start achieving valuation figures.

We bought the land for this development at the end of 2003 for $2.8 million plus GST ($3.2 million). It was 1.5 hectares that was zoned residential. The building will be finished by Christmas 2005. We are doing the development in four stages; the first six homes were finished by end of February 2005.

These are managed homes, with a tennis court, swimming pool, gym and all the houses around are rural residential, so this will be the only high density

I moved this three bedroom house onto the spare land at Wellington Street, Christchurch. After moving and renovations it cost $105k.

housing in the area. We've had a lot of write ups on the development as we released it in Easter 2004.

One that didn't work

In February 2003 I found another house in Kilmore Street in Christchurch called the Vestery, a prime part of town. I contacted Chris and we put a concept together and sent it out to people who might want to put up $75k.

Our plan was to build a 16 unit apartment building; the price of the properties at that stage was $295k. The investors' total contribution would be $140k with a net profit of 118% return on their original investment but we couldn't find enough people to put up the money. So in the end Chris and I bought the property for $355k in May 2003. It's in three flats, which we rent out for $385 per week. It valued up to $490k in May 2004. We aim to hold on to it and to eventually develop it into the original 16 apartments we planned and to hold them.

Development is difficult, and you have to be careful. We've got a good group, but I am not a developer; I am just taking advantage of some opportunities that have arisen. Anything to do with property I love.

Positive purchases

After the Kilmore Street experience, I did the Richmastery Property Academy in May 2003 because I wanted to learn more. I had second thoughts on a property I was looking at (a group of three homes in St Albans) and let it go. I had heaps of contracts and I was making loads of offers, I had agents calling all the time and I was putting contracts on places left, right and centre. I have slowed down since then; because of the Arrowfield Mews development time has been tight but I will be back in to it soon.

In July I bought a house that was in two one-bedroom flats in Wellington Street, in Linwood, Christchurch. The purchase price was $120k. I turned the lounge of one flat into an extra room and rent the flats out for $320 per week, giving a 13% return.

This property also had a block of land out the back that was big enough to subdivide. So I relocated a three bedroom house onto it that I purchased for $18k; it came from Wedons and was an old air force base house (Wedons is near Rolleston about 15 minutes out of Christchurch). After all the expense, the new driveway and the carports, the property revalued at $345k plus. I didn't subdivide in the end; it's all on one unit title and has been surveyed for subdivision. I fully renovated the house after moving it and this plus the cost of the house and moving it was $105k. I have both houses rented now for $615 per week, which is $32k per year, and it owes me $225k, giving a 14.2% return.

In June 2003 I purchased a block of six flats in St Albans, 5 km from the centre of Christchurch, for $365k; they are now valued at $546k. I bought these before they hit the market, and they were asking $400k. I bought them through real estate agents who were actively looking on my behalf and I just made my offer on the numbers. They are brick and tile with aluminium

New warehouse purchased off the plan to accommodate my business. Bought for $1.55 million, when tenanted it will be worth $2.1 million.

225

windows, so are very low maintenance. I didn't need to spend anything and some of the tenants have been there for 15 years. They are rented for $140 per week (which is under-rented), giving an 11.9% return.

Next I purchased a commercial building in October 2003. I had no cash so I put $2000 on my credit card. The vendor was asking $240k plus GST. I bought the building for $185k and got a valuation of $200k; I sold it just over a year later at the end of 2004 for $260k.

I then bought a new factory off the plan off a developer for my company Independent Doors and Southern Doors to use. I got this for $1.55 million and it is currently being built. It's a 2000 square metres warehouse on 3000 square metres of land. When tenanted it will have a market value of around $2.1 million. The company will rent it off me for $176k per year.

Love the game

I have a reason for doing all this – I get a huge buzz out of the property game. I have a great bunch of people around me and enjoy working with them. I sometimes get asked for advice or offered to partner up in deals, and it is great helping people achieve their goals also. I get bored if I sit still.

My goal was to make a $1 million a year in profit and now I've achieved this I have re-set my target to make $1 million passive income after costs from property over the next five years. I have also started investing in shares and other businesses.

My goal for 2005 is to spend more time with my family and leave work at the office; I'm not sure how I'll go! My partner Kathy is also starting to look for opportunities so it would be great to do something with her.

My property portfolio is now worth $5.085 million. My total debt across the properties is $3.195 million, making my total equity $1.9 million.

I have no debt on any of my businesses and will be carrying a total debt on my business development of $7.2 million over properties worth $16.4 million.

TOP TEN TIPS

1. Always buy under value; you make your money when you buy.
2. Always look for a twist or angle: is the section subdividable or is there more than one income stream, such as with flats?
3. Honesty and integrity — I only deal with people with those values; I don't deal with dodgy people.
4. Set up your structures before you start.
5. Look for loyal real estate agents. I have a brilliant agent who goes the extra mile for me so I look after her. Look after people the way you want to be looked after yourself.
6. Get to know the area.
7. Set your rules and don't step outside them.
8. Work out how you want your portfolio to be before you start, and work out how you are going to get there.
9. Definitely buy more positive cash flow to support your negative cash flow.
10. Get a good team around you like good property managers, accountants (I have fired a few) and lawyers.

Chapter 24

An eye for a buy

'I'm just glad we have created options for ourselves through investing in property.'
— **Dennis Cashman, Sydney, AUS**

I live with my wife Anita and my two children in Sydney, Australia. I have six investment properties: three in Sydney, two in Tasmania and one in Queensland. In just five years I have built a total portfolio of $2.5 million and total equity of $1.1 million.

In 1998, I was working full time as a marine engineer, spending five weeks on at sea and five weeks off. I sat down with my accountant and looked at what my retirement was going to be like. I was 48 years old. At that stage we owned our own home, which was a 32-year-old house in Mt Colah, a suburb of Sydney, 22 km from the CBD. We had around $300k projected in a retirement fund.

Taking a loss

We also had an investment property in Pitt Street, central Sydney. This was a 75 square metre, one bedroom unit that I had bought in 1995, for $175k. When buying this we had followed someone's advice, which I know now wasn't a very good idea. It was rented out for $250, then $350; the vacancy factor was only days in a year. However, it didn't have fantastic depreciation, was high maintenance and it was a dull design.

We decided to sell this unit when the bathroom and laundry needed upgrading at a cost of around $30k or $40k, which would have caused us a cash flow crunch. We sold it at a loss for $171k in 2000.

> I learnt a good lesson here, which was not to listen to advice from others unless they are professionals, experts or people who have done it several times before.

At this point I became very concerned about our retirement situation and felt things were not looking good at all. I know the figures for retired folks for this country: 83% of the Australian working population retire with less than $12,000 a year to live on and 50% of those have less than $8000 a year to live on, and I didn't want to end up in that situation.

I had been working for 25 years and could see I was in the trap where my income was just covering all my expenses even though I earn well over $100,000 per annum (the average wage in Australia is $37,000). This also meant I was in the top tax bracket of 49.5c in the dollar, which means the government is taking half of everything you earn over $35,000.

How to get ahead?

I asked my accountant what I could do to improve my situation. He suggested a couple of things: buying property through negative gearing and self funded superannuation. So I decided to take on both things at the same time.

Anita and I invested in shares in the stock market. I went down to the stock exchange and listened to a couple of seminars, then bought stocks in companies that I use every day. I only learn by doing things and felt this was low risk strategy.

I also use the squirrel mentality: if you buy a share and it doubles in value, I then sell half. In the share market in Australia you have to pay 49c in the dollar on any profit you make.

Crazy buying?

We also bought a property in Manly in 1999 off the plans. It was a 65 square metre studio apartment. I paid $220k and put down a deposit bond of $22k from the equity in my own home. It settled in August 2000 and I borrowed the rest off the bank. People laughed at me and told me I was stupid to pay that much for a hole in the ground. However, it is located in the centre of Manly and now rents for $380 per week. It's not quite positive cash flow, but after tax (depreciation is $8000 a year as it is brand new) it puts money in my pocket at the end of the week. It's now valued at $390k.

We sold our Mt Colah family home in May 2000 for $325k; we had purchased it for $139k in 1992. We bought a new family home in August 2000. This was a 90% complete townhouse in Hornsby, a suburb of Sydney 20 km from the centre of the city. It is five minutes' walk from the rail line and right beside the site where a planned Westfield Mall was being built. I purchased it for $510k; people thought we were crazy and had paid too much, but it is now valued at close to $1 million.

In March 2001, we purchased a brand new one bedroom unit in Crows Nest, 8 km from central Sydney, for $299k. It is in a block of 48 units, six floors high, with eight units per floor. It is air conditioned and beautifully fitted out. It is walking distance of the railway, shops and over 200 restaurants. It rents for $340 per week. I put down a 10% deposit using the equity in the Manly unit. This is now valued at approximately $350k, which isn't positive but it breaks even after depreciation. Unfortunately, the view has been since built out by another development that the council promised us faithfully would only go to two storeys. It went to four.

An eye for property

I was finding it easy, the one thing I have is a good eye for property; even off the internet I can pick a good property. When I buy, the numbers have to add up; if they don't make sense I won't do the transaction.

> I interviewed accountants to find one who had investment properties as well as self funded super. I do this so I know their heart and head are going in the same direction as mine. Don't have any hesitation in changing members of your team to make sure you have the right person – it is your money.

The next one we bought was in Queensland at the end of the 2001 just before the boom. I was told by colleagues that you can't make money out of Queensland. There'd been no growth in Queensland for eight years. We bought the house for what the vendors had paid for it eight years earlier when it was brand new.

Our one bedroom unit in this block of 48 in Crows Nest will always appreciate in value — it's new, close to the city centre and handy to everything.

The property is an immaculate three bedroom house with double garage in Mermaid Beach, 85 km south of Brisbane. It's a 10 minute bus ride north of Coolangatta, a 2 km flat walk to the beach and 400 m from a major shopping centre. We purchased it for $265k.

Five months later property values in Queensland started going up in. We were contacted by many agents who all wanted to sell it for us. Some 20,000 people per year are now shifting to the Gold Coast and there's no land available. The house is now worth $410k and it rents for $310 per week, which means it breaks even after depreciation.

Dealing with the banks

I have my loans split between two banks and in total I've used three banks; I left one due to a lack of service. I have been able to negotiate interest rates down by 0.5% and I play them one off against each other. I go direct and haven't used a mortgage broker. I felt comfortable and confident enough to go and front the banks myself so that's what I did.

You can ask the bank to revalue a property a year after purchase and then if the equity is greater than 10% the bank can make the property sit on its own so it is no longer incumbent on other properties or the property you borrowed against for the deposit. You can achieve this as long as you present yourself professionally and go in and let the bank know exactly what you want – you need to be a bit aggressive with them.

Opportunities in Tasmania

I then used the equity in Queensland to buy a property in Lutana, a suburb of Hobart, Tasmania, 4 km from the CBD. It's a two bedroom townhouse on 320 square metres of land. It has views of Derwent River, which is where the Sydney to Hobart yacht race finishes. I purchased this for $105k in March 2002. I rent it out for $185, so this property gives us positive cash flow.

I had begun looking in Tasmania because there were no opportunities in New South Wales to buy good property at a decent price. Also my wife and I can claim travel allowances of $1000 each per year to travel to Queensland and Tasmania to inspect our rental properties. I also claim mileage to inspect my local properties plus office expenditure and my computer chair and desk.

The next property I purchased in Tasmania was in Penguin, a small town near a penguin colony, situated between Devonport and Burnie, 300 km from Hobart on Tasmania's north coast. It's a brilliant spot right by the sea on the Bass Strait. It's a three acre rural property with a large double brick house with three bedrooms, one bathroom and a four car garage that we are going to convert into an art studio, en suite and theatre area. It has solid Tasmanian oak flooring and is immaculate inside. It has two dams and its own water supply, protected from the weather. I plan on growing my own fruit and vegetables.

It is a reasonable distance to town and is good in terms of size for a rural block (if you buy more than three acres of land in Australia you pay capital gains tax on it when you sell).

We purchased it in May 2003 for $175k. We put down a 10% deposit of $17,500, which we raised from the combined equity of the other properties. We had been looking for a property for us to retire to and I had looked at 1100 rural properties on the internet before we found this one. I was able to rent it out immediately for $175 and it has since doubled in value; it is now worth $350k.

Options created

I've had three doses of cancer and recently I smashed my foot in six places; I'm finding work hard. Anita is a nursing sister and had a patient fall on her and injure her too, so we want to call it quits. I want clean air and clean living and to prolong my life and am just glad we have created options for ourselves through investing in property.

Our plan is to sell Hornsby, Manly, Crows Nest and Mermaid Beach, which should leave us with about $800,000 cash that we will invest in the short term money market and go from there. We will move to Penguin in 12–18 months' time to retire and will keep the rental property at Lutana. The farm at Penguin is now worth $450k.

Investors always needed

Remember to have landlords' insurance and get the depreciation allowance on your properties. Most (85%) landlords don't do this. Some 6% of real estate investors house 23% of the population in Australia, so that's why the government can't get rid of negative gearing. For example, at Mermaid Beach, on our loan of $270k the government gives us an $8000 tax rebate and depreciation each year.

> The government can't afford to house people so the market will always need property investors. The number of people renting is increasing. In Sydney, 60% of the working population own their own homes and 40% rent. In Brisbane 65% own and 35% rent and this is the average for the rest of the mainland. In Tasmania 67% own and 33% rent.

I find it's better to pay a property manager and let them go to court on your behalf on any tenant problems. I keep in close contact with my property managers and get them to feed me information on the market.

I have read about 10 or 12 property books. I used a very simple but great guide, *Successful Property Investing*, which became my Bible. I have attended many seminars, seven or eight about shares and about 40 or 50 on property. Each time you learn a little bit more, pick up on depreciation allowances and things, and other ways of doing things.

I think wraps are highly dangerous and I found that what I was doing was working for me so I stuck to it.

TOP TEN TIPS

1. Trust your own gut feeling, and believe in common sense — don't listen to the media.
2. Do your own research; for the share market go to the stock exchange, for real estate go to seminars and read books.
3. Understand the market you want to buy in; go to open homes, find out what properties are selling for.
4. Don't buy through emotion; a good investment is not what you want but where the need is; e.g. on average there are 1.4 people per household in Australia. People want small places, easy to keep clean, close to transport on small sites with low maintenance.
5. Understand and look after your cash flow, keep your bookwork up to date.
6. Set your goals and make them hard and high and go for it!
7. Have landlords' insurance and get the depreciation allowance on your property.
8. Don't be an expert on everything — you can't be.
9. Everyone's scared; we were. I'd never had a huge loan before but as time went by I understood the mechanism that worked. Use interest only loans fixed for three years.
10. Always have a cash reserve of $15k to $20k for vacancies or if something goes wrong. This is so you can survive if your insurance company doesn't pay out and avoids a position where you have to sell.

Chapter 25

Goal driven

'Our goal is to choose when we work. We are creating our lives, jobs, families around that goal.'
— **Rustica Lamb and Garry Butler,** Auckland, NZ

I live with my husband Garry in Browns Bay, a suburb of Auckland's North Shore. My father is a property investment guru and has always encouraged me to get into property investment. He has always said don't get a Just Over Broke (job) and never pay off your mortgage. Instead get your tenants to do that for you.

However, it wasn't until after I turned 32 and met Garry that I decided to take his advice. My father has become our mentor, along with Robert Kiyosaki, as we have read all of his books. We have also gained some valuable tools and were spurred into action by attending the Richmastery Property Academy in May 2003.

Living the high life

When I met Garry, he had two main bills, his credit card bill and the hire purchase on his TV. This was the only debt he had in the whole world but he also owned nothing; all his money went on entertainment. Garry had had an awesome time for 20 years: he had a gold card for the Loaded Hog (a pub at Auckland's Viaduct Harbour) and had spent thousands training and competing in three Ironman competitions. I was the same; I had been earning a good income and living the high life but had no assets.

My parents had a different life to us. They got married when they were very young and were always hard working and spent their money wisely.

Our first purchase in Woodlands Crescent, Brown's Bay, has been a home, a rental unit and equity provider.

Mum worked two jobs to put my brother and me through private schools. I remember nights when I was young my parents had bought flats and were painting them up and doing them up for their tenants. My father worked hard all his life making money; at 32 he bought a Mobil service station, and worked long hours. Then when New Zealand's import laws changed he took the opportunity it allowed him to set up a rental car company called Pegasus, which is very successful. My parents live in Nelson. He's sold his rights to Pegasus in New Zealand now for his own passive income.

Changing habits

My father has always been into property and wanted me to get into it too. Three years ago I decided to do something about it, I was getting a bit older and when I met Garry in April 2001 we decided our aim was to save up to buy our own home.

In November 2001 we found a four bedroom house in Browns Bay with sea views; it was a do-up on Woodlands Crescent. The house was on the market for offers from $267k. We offered $220k and eventually negotiated a purchase price of $250k, when we offered we had an initial deposit of $5000 and negotiated a delayed settlement of six months so that we could save the other $7000 for a 5% deposit. The market valuation of the house at the time was $285k but we got it at a discount because the vendor had been overseas for two years and the tenants had wrecked the place. (The house is now worth over $480k.)

Prior to settlement in July 2002 we had to save $1000 each month so that we could pay the $12,000 deposit when we settled. We found we had to work very hard to save that money, and had no leeway to go outside our budget. If we did not have a deadline it probably would have taken us 10 months to save the same amount.

We knew to achieve this we definitely had to change our spending habits. I was used to spending $600 a month at Cin Cin, an upmarket bar in downtown Auckland, and Garry used to spend $100 every night at Auckland's Viaduct Harbour drinking in upmarket bars. So we had to significantly change our lifestyle too.

When it came time to settle on the house we had to get my parents to guarantee the loan because I was self employed. Only Garry's income of $55k could be taken into account.

Setting some goals

During this time we began reading Robert Kiyosaki's books which helped motivate us and because I could tell the market was going to go up that gave us a sense of urgency too.

> We got engaged in April 2002 and set some more goals. We decided we didn't want to work for other people for the rest of our lives. We are lazy; we want to be able to spend time with our kids without having to work. We would like to travel for months of every year, living in different countries. This year we are beginning to live our dream, and we are off to the Greek Islands for six weeks.

Once we settled on the house at Woodlands Crescent, we spent several months recarpeting and painting the house. In total we spent $8000. We lived there for 12 months and then we went house sitting and rented out the house.

We were house sitting right next door to our tenants and found ourselves watching them party into the wee small hours every night. In the end we had to give them a warning letter and they quietened down.

Since then we have moved back to Woodlands Crescent and put in a new kitchen, repainted the feature walls, and put wooden flooring throughout. This cost another $10k.

On with the plan

Our property plan was to buy one property each year. So we wanted to get one before July 2003 as this would be a year since our first purchase.

One day we went to an open home in Rangitira Avenue, Beachhaven and overheard the real estate agent trying to sell a property down the road. We told the agent we'd be interested in seeing it. It had not been listed at that stage and we ended up being the first to see it.

It was a three bedroom house and the vendors were asking $187k. They desperately needed to sell. We offered them $175k and said that was our best offer. They wanted more because they had renovated the house: it had new carpet, new walls and fresh paint. They had purchased it for $169k two years earlier. The valuation came back at $180k.

> On 3 April 2003, the day before our wedding, we learnt that we had purchased the house for $175k. The conditions were four weeks to arrange finance and a six week settlement as we had a honeymoon to go on. We also negotiated early entry to secure tenants. But in the end we were happy with the existing tenants and allowed them to stay on. We put the rent up by $20 per week, as it was under-rented.

We got the deal 'no money down' as we had our Woodlands Avenue house revalued at $325k and used this new equity as our deposit. We rented it for $320 per week and it has a positive after tax cash flow of over $3500 per year. This was a great step towards our goal to create a passive weekly income.

Buying a business

Another goal we had was to buy a business. A year later we saw a for lease sign on a shop window in our neighbourhood. We spoke to the owner who said he was closing down and that this was going to cost him money. The shop was a specialty printing and paper shop in Browns Bay, specialising in wedding invitations. We liked what we saw, and felt it was incredible how this opportunity had presented itself; it made us realise that luck is when preparation and opportunity come together.

So in early May 2003 we purchased the printing and stationery business for $26k for the stock and $2000 for goodwill. We borrowed $5000 off the bank and worked out a payment schedule with the vendor to repay the rest over the next 12 months. We then renovated the shop. The business has been there for 13 years so is very established. While we renovated we put paper up on the windows and then on 10 May had a shop re-opening.

Expanding our minds

Around this time we decided we wanted to learn more about property investment. We had seen ads for the Richmastery Property Academy in Kiwi Property Investor (KPI) magazine (available through www.richmastery.com). We had heard about what people had achieved after attending the course on a Richmastery CD that came with KPI magazine. Also, some of our friends had bought four properties in a very short time using the Richmastery Property Deals website. Garry was not keen at all but I reminded him that there was a guarantee that he could get his money back if he didn't get value for money. He finally agreed and we both attended the Richmastery Property Academy in May 2003.

At the end of day two, Garry was ready to ask for his money back until he saw Brad Sugars and from then on he got it.

We both got a huge amount out of the academy. It really expanded our minds. We knew much of the content, having seen, read and heard it before at other seminars. I learnt the most from playing the simulated 'Property Game'. I worked the figures at home late at night and just missed out on winning the top passive income by a few thousand dollars.

> I also learnt that if you're not first in line to buy properties you miss out. The winners knew how to play the game; we now can see the potential and opportunity that is there for those who know how to play the game in real life and how they will win every time.

After the Richmastery Property Academy I went to my employer and said I wanted to work four days not five. (In November 2004 this became my reality so I now have time to work on our existing properties and search for more and work on our business.) We were brainwashed. It made our possibilities seem endless and it was fantastic as it helped us move forward.

The day after we finished the academy Garry quit his job so he could run the shop (we had an employee but decided we could pay Garry this wage and he would have time to also look for property).

Garry says of attending the Richmastery Property Academy: 'I was so fired up, I absolutely got it; I just wanted to buy properties and renovate them.'

Going shopping

Our latest valuations show that we have turned our original $12,000 into $235k in 22 months. However, starting the business and me reducing my hours has affected our debt servicing ratio, so we are working on how we can amend that. Garry's income in the business will not be recognised for two years.

The house at Woodlands Crescent in Browns Bay is now worth more than $480k and we owe $235k against it. Our Beachhaven property is worth more than $235k. After the academy we refinanced and put our new equity into a revolving credit account to create a line of credit. This came to $112k.

We then went shopping. We found a place in Salisbury Street, Birkdale, a suburb on Auckland's North Shore. It was a three bedroom do-up with plans approved for a 70 square metre minor dwelling in front of the house.

We learnt a valuable lesson when we bought this property because we didn't stick to our own rules when a savvy real estate agent put us under huge pressure. I had seen the property on the internet and was the first to see it. The real estate agent said we'd get it through faster if we were cash buyers so she crossed out the finance condition on the agreement and said we would be protected as it was conditional on full and final approval from our solicitor.

But in fact it meant we had gone unconditional without confirmation of finance. We also forgot to instruct the lawyer not to approve the contract within the three days until we had our finance.

Rangatira Avenue, Beachhaven house bought 'no money down' with equity from our first house.

However, we got finance and purchased the property for $265k, which was the initial valuation; the vendors had been asking $275k. We settled in September 2004 and used $50k from our line of credit account for the deposit. We immediately rented the house for $320 per week.

Our plan is to build the minor dwelling for $110k and spend $10k on landscaping the property. Construction on this is due to begin very soon. The estimated valuation once this has been done is $495k and we will get between $660 and $690 per week from renting both.

Fitting life around our goals

Education is very important. You cannot put a value on the urge to take action that we got from doing the Richmastery Property Academy and also from all the books we have read. Some we recommend are Robert Kiyosaki's *The Cash Flow Quadrant, Retire Young, Retire Rich* and *Rich Dad, Poor Dad*.

Our goal is to choose when we work. Garry says that we have decided that we don't want to be victims to our circumstances. Our 'why' is that we have a goal to spend two months (June and July) of every year in another country, living as locals; Italy, France and Greece are first on our list. So we are creating our lives, jobs, families around this goal. For example, I am aiming to work two four-month contracts per year, February–May and August–December, when the shop sales are in a slow period.

We've achieved our goal of owning a business — our specialty printing and paper shop in Browns Bay.

We do find we have to be careful who we speak to about our goals. In New Zealand if you say you just want to make money then that's looked down upon. We want money to create choices, not have money for money's sake.

We have sourced statistics on property around the country and looked at projected growth areas and are now focusing on these places. Our plan now is to buy one more property in Auckland and next year we will focus on areas north of Auckland.

The market has continued to rise and our total portfolio value is now $1.25 million, our total mortgages are $867k, which means we have increased our total equity from our original $12k to $378k in 2.5 years. Our total after tax cash flow is about $15k and that is because we are currently living in one of our properties.

TOP TEN TIPS

1. Have the attitude 'you can do anything' and 'don't ask, don't get'. Start small if you need to and try things that you wouldn't normally do.

2. Know what you want; ask yourself why you are creating wealth.

3. No matter what you hear at seminars, some people do have a better debt servicing ratio than you (bigger incomes, more equity, other business income) and you do not always hear this. Don't be discouraged when you go to a mortgage broker and discover this. Know your own debt servicing ratio and take steps to improve it, e.g. buy a passive income producing rental property before you buy your own home.

4. Be creative with your deals, sign them up to suit you. Legally, real estate agents must present all offers.

5. Look at property every weekend, or at least read the property press and look in the local paper and on the internet so you know your market. Use sources such as www.reinz to track property median changes and other data that helps you decide what is a deal and what is not.

6. Know your numbers, purchase computer software that tells you the rental return and passive income after tax. Make rules and stick to them.

7. Know why you are buying each property: passive income or capital gain?

8. Get a good team: mortgage broker, accountant, lawyer, handyman.

9. Be firm in your sale and purchase agreements; don't let the real estate agent pressure you. Know the clauses you use.

10. Get a chattels valuation every time you buy a property; this allows depreciation.

Chapter 26

Minimal outlay

'Our outlay was minimal ... property investment is not as scary as it looks.'
— **Don and Sharon Rankin,**
Brisbane, AUS

M y wife and I have done extremely well out of property investment in a very short time.

We have owned our own home freehold in Wynnum West, a suburb of Brisbane Bayside, since 1990. We saw the house advertised in 1986; it had gone for auction. I saw the sign outside the day after the auction and discovered it had been passed in, and the reserve was $58k. It was the worst house in the street. In Wynnum West the houses are brick so they are lower maintenance than the Queenslanders in other parts of Brisbane. That was in the days when interest rates were 18%, which was pretty frightening. I had a business, a fishing tackle shop, which owed me a lot of money in stock. The bank suggested I take out a loan for the company to pay me back for the investment in the business, so I borrowed $45k. The good news was that, because it was a mortgagee sale, and the date for settlement was 1 July, they called us and said, 'If you settle on the 30th we will take $500 off.' So we paid $57,500 for the house.

In 1990 I sold my business and paid off the mortgage; I was only 30 years old at that time. We also had some money left over and my wife and I travelled around Australia for a year. It was a trip of a lifetime.

We returned in 1991. My wife went back to working in a retail jewellery shop. I had a carpenter's licence and I worked with my cousin who was a builder and applied to get my builder's licence in 1993. I then started my own business as a bathroom renovator, called Bayside Bathrooms. The business went very well; it was a lifestyle thing, I would do two bathrooms, about eight days' work, a month and the rest of it was getting in subcontractors and quoting for jobs.

Everything pointing up

My wife and I decided to start to buy property in August 1998 as a way of building wealth for our retirement as I am 44 and my wife is 42 and we have two children under 11. Sharon wasn't scared by properties, even though we have friends who thought we were game investing in property. They're now the ones that haven't got rental properties and they're the ones that will be working until they are 65.

The market had been dead here for so long; people couldn't sell houses. We'd already seen the previous property boom in the late 1980s and we felt we were well and truly due for a property increase. I'd read articles that said Brisbane was running out of land and with GST coming, I'd read reports that New Zealand property prices had gone up when GST had come in. Everything pointed up.

Offering low

We bought a three bedroom brick house with inground pool and double garage on the bayside in Manly West, in Hinckley Street, for $124,500. It had been on the market for over a year, a deceased estate with an original list price of $180k. The day we inspected the property, the agent told us they had been instructed to present all offers. So I offered $120k, the agent said, 'No, they're not going to take that.' I said, 'Just give it to her.' They knocked it back, but the agent said they'd probably take $130k. I said I would offer $124,500 and the agent almost fell over in disbelief when the vendor took it.

We spent another $9000 on renovating the property and purchase costs. We borrowed $135k (by then interest rates were lower) on a principal and interest loan. For the deposit we only needed $2000, and we paid $5000 in legal costs and stamp duty and another $4000 for the renovations. We tiled the kitchen and dining area, did some minor renovations to the bathroom, put up a new pergola outside, and fenced it as it was a corner property. We did some of the work ourselves and also got my business subcontractors to do some of the work.

We quickly had it rented for $220 per week and our outlay per year was easily managed. We paid the letting agent 6%.

Double whammy

We then bought our next property in November 1999. We noticed that it was harder to find a good property at the right price as more people had started buying. We were looking for a double block with views; my rationale was that if you're going to get appreciation you get a double whammy with a double block.

We were lucky that we found what we were looking for by accident through a friend who wanted to sell his rental property to release funds for his business. I had done some renovations for this friend over the years and his father had Alzheimer's. While I was driving to look at a property with an agent, I saw his father walking up the road with one shoe on. I took him home; his wife was beside herself, and she thanked me profusely.

My friend phoned me and thanked me for helping his father. I told him the reason I happened to see his father was that I was looking for a rental property. He asked what I was looking for, and I said, 'A double block with views.' He replied, 'I've got one. I only listed it today.'

So I went to look at it. It hadn't been painted, the gutters were running off, so we went inside just to be polite, thinking we wouldn't buy it. But it was incredible inside. They'd spent $10k inside and it was perfectly done up. It was a three bedroom house, with bathroom and a carport. It was sited on an 800 square metre block and was already in two 400 square metre blocks on separate titles.

It was located in Wynnum West at Sibley Road on a hill with unrestricted views. My friend had only verbally given the agent the contract so he took it off the market and told us that the agent had said he could get $130k. I said I can only spend $120k so we agreed on that price and did it through solicitors. He had paid $120k and spent $10k on it, so he went backwards but he was in a hurry to sell.

We purchased it for the $120k plus $5000 in stamp duty and legal costs. Then we spent another $10k renovating. We had new gutters put on and repainted it. I paid a subcontractor to replace six concrete stumps (piles) that the house was sitting on, it was a low stumped house and we closed it in to make it look more presentable (I did this myself). We fixed windows that wouldn't shut and put in a new pantry. We put a fence up the back, I got a bobcat and a truck into the backyard and cleaned it up, and took about five loads of junk to the tip, so it would be easier to maintain. It looked fantastic.

Tenancy tribulations

We rented it out for $175 per week. We had one bad tenant who didn't look after the property. Our property manager hadn't done much; he did the inspection and I wasn't happy with it. The tenant was behind on rent a lot; we had her for a year and when the lease ran out, I decided to get rid of her. The letting agent almost had to get the police to get her out; they had to issue her with a summons, and she was saying she couldn't find anywhere. We took her to the tenancy tribunal to claim damages and we got the bond of $700 back. We had to spend $1000 cleaning up the place: there were holes in the wall, curtains ripped off, had to get the place fumigated for fleas.

We then got a great tenant who paid $180 then $185 per week, and they were there three years.

Having to sell

I had an unfortunate accident in 2000 and had to stop work. We decided to sell one of the properties as I was not working for 13 months. We wanted to sell the three bedroom brick house and keep the double block as we knew it was the one to keep. Properties still had not moved much in price then and we were fortunate to sell the brick house with a $10k profit after expenses. At the time it was a big help, but had we known what properties today are worth I guess we would not have sold. We did it for peace of mind. I was struggling on my insurance as I hadn't been reviewed, so it wasn't as much as it should have been. Luckily we did not sell our other property and held it till January 2004.

Moreton Island dreaming

The next property we bought was on Moreton Island, a place we love. It's a sand island 35 km off the coast of Brisbane Bayside that includes a national park and so has very limited housing. It takes one to two hours to get there

We begged and borrowed to get our Moreton Island property — a blue chip investment.

by barge. Its beaches are like Fiji. We had been going there for 20 odd years, staying in a family holiday house, and had seen prices continue to rise every year.

We had always said we didn't have the money to buy a place but one was for sale so we called the agent. The asking price, around $600k, was too much for us. But he said a block of land had come on the market the day before for $320k, all it had was a garage with a toilet and shower. It was three houses back from the beach. At the time there were only about three vacant blocks of land there and the other two I knew the owners would never sell, so this was our chance.

We offered $275k on the condition that we could sell our rental property. They accepted and we were flabbergasted; we got it for $285k with costs. We settled on the property two weeks after signing the contract in mid December 2003. We decided we wanted to pay cash for it, so we bought it in partnership with our super fund (in which we had $66k). After the first two weeks we went unconditional by borrowing the money from a millionaire friend and putting down a deposit of $10k, which we had in savings. We didn't want to lose the deal, and there were back up contracts on it, with 10 people wanting it. Offers of $360k cash came in after we signed the contract with the vendor. Statistics show that growth in people moving to islands is increasing at a rate of 26.4% since 1997 in this region.

The market was dropping so we wanted to sell our rental property at Sibley Road as quickly as possible to pay my friend back (even though he'd given us six months to pay him off). When we sold to a developer for $390k three weeks later it settled a month later in January 2004.

Not as scary as it looks

In approximately six years we have gone from virtually no investments to owning a blue chip investment property outright. We currently have it listed with an agent for $600k and have had 40 inquiries and a couple of inspections in less than a month; the agent is confident it will sell.

One of the investment strategies we followed was that we were not overcommitted and that our outlay was minimal. Once we had our investment properties rented everything usually went smoothly, so property investment is not as scary as it looks. As long as the property covers most of the loan, usually you cannot go wrong as long as you do your homework. If you don't have to sell like we did on our first property, properties will eventually go up in price.

I hope our story helps inspire others to have a go with property investing.

TOP TEN TIPS

1. Position.
2. Check with real estate agents for rental prospects.
3. Talk to neighbours about the house.
4. Get pest and building inspections.
5. Try to buy a cash positive property or low negatively geared one.
6. Try to buy a property with either views, multiple blocks of land or in an area that is tightly held.
7. Study the area you are going to buy in for prices.
8. Don't be afraid to offer a low price.
9. When selling don't go with one agent unless you are confident of a quick sale.
10. When selling have a bottom price and don't let an agent pressure you to sell below your reserve.

Chapter 27

Pass Go

'Now I have a huge mortgage and look on buying and selling as a type of Monopoly game.'
— **Tom Connelly,** Christchurch, NZ

I live in Christchurch, the largest city in the South Island of New Zealand. I have four children and have been divorced for nine years. For the past six years I have been re-educating myself while working as a Lecturer in Professional Studies and Practice and as the e-Communications Coordinator at the Christchurch College of Education. I am a boilermaker welder by trade, and have had 22 jobs since leaving school. I have since gained a Bachelor's degree in teaching, a diploma in ICT, a certificate in Maori language, papers in web design and two-thirds of a Masters degree.

I am originally from Cromwell, a small town in Central Otago. The first house I bought was in Christchurch when I was an apprentice boilermaker. I purchased it in 1982 for $18k. My company loaned me the mortgage under their superannuation scheme. I had to sell it after I received a back injury and got $26k for it. I used this money to move to Australia where I travelled and worked for two years. I then began on my big OE and travelled for a further two years.

An off-putting experience

I returned to New Zealand with my wife whom I had met in Canada. In Dunedin in 1992 I bought my second house for $33k. We sold it for close to $50k three years later because I had moved to Christchurch to attend teachers training college. First we rented it out and then we decided to sell,

250

because we were going to stay in Christchurch but also because we were having hassles with tenants not paying the rent, and I was a student with a young baby having to top up the mortgage. This experience put me off investment property for some time.

Some key skills

While studying in Christchurch I also ran my own business, Tommy's Toys Educational, a party plan system selling educational toys, manchester and books. After six years it had expanded to employ six staff selling educational toys for me around Christchurch and had evolved from a home based business to a shop.

A lot of the things I have done in my life have given me the skills for what I am doing now. When living in Australia I worked as a prison officer at Pentridge Prison, Melbourne. This taught me a lot about dealing with people – and diplomacy.

I learnt that you need to set firm boundaries, both for yourself and those you work with, and that you don't compromise on your principles but that you have to be diplomatic in how you don't compromise. You also need to learn which battles are worth fighting for and which ones you can simply walk away from.

Teaching has also taught me a lot, including management and organisational skills (including research skills) and confidence.

In 1989 we bought a house in Christchurch in Linwood for $55k – it was a family home. We lived there for six years until my marriage broke up. When this happened, I was forced to close my business, and my wife got our family home as part of the settlement. I look at this as a learning experience. You can sit back and look at everything that's gone wrong in your life or you can ask, 'What do I learn from it?'

A new castle

In August 1995 I bought my next house in Newcastle Street, Linwood, Christchurch for $75k for me to live in with my kids. I lived here until February

2002 when I moved to Rangiora to live with my girlfriend. The property in 2004 is valued at $131k. Over the seven years I lived there I slowly renovated it to achieve a good sweat equity. I had also been working as a Workshop Technology teacher at the local intermediate school, had been running another small part-time business from home and looking after three of my children 50/50 as a solo dad (two weeks on and two weeks off).

When we moved in to Christchurch from Rangiora in October of 2002 we bought a house for $112k at Breezes Road, Aranui. It remains my family home it is now valued at $160k. It's a double storey house with the top storey being the master bedroom. I am building an extension to the top storey to include a studio, kitchenette and en suite.

Buying rentals

When my relationship broke up in 2003 I decided to refocus on my work and property acquisition. (To others I am a workaholic but I do not find work a drudgery – I find it fun.) This is the point at which I decided to buy rentals. It seemed a bit silly having my house at Newcastle Street empty, but the renovations hadn't been finished. My mortgage broker suggested I keep it and rent it out. He also convinced me that I had enough equity to use as a deposit to purchase another place; this was an eye opener for me.

> Prior to that a friend had been telling me to use the equity I had in my properties and buy again, but I still had the idea of paying off the mortgage and being debt free. Now I have a huge mortgage and look on the buying and selling as a type of Monopoly game. (This helps you distance yourself from the big numbers!)

So my former home on Newcastle Street became my first rental.

Car wreckers' home

In June 2002 I bought my second rental in Barbour Street, Christchurch. I found this by a fluke because I went to the wrong address! It was valued at $86k and I bought it for $71k because no one could sell it because of the uncooperative tenants. There wasn't even a sign on the fence or any advertising being undertaken.

I look for houses that I can add value to — there was plenty of scope for that in the dope growers' pad in Charles Street.

The tenants owed three months' rent and wouldn't let anyone look at it. They had stripped down motors in the lounge and three partially wrecked cars on the front lawn! It has two bedrooms, two lounges, a sleep-out which is the original cottage on the property and an outside toilet. In the last three months I have built a connecting porch to move the toilet inside and it is rented on a fixed 12 month lease for $225.

I redid the kitchen, painted the bathrooms, relined the whole house, repainted the inside and polished the floors. I rented it out cheaply for $140 while I was renovating it and then when I finished I put the rent up to $190.

Three months after I bought it I had it revalued to get the equity out to buy another place. It's now valued at $148k.

Drug growers' house

I bought my third property in Charles Street, Charleston, Christchurch in early 2003. The government valuation was $85k; I offered $68k, and I got it for $76k. I got it revalued at $90k three months later and repeated the rebuilding thing. It is a single unit split into two so while I was renovating Flat 1 the rent from Flat 2 covered the mortgage and outgoings on the property. It was in two one-bedroom flats, but I have made it into a one bedroom and a two bedroom.

It was a drug house: they were growing dope in one of the flats and due to the hydroponics it was full of black mould. Again I had to renovate extensively. In total I spent about $10k and because I had no cash flow at the time I put everything on the credit card. Because of lack of time and actual 'cash' the renovations took me two years. The whole time I had Flat 2 rented for $120 per week. Once I finished the renovation on Flat 1, it was rented for $160 per week on a one year fixed term. Once all renovations were completed the property was revalued at $151k.

Doer uppers

I look for a particular kind of house, preferably a rundown rough cast or secondly weatherboard exterior, a minimum of three bedrooms, no garage and no formed gardens. These are the things I can add value by putting in. I put in bark gardens with native shrubs. They are doer uppers. I look at how much I have to spend on them, what I think it they will be worth once I've done the work and take the cost of the renovation off that.

I use trendy colours on all of my renovations: I have a five colour scheme that is the same for each property.

I do all the work myself but can now afford to get in a plumber and an electrician. I used to employ friends on weekends to do it but it's much cheaper in the end to get it done quickly and get the rent coming in faster. If I don't have the cash I put it on my credit card.

Best buy

I purchased my fourth rental in Cecil Place, Christchurch in October 2003. It was an emotional buy and I wanted to buy something quickly as I could see the market moving up. They wanted $105k; I offered $95k. Initially I thought I paid too much. In truth this has turned out to be my best capital growth property: the valuation is now $163k and the renovations have not been taken into account.

I had to evict the tenant after she abandoned the place but left her possessions there when she owed me rent. I don't take things like this personally. When you own several houses the failed rent is not as serious as if you only owned one property. I took her to the Tenancy Tribunal and got my $600 bond back and another $1200 for cleaning/damage/storage of goods. It is now rented for $225 per week on a one year fixed term.

> All my houses generate positive cash flow and profit. I re-invest the generated rentals and tax breaks I make into further purchases and renovations. My advice is to turn the stress into a challenge.

Five and six

I purchased my fifth rental in December 2003 in Wildberry Street, Woolston, a lower socio-economic area of Christchurch that has boomed because there are lots of old character houses. The vendors were asking for offers over $112k. I offered $105k, I went up to $110k and supplied a list of faults and costs to fix and he accepted. It was valued at $145k one month later and I had done nothing to it. It is now rented at $235 per week on a six month fixed lease and the valuation is $144k. Houses in this street that have been renovated to a good standard are now selling for around the $200k mark.

I then bought my sixth rental in Mackworth Street in Linwood, Christchurch in June 2004 at an auction. It was empty and needs a lot of work. The reserve was $105k and it was valued at $115k but was not liveable (the valuation is now $131k). This is my next project and I will spend about $6000, reinvesting the money from my other rentals. This will value up to around $140k and will get $230 per week in rent.

Goals

I have put the house in Newcastle Street on the market and have turned down the highest offer to date of $154k. I'm in no rush to sell as the yield from this property is 13% on the money borrowed against it. I want a minimum of $150k in the hand. Because of the improved valuation on all properties I am able to borrow equity out of them.

I am in the process of forming a trust and company to buy and sell properties and am now only working part-time for the Christchurch College of Education as planned so that I can concentrate on this project.

My aim is to buy, renovate and sell a minimum of four houses a year with a minimum $10k profit margin on each one. That pays off the rentals, which are interest only loans, and then they become full rental income units to support my lifestyle. I have cut down to three days a week at work.

My original goal when I bought Barbour Street was to own 10 houses in 10 years partly due to the fact that the key tag organiser I bought had room for 10 key tags. I have already acquired six rentals and seven income streams in less than three years. I have put approx $20k in to buy a portfolio of more than $1 million over the past three years. My aim now is a portfolio of $6–7 million of property with a 10% yield five years from now.

Getting fresh perspectives

You can never learn too much and will always get another perspective on a theme each time you hear someone speak on the issue. Every property seminar I attend I get some more ideas as to what I want to do.

I read *Kiwi Property Investor* (KPI) magazine (available from www.richmastery.com) from cover to cover each month and I use the Richmastery Property Analysis software and have just recently purchased their new software product REVIQ. All these tools help me focus on and plan for future activities.

I attended the Richmastery Profit from Property seminar in Christchurch in 2003. Going to the seminar gave me confidence when it became obvious that others had successfully done what I was doing and if I continued to do this with care it would become a profitable 'hobby'. I gained confidence mixing with like minded people. I have attended two further Richmastery seminars since that first one.

My sixth rental in Mackworth Street is a typical do-up project for me, reinvesting the money from my other rentals.

Attending seminars and reading books reconfirms the information and it becomes ingrained in what I know. I also read anything in magazines, newspapers and books related to property, business and self-improvement. Plus I read about other issues that impact on property to get a variety of perspectives on trends to formulate my own plans.

Some of the books I have found useful are: *Real Money Real Estate* by Phil Jones, *Selling a Home Privately in New Zealand*, *Real Estate Investors' Secrets*, *Building Wealth through Investment Property*, *Real Estate Riches*, *Your Investment Property*, *Retire Young Retire Rich*, and *The Inner Edge*.

I manage all my own properties and my biggest problem is cash flow to develop and to make sure I don't overextend myself.

I did have all mortgages with one bank, which was a bad idea. Now I have divided my portfolio over two banks. My mortgage broker does all this. In fact, my best investment is my mortgage broker (at Mike Pero), whose financial advice has kept me in the play, and my solicitor who always points out everything that could go wrong with each deal – and then I do it anyway, but it's great to have a critical eye over your shoulder.

People ask me why own all these houses (and the problems that go with them) when you only own 10% and the bank owns the rest. My answer is that if the value of my property portfolio goes up by 10%, I double my money – a fact that many people fail to grasp.

In fact my rental portfolio (excluding my own family home) has increased in value by around 60% in three years. The rental yield on the price paid is about 11.5%. The rental yield on money of my own that I have invested works out to be over 300%!

I began with $20k of my own money and in just three years have bought a rental property portfolio of around $1.15 million. My total mortgages are $700k so I have created a total of $300k in equity and a pre-tax cash flow of $403 per week.

TOP TEN TIPS

1. Have a good mortgage broker and solicitor.
2. Divide and conquer the banks by using different lenders.
3. Get to know your clients (your tenants) but keep a professional distance. I aim to have one year leases. Be firm but fair.
4. Do your homework. Present the property to the bank. Use facts and figures, not emotion.
5. I do renovations myself and employ others only when essential. I get 10% discount on my own materials. Always pay tradespeople first; you will generally get service when you need urgency.
6. When I buy a house I look for potential: how can I turn a future dollar here?
7. Read anything about real estate. You don't need qualifications, you need goals and knowledge. Know what you want to do and where you are going.
8. Look and compare. You need to be able to spot a bargain. I stick to a certain area of Christchurch that I know well.
9. Be careful of real estate agents: they work only for themselves.
10. Play the tax game, and make sure you understand how tax works.

Chapter 28

Getting time back

'I was amazed that so much money could be made so easily without having to put in an enormous amount of time.'
— **Graham Thomas**, Ulla Dulla, NSW, AUS

I am married with four children, and I am in my fifties. I have been in the furniture game for about 30 years, upholstering and manufacturing furniture, and also had a great interest in the building trade. I've always tried to develop something every three to five years, different projects from house renos to commercial developments.

Knowledge and networking

For me, the Richmastery Property Academy was a great time, but you've got to do the Richmastery Personal Property Mentoring Programme – that's the side of it that really kicks you along. Not that the mentoring gives you greatly different information than what you are shown at the academy, but you're dealing with 20 to 30 people who are doing different things and this can open 20 to 30 different doors. It's all about the networking.

One of my relations sent me the information about the three day Richmastery Property Academy from Japan and said, 'You should do this.' Something just clicked with me. I knew it was what I needed. I'm a great believer in clichés. The saying 'the difference between a rich person and a poor person is their knowledge' is one I've heard a lot and it's very true.

I made the decision to pay for my son and myself to go up to Queensland to do the three day Richmastery Property Academy in October 2002.

I got a massive amount of knowledge out of the course. I came back totally focused on what I wanted to achieve. My son actually went out and did some work with Richmastery in Sydney; he put a couple of deals together and that helped to keep me focused too.

> The biggest thing I've learnt is the sharing of information and knowledge. I am a great believer in never dying with your knowledge; that's why these types of organisations are so good because it's sharing knowledge. Some people have the attitude that if you're sharing knowledge that person can take something off you – it's not like that. Understanding all areas of the industry is valuable.

Changing direction

One thing about doing the Richmastery Property Academy is that it has given me the time to go back and coach soccer, because it helped me changed direction. I sold my furniture business and began concentrating on getting income from different sources. My business was taking up a lot of time, but was not a great return against the hours required to keep it going.

The knowledge I gained from the Richmastery Property Academy has given me my time back. I can now spend a number of hours on the computer looking for property deals when before I just didn't have the time.

The Mentoring Programme

After the academy I decided I wanted to join the 12-month Richmastery Personal Property Mentoring Programme based out of Sydney. I remember asking myself whether I should spend the money. Looking back with hindsight it was a hard decision but well worth it for the knowledge I gained. It is hard to spend that kind of money on education especially when you're my age and not used to re-educating yourself.

I started the mentoring programme in February 2003. Once I began I found it was hard to find time to look for properties and I realised I was still lacking time and lacking cash flow to get that time, which is what a number of people in the mentoring group had problems with to start with.

I decided I needed to get out of my furniture business. I verbally put the business up for sale, but it took 12 months for it to sell. In the end I only got one offer for the price I wanted and I took it, as it was a specialised business. During that year I worked very hard to get the business viable for someone to buy. Once I had sold it I used the collateral to survive as income to buy me some time.

Too green

I started looking for properties but couldn't find any houses that were positively geared. Then I noticed that the local council had proposed zoning changes on a number of coastal rural properties to medium density, near where I live in the south coast of New South Wales.

I started knocking on doors of landowners. In December 2003, I found the owner of an 11-acre block and looked at some plans that had been drawn up for the block. I tried to assess the value of the lots and work backwards from there with a view to developing the site.

I was in the middle of the mentoring programme and took the deal and plan to my Richmastery mentor, and with further help we worked out a price from there. I went round surveyors, architects and found out the costs involved in road works, sewerage, electricity and water. I worked out that I was looking at about $50k a block to develop plus purchase price. At that stage I estimated that the blocks would have sold for about $170k each. The plans had about 100 lots so I would need $6 million to put in, plus the purchase price.

I was still dealing with the owner, and she said to submit an offer. She actually told me the highest bid but I didn't believe her, so put my offer in lower than what she had told me, thinking that there was not enough value in the development at my selling prices.

My offer was for $5.9 million but it was too low; another other developer had put in a higher offer. As it turned out it was the figure I was given by the vendor. The market had started to turn. I'd valued the blocks at $170k while the successful purchaser put them on the market at between $220k and $330k and some were sold off the plan for theses amounts. This lack of foresight into the market was all due to the fact I didn't have enough knowledge at that time.

Looking back now I'm glad I didn't get the deal because I would have gotten burnt, it was too early, and I was too green.

Second bite

The new owner listed it with one of the local agents and I saw the property for sale on the Friday afternoon showing a development for 100 lots that the new owner had had drawn up on this same site.

Saturday morning I went to the real estate agent and tried to put a proposal together for an expression of interest – but the agent had no idea what I was talking about. I spoke to my business partner, Corie Stone. I met him through the Richmastery Property Academy and then began doing business with him while we were both attending the Richmastery Personal Property Mentoring Programme. He called our mentor about it, who advised going back in and putting a deposit down on the deal so as to have some control. So I turned around and went back in and wrote a cheque for $33,000 and received a receipt, knowing that it would be returned if no deal was struck. Within two hours the developer had called me and arranged an appointment and Corie my buisness partner and our Richmastery mentor met with him a couple of days later.

The developer had never heard of Richmastery. Our proposal was that we would sell the sites on the Richmastery website. But the developer only gave us 14 days in which to sell them, which was not enough time to list them, so that part of the deal fell over. This worked out better for me as

I may not have got the knowledge out of it that I got, had they been sold in that manner.

It took almost four days to get the paperwork through, so Corie and I ended up with only 11 out of the original 14 days to sell the blocks.

The contract was over 33 of the 100 blocks. The asking prices were between \$220k and \$330k depending on the size. We asked for and received from the developer a 5% discount off his listed price with a 5% deposit if we could sell them in two weeks.

We had a put and call option on the whole deal with a clause added that if the project did not go ahead or failed to reach medium density all monies would be returned – people could buy and on-sell without paying stamp duty, because there was no title at this stage – we were just selling the deal not selling the land.

Selling blocks

So I set about trying to sell some blocks. It's funny, I was up town getting the car fixed and I saw a builder. I didn't know him that well but because I was three days into the 11 day period I knew I had to sell some of the blocks. I'd written myself out a sheet explaining the deal with a plan of the development so I gave the builder a look at the deal; he immediately took two as he could see it was a great buy. So I then got on the phone and started calling other builders. Word got out that I had these properties for sale. When I was really running out of time, I stood in the main street of town just talking to people I knew and sold another three in one morning.

Corie was working on selling them through his contacts as well, but the structure of the deal did not give people enough time to think about it as time progressed into the remaining days.

At the end of the period we had sold 29 blocks; some of these fell over and the developer let us resell them so we went back and sold them again. The contracts still had not been processed by April the following year so no money was paid out by the new owners for four months and they were still increasing in value.

The developer increased his prices on the remaining blocks that we did not control by 30% and the agent was selling his blocks at these new prices.

Options

Corie and I managed to secure five blocks for ourselves from the 33. We are able to develop a total of 16 separate housing units on these. Each unit is currently selling for $160k each in surrounding locations.

We have two options available to us: either to build the units and then sell them or do a DA (development application) and on-sell that with the land. We could possibly sell our land (the five blocks) for about $2.5 million. We paid $1.1 million for them and the only costs out of our pocket totalled about $55k, most of which we recouped from the sale of the 29 deals. Plus we have control over the five blocks until at least 2006 or until the development is finished.

The subdivision itself is still not signed off by council and the developer himself doesn't expect the subdivision to be completed until July or August 2006. However, as it's already approved on council rezoning plans, we are nearly 100% sure it will go through.

On all the contracts over each site we sold, all money will be refunded if the rezoning doesn't occur. That's why it's a good deal because if it all fell over tomorrow everyone would get their money back and just have the experience.

Great deals everywhere

I was amazed that so much money could be made so easily without having to put in an enormous amount of time. The biggest thing you have to have around you, which is something that they teach you at the Richmastery Personal Property Mentoring Programme, is a good team of support from Day One. Good solicitors, architects, accountants, Richmastery mentors and like-minded developers.

Since then Corie and I have been looking for new properties. Initially I was going to buy houses that needed renovations, but now I'm looking at doing more of these subdivision deals. We have both locked a number of deals up since this one, using options to take control before buying or on-selling them.

We are now looking at childcare centres, which will bring in more passive income. We also plan to purchase properties with the childcare businesses as the lessors and on-sell the childcare centres.

Our aim initially was to double our cash flow in a 12 month period and we are going to more than achieve that.

It's been great fun, it's been a big eye opener, and we now can see great deals everywhere. None of it would have happen-ed without going to Richmastery and meeting all of these men and women all working in different areas. We both assisted on the Richmastery Property Academy in Sydney last May 2003, which was a great opportunity to hear and revise the information again.

TOP TEN TIPS

1. Gain knowledge in whatever field you choose to concentrate on — choose only one or two fields until you get your cash flow. Don't spread yourself too thinly.
2. Set clear investing and business rules and goals.
3. Fight your own fear factors.
4. Be prepared to share your knowledge to get knowledge back — you tend to find out a lot more when you network with like-minded people.
5. Read books.
6. Take action; don't be afraid of making mistakes.
7. Believe in yourself.
8. Use the knowledge by putting it into practice.
9. Create a good team around you from Day One and don't listen to people who are not working in the field.
10. Don't be scared to spend money on your education, and enjoy what you are doing.

Chapter 29

Sky's the limit

'I have learnt that it's worth spending $10k on an education that's going to set you free.'
— **John Teviotdale**, Queenstown, NZ

I bought my first home in Queenstown in 1984 with my wife, just as the market was starting to sky-rocket. I said to the real estate agent that I wanted a sunny spot with sheds that was reasonably priced, i.e. under $100k. He said I wouldn't find anything for that kind of money. About three weeks later he turned up in a sweat outside my workplace, he jumped out of his car and said, 'I've found the house for you.' I said, 'I can't leave the joinery factory,' but he insisted: 'You'll have to. You have to come with me.' So I went with him out to Frankton.

One of my goals had been to have a lakefront property. This was a quarter acre site with sheds and a transportable house. They were asking $60k and I said I'd take it. I asked the agent why it was so cheap and he said the vendor was desperate to sell. It was in a sunny spot and in Queenstown this is a very good thing, but it needed a lot of work. I replaced the rotten wood and mowed the lawn, which was up to my waist. A week later the same real estate agent came around and told me the place would now be worth $90k.

Next I put in a new kitchen, new bathroom and laundry and painted throughout. My wife and I stayed there for four or five years, then the market went up and we decided to move to Australia. In the meantime we wondered what we should do with the house. We were all set to go. We were leaving the next day so we decided to get a tenant in as it hadn't sold in three weeks on the market. But just before we went someone made us an offer of $125k.

I was very happy with that, and we then bought a section in Kelvin Heights straight away for $58k. We anticipated doing the same thing in Australia but didn't. We lived in Australia for about five years on the Gold Coast and then decided to return to New Zealand in 1992. We put the Queenstown section on the market but it didn't sell, as the market had gone flat. We moved back and got an offer of $58k so we sold it. We learnt the lesson then about buying bare land.

The end of the world

Our next purchase was an old character house for $58k in Winton, a small town 20 minutes from Invercargill, New Zealand's southernmost city. We mainly just dollied up the kitchen. We sold it for $125k about five years later because my wife and I were getting divorced. We had two children. I felt like it was the end of the world. My wife had walked out on me and I had lost my two kids whom I adored.

I had been a timber joiner for 30 years, but after my joinery business in Invercargill failed and my marriage ended I moved to Queenstown at the end of 1997. I ended up sleeping in a backpackers to begin with. In Queenstown I could not get work in joinery after six months of trying so I decided to get out of the trade. I felt it was time to do something different anyway and after 30 years in an industry I didn't have much to show for it. The only thing I'd gotten out of it was the skills, the knack and know how to do up houses. I seemed to be attracted to wooden houses even though I swore I'd just go for low maintenance brick and tile places.

Doing the right thing

My mother passed away soon after and I inherited about $50k. I thought I have to do the right thing or else I would lose that as well. So I looked around, talked to real estate agents – all the while living in a cabin at the Queenstown Motorpark.

I decided I needed to learn more about investment and read some books. I read *Rich Dad, Poor Dad* and was quite inspired by that. I read the rest of Robert Kiyosaki's books too and learnt about the equations, and I received all of their newsletters and attended a Robert Kiyosaki seminar in Christchurch. I got a few books out of the library on real estate.

> I realised that while the bare land I had bought in Queenstown had sky-rocketed in value, it was hard because of having to pay the rates and having no return, so I saw it as dead money. I also realised that I really enjoyed the process of doing places up. In fact, I was stuck in the mindset of looking for houses just to do up. I did think perhaps I should rent them out but was told I wouldn't get a good enough return.

On the waterfront

I noticed that prices were creeping up. It was August 2001. After getting rather disheartened, looking at the adverts for 80–100 properties in agency windows downtown, I went to another agency that was reasonably new and out of the way.

After telling a real estate agent my limit was $150k, he laughed! Telling me about a house (their cheapest) at $205k, he convinced me to have a look. I was put off with one or two things. The ceilings were all hanging down as the water pipes had burst. But I thought I could fix it up and rent it out. The agent told me the owner was very depressed and just wanted to get it sold as it had been on the market for a year and his wife was already in Auckland.

I then became quite excited, went home and did some figures. The house was on the lakefront with lovely lake views. It had a bedroom and an en suite upstairs, three bedrooms downstairs, two bathrooms and two toilets and a double lock up garage. The section was 900 square metres.

I called the agent and said I wanted to go back and see the house without the owner there. I checked it out and thought that, apart from the obvious problems, the house was sound. The agent suggested I put in a silly offer of $175k. The vendor counter-offered at $185k. I then went around the other real estate agencies, quizzing them on 30-year-old properties as large as this, with similar zoning and in a lakefront position; they all replied that there was nothing under $300k.

Reassured, I went straight around and the deal was done. I signed subject to suitable finance. The figures looked better with only 10% down but the banks told me I had to put 20% down so I almost walked away, but then

The Queenstown waterfront property – bought for $185k in 2001, valued at $380k three years later.

remembered the real estate agencies saying that I wouldn't get anything like this house for under $300k.

I purchased it in September 2001, and after that property prices just went ballistic. I did up the house and got rid of all the trees so there was a lake view from both storeys not just the top storey. On possession day all the water pipes and ceilings had been fixed and were brand new – it was an insurance job. Three people tried to buy the house straight after me; it was luck really that I'd stumbled upon it.

The purchase price was $185k, with a deposit of $37,500. The rental appraisal was $320 per week. (The latest valuation in 2004 was $380k.) I was told that the place I was living in at the motorpark was being pulled down so I moved into the house at the end of September 2001.

Getting the knowledge

I continued to read more on real estate. I began to buy *Kiwi Property Investor* magazine, which is where I heard about Richmastery. I also started reading Dolf de Roos and thought if I did further seminars it would be either one of his or another one of Robert Kiyosaki's.

The lady I was seeing arrived back from a trip to England and said she was keen on property. She said she was going to a Richmastery seminar in Queenstown. So we attended the Richmastery Profit from Property seminar, and found it to be fantastic. It was almost like reading the books but having the information presented on stage. Everything the presenter was saying made so much sense. I had gone to a lot of other seminars but they had presented negative-geared ideas. I had gone to the Investors Forum and joined up with that and quite enjoyed it but the Richmastery Profit from Property seminar was by far the best. We went ahead and bought tickets to attend the three day Richmastery Property Academy in May 2002.

> I got a lot out of it; I really got the thing about buying at a discount and all the options real estate does give you, buying do-uppers at a discount and refinancing so you can recycle your equity and do it again and again.

I wished I'd learnt all this 10 years earlier, which would have meant I had kept my first home in Frankton, now worth $400k. I could see that I would have paid off the $60k I'd bought it for and be getting $400 per week in rental for it, which would be mostly profit.

Buying by the rules

We followed all the Richmastery rules and in Dunedin purchased a five bedroom house in Dalmore, which is close to the university. We got it at a discount, it was in the right area and it had over $4000 after tax cash flow. They were asking $198k; we got it for $185k after much negotiation, and with a delayed settlement. We put down a deposit of $8000 – which was another Richmastery tip that you don't have to put down 10% as a deposit. We settled in December 2004 and now rent it for $80 per room.

We purchased another property here in Queenstown. We found this one through an ad (another Richmastery technique) that said the buyers had already purchased and needed to sell fast. It had been on the market for $349k. It was a three bedroom apartment with a lock up garage. We went to the open home. The place was a 20-year-old duplex that was a bit outdated. I called the agent a day or two later to enquire if there had been any interest in the property and he said I'd better come into the office and make an offer. I offered $240k, verbally, and the vendor turned it down immediately. I rang again a week later and discovered there had been no further offers. I declined to improve my offer. The real estate agent phoned a few days later and said the owner was prepared to go down to $290k, and after the following Tuesday it would be going to the highest bidder over $290k. So I offered $280k. In the end I got it for $285k.

The property is one of a block of two flats; the unit next to it of the same design recently sold for $320k. I have had it valued at $310k. At present it is 90% financed. It's rentable at $360 per week, which makes it cash flow positive ($11 after tax cash flow) and in a high growth area. The bank contributed towards solicitors' fees and is paying the first year's insurance cost.

Onwards and upwards

I have used the equity in my home to purchase all my investment properties. My own home is now worth $360k. I plan to convert my place into two flats. I will live upstairs and rent the bottom as a three bedroom unit for $360 to $400 per week. I need a permit to do this but no extra resource contents are required; it just needs fire-rated lining put in downstairs. I could also turn part of the L-shaped lounge into a fourth bedroom.

My goals are to keep doing what I'm doing now. I have a buy and hold strategy so that I can knock off the night shift and bring down my hours. I work 70 hours per week driving a nine-seater tourist van. This would bring me down to a week-on, week-off scenario so I can spend more time looking for property.

I have always been advised by real estate agents to keep to my own area but through Richmastery I have learnt to look everywhere and that the sky's the limit. I've made over 100 offers further south. My logic is that something will happen and if I can quit work and do up the odd place and spend more time with my girls, who are now 10 and 14, then it's all been worth it.

My partner Ellen is an accountant, my nephew is a lawyer and I see Richmastery as my mentors. I have never spent money on education before and this has been so worthwhile.

I felt like giving up when I got divorced. When you're on your own you wonder why you should make the effort. It took me a while to get back on my feet, losing my business, my home, my vehicles – a total worth of $400k. I had bought the joinery business for $200k and when it was sold all I got was $28k. I have learnt that it's worth spending $10k on an education that's going to set you free. I am passing on my newfound knowledge to my daughters too.

I have set up an LAQC with Ellen's help, and this owns both our Dunedin and Queenstown investment properties. In two years I've created as much equity as I had previously achieved in 15 years. Really, all of this has happened because I've educated myself. My total portfolio value is $925k, including two high capital growth properties in one of New Zealand's prime locations. My total mortgages are $573k, giving me total equity of $325k. My after tax cash flow is around $5000 per year.

TOP TEN TIPS

1. Follow the rules.
2. When I started doing up houses I was very particular, but now I don't spend as much on materials. Buy second-hand, and do things on the cheap where possible.
3. Make sure you buy at a discount.
4. Do the figures and make sure the deal provides positive cash flow.
5. Stay focused.
6. Don't get emotional.
7. Invest in yourself, do seminars, read books, go along and keep learning.
8. Don't be afraid to ask questions.
9. Look for positive cash flow before growth.
10. Be creative with how to make properties positive cash flow — learn from tossing ideas around with others.

Chapter 30

Starting early

'I bought my first property at 21; I'm now 27 and I own eight properties valued at around $3 million.'
— **Ivan Gunarajan**, Sydney, AUS

I'm a big fan of positive geared properties. Property investment can hit you hard when there's no capital growth if you are paying for a property that is negatively geared in those times, but if it's positively geared it doesn't matter if you are not getting any growth at all. Basically you make the money over time and get the return. I have tried to buy some negative geared, high capital growth property and then offset this with the positive cash flow property.

$70k by age 20

After high school I took two years off and worked and partied. I studied for a Diploma in Real Estate Business Management, which was a year and a half long, and at the same did part time work and managed to save some money. I was still living at home; I had started working when I was 12, and had been saving $150 a week since then, so I had about $70,000 saved by the time I was 20.

I have recently graduated with a BA in Applied Finance and a Masters in Finance and currently work for Perpetual Trustee. When I started university, I had already bought one property at the time, which my father had mentored me to buy. It was his suggestion that I invest in property.

I purchased this for $160k in March 1999 and put down a 20% deposit of $40k. The house was in Chiefly Avenue, Sefton, in Paramatta, a suburb of Sydney approximately 30 km out of the city centre. It had two bedrooms. It was on a section with a wide frontage and my father said it would suit a duplex in time. Its market value five years later is now around $400k. I wasn't really interested in property then.

Shares versus property

Applied Finance is all about the stock market, so I put the rest of my money into the stock market, and I thought I was doing well when the market as a whole was going up. I did eventually realise there was more to it than meets the eye, and small investors are the last to know when things change.

I learnt this lesson the hard way when I lost close to $45k in the same year I bought my first house. With the dotcom boom, in a matter of months my shares were worth $88k, but then when the crash came they were worth nothing.

When the crash came I took a bigger interest in property as I realised it was much safer. It takes much more time but if you stick to it, in the long run it gives great returns. If you set yourself a goal in real estate you will achieve it. If you say you want to buy one property every year in the long run, you can go to bed and not have to worry.

Because I was so young the share market seemed challenging and much more exciting than real estate but now, if I had the money, the majority would be in real estate. I am still doing the stocks and now am trading currency. It is such a large market that no one gets the information first. I aim to make $200 with every trade, so if I do three successful trades a week then I'm making money.

Snowballing equity

The hardest part with property investment has been getting the finance to buy consecutive properties and the hardest thing so far has been saving the initial deposit on my first house. Every deposit after that has been from equity in the existing properties. Each year I get my properties revalued and they go up, so I can buy on the newly created equity. It just snowballs and you don't stop.

Two-bedroom duplex just 10 km from Sydney CBD, bought in 2000 for $602k, now worth around $500k each.

I purchased a two by two-bedroom duplex in Croydon in March 2000 for $602k plus $22,500 stamp duty. It is located 800 metres from the railway station, close to the bus route and just 10 km from the centre of Sydney (15 minutes' drive at off peak). They are old Art Deco brick and tile semi-detached houses under one title each with two bedrooms and a sunroom, plus a lounge, kitchen and dining and a backyard.

I put down a deposit of $120k, which I had earned from the stocks again (my father kept saying, 'Don't leave it in there.') and I borrowed the rest. I was working part time earning close to $28k per year at Star City casino bar tending and waiting. My dad is a bank manager so was able to help me get the loan. The rental return is $560 per week so I still have to pay $200 a week out of my own pocket for this property. The bank revalued it at $860k in 2002, so now each semi would easily sell for between $480 and $500k each. I did have a property manager but now I collect the rent myself and it's just around the corner from my house so it's convenient.

I polished the floorboards, repainted, resurfaced the ceilings and put in new blinds. I have spent about $3000 on each in the time I have owned them and have had the same tenant in one for three years.

Brisbane buys

In July 2002 during the university holidays I took a week off and went up to Brisbane. I used the equity in the duplex to purchase a block of three units and a house in Asply, a suburb of Brisbane, 10 km from city centre. I purchased the three units for $325k plus $10k stamp duty.

The flats are not even a kilometre to the shopping centre, rail and a bus route. Asply has a shopping centre and the flats are surrounded by houses and located near a primary school. All the tenants are teachers that work for the school. The two bedroom units rent for $195 each per week and the three bedroom unit rents for $220 per week.

So this was a positive cash flow deal; the interest rates were 6.6% fixed for five years on interest only (all my loans are interest only, something my dad advised me to do). Two years later they were worth $650k. The same tenants have been in there the whole time. So far I haven't had to spend a cent on maintenance but I have had to redo the concrete driveway.

I also bought a three bedroom house with mountain views in Duneedoo Street, Stafford, which is 7 km from the Brisbane CBD. I bought this for $285k, and two years later it was worth $400k and rents for $320.

Waterfront commercial

In July 2003 I purchased the best buy out of all of my properties at the time that Sydney was cooling off. It is a three bedroom house in Main Road, Speers Point, New South Wales. This is 25 minutes south of Newcastle and two hours north of Sydney. It's right on the water at Lake Macquarie. It's also a commercial property, on 809 square metres of land, with a 22 metre frontage.

I knew developers owned a site three doors down on the same zoning (density 3C) and they were already building nine storey apartments with a view of the water of this inland lake. This had potential, it was 100 metres from the water, and zoned high density. I knew if I purchased it I could sell it off at a premium or develop it. I got it for $310k at auction. A deceased estate of my girlfriend's aunty, they just advertised privately and it didn't go through an agent. I just said whatever price you get I will give you $1000 more. It's now valued around $550k.

From doom to boom

I had one major concern, which was that Pasaminco, an old Australian mining company (which went into receivership at the time I purchased last year), had a site for mining lead and sulphite only 1 km from this property at Speers Point and Boolooroo and the wind used to blow dust over the houses, so no one wanted to buy there.

Three bedroom house in Speers Point, NSW, on a commercial site opposite Lake Macquarie — it has to be a winner.

Values in the surrounding suburbs were considerably higher and I knew Pasaminco might close due to their financial difficulties but didn't know this for sure when I bought the land. But just after I bought it, the mine did close down so there is no more toxic lead or sulphite.

The suburb has boomed since. At the moment my biggest problem with the site is mowing the grass. So far I have also spent six months renovating it and have spent $50k but it's still not finished. I've saved on the house by doing the work myself.

All the wallboards were rotting off, and I changed all the windows and doors. I made the timber windows myself. The bathroom has been done but I still haven't put in the basin and the shower screen in. I still have to put the guttering up and am still painting. Then it will need blinds and the floor boards polishing. I have put up a new fence and have painted the outside.

I have rented it out for $260 per week; as I anticipate capital growth I am happy to hold on to it even though it is negatively geared. I will try to get a commercial tenant in there so I can get more in the way of rent. This property is now worth $550k and more if I can get some units approved on the site, but it is costing me as it is still not rented after more than a year. I had just finished university in July when I bought it but since starting a new job I haven't had the time to do the work.

One a year

I am now looking to buy again this year, following my father's advice of purchasing a property a year. I have also learnt from his success that buying in lower valued areas and having positive cash flow can pay off. He did this in Brisbane and the properties doubled in value there. Even if it doesn't it's not money coming out of your pocket so capital growth is the bonus. I regularly look for property on the internet; it's so much easier. I search on www.property.com.au

I have targets of buying positive cash flow property in Rockhampton, six hours north of Brisbane, and in Warwick , two hours south of Brisbane.

TOP TEN TIPS

1. Know your suburb and market. Do your homework if you are purchasing out of your local area.

2. Set your goal for each property and make sure you achieve it.

3. You need to have a mentor, to follow and build on their advice.

4. Purchase something that you can add value to, develop, or do up, it makes it more fun and challenging.

5. Buy a block with units. Try to purchase blocks of flats surrounded by normal residential houses rather than others blocks of flats — it's more appealing to the tenant and to purchasers.

6. Important! Don't default, keep up to date with your bank repayments

7. Don't worry too much: if you don't take risks you don't make money. The risks in real estate are less than in business or with stocks. Educated or calculated risks are good.

8. Keep away from swimming pools, especially if you're renting out. They are dangerous, incur water rates, need fencing, pumps, pool cleaner, etc.

9. You need plenty of cash; always put money aside.

10. At the end of the day you have to take an interest in property if you are going to invest in it and you need to be passionate about it. Master it and make it your hobby.

Chapter 31

Eight houses in five months

'We love purchasing property, we love being landlords, and we love knowing that our future will be great.'
— **Corrina Laird**, Hamilton, NZ

Phil and I are married with three boys aged two, six and seven. We live in Hamilton, which is a city of about 150,000 people an hour and a half south of New Zealand's largest city, Auckland. Phil is the foreman of a stainless steel engineering company and works full time between 50 and 60 hours a week. I'm a qualified baker although I am too over-qualified to work any-more. So between loads of laundry and kids' stuff I dreamed up a crazy idea of becoming a millionaire residential property investor. Although being a mother is my first priority and something I truly love, property investment has become my new passion!

Learning the hard way

In October 2001, Phil and I decided that we needed to upgrade our house as our first home was too small for our growing family. We soon discovered that we would be better off to rent out our home and purchase a bigger one. It became a business decision as the market was in a lull and it made better sense. We had paid $113,500 in 1997. We had $40k equity and a mortgage of $75k. So we rented our home for $190 per week, and purchased our new home using the equity as a deposit.

We purchased our dream villa in one of the best areas of Hamilton with a quarter-acre section that has provided the boys with lots of room to move. Three days before Christmas in 2001 we paid $143k and got 100% finance, by securing the new house against our other home, and moved in.

The Dinsdale cottage provides good positive cash flow and development opportunities.

We soon discovered that the structure of our properties was all wrong. Our original home was in a family trust. We didn't understand about tax and purchasing structures, and I'm not sure anyone else did either at that time. We learnt the hard way after our first tax return was filed and ended up with a big tax credit with the lovely IRD. Our accountant explained that as a family trust doesn't earn any money, it doesn't pay tax therefore we can't get any tax back. So we looked into other methods for purchasing property and the correct tax structure for this by talking to our bank manager, lawyer and finally our accountant.

I felt like I needed to know more but had no idea where to look so I talked to a friend of ours who is also an investor and he suggested we attend a Richmastery seminar. After checking them out on the internet we enrolled in the Richmastery Profit from Property evening seminar and in June 2003 we attended our first seminar. It was really informative – the purchasing structure was such a biggie as not many people really knew much about LAQCs. We knew that a family trust was not working so we were on a mission to find out what would work for us. I decided to go along to another seminar next time they were in town to buy the Richmastery Property Analysis software and to fill in the gaps from the first time around. We felt at this stage we had enough knowledge from the seminars to move forward with our investing and we felt the software was such a valuable tool to have as it takes all the guesswork out of deciding if a property is a good buy or not based solely on the figures.

Starting again

We decided to sell our first home, set up an LAQC and start again, doing it right this time around. We sold that property in October 2003 right at the height of the boom. It was the perfect time to sell; we achieved $119k, which was a good price for the market and area, and we had bought the best house in the worst street.

At the end of October 2003 we decided to get married. I got a little bored organising the wedding, so I called my real estate agent and told her that I wanted to go shopping. By then our new home was valued at $200k so with our $80k equity I started our buying spree. Our first house was bought, and settled on 9 January 2004. This was a three-bedroom, Hardiplank home with a single garage, in Thoughting Estate, a suburb 10 minutes from the centre of Hamilton. We paid $135k for it.

The agent came to us explaining we had gone into competition, the other offer was more than ours and she tried to talk us into increasing our offer. But we were adamant that we would stick to our price even if the deal fell over – we were happy to put it all down to experience.

Later the agent called to say that we had got the house because, although our offer was less than the other one, we had basic clauses in the contract and the deal was less likely to fall over. Phil hadn't even seen the place at this stage, but the figures worked and it was the first of our positive cash flow properties rented for $250 per week.

A few days down the track I had a knock on my door by a new real estate agent, asking if I wanted to sell our house. I said, 'No but I'm looking for an agent who wants to work for me as I would like to buy a house every month for the next year and my husband wants to buy a block of flats.' He took a step back; his eyes popped out of his head and he said, 'I am glad that I knocked on your door.' So that was the beginning of a great relationship.

We purchased our next property two days before Christmas, and it settled on 14 January 2004. It was around the corner from the first house and was the same kind of house as the previous one. We paid $118,500 for it and rented it for $230 per week. The house wasn't even on the market when we

Ulster Street house bought sight unseen at $15k below asking price.

bought it; the owners had had bad tenants and had decided to sell, but while doing it up they decided to keep it. Our trusty agent put an offer in while the vendor's husband was at the movies; over the next few hours of haggling we came to a great agreement. We had to put new carpet and vinyl throughout, which cost around $2500. We also painted the fences and added some gardens. I later found out we paid only $2500 more for it than the previous vendors had paid three years earlier. I was getting more confident and we were very pleased with our purchasing.

A steeper learning curve

Our biggest learning curve was a property in Maitland Street. We decided to purchase through our original real estate agent, although I felt she had lost some of her fire and passion. She raved on about the property, which was for a reasonable price, and she managed to mask and direct us away from a few water problems in the bathroom. She explained that there were some issues with the bathroom and toilet but the vendor's insurance company was going to fix it all up. We waited six weeks for a resolution before I instructed our solicitor to get us out of the deal no matter what. He ended up threatening to sue the real estate company for misrepresentation if they wouldn't let us pull the contract because it soon became apparent that the vendor's insurance company hadn't even assessed the house and the vendors didn't appear to have any intention of fixing the major damage. I became a little stressed (actually a whole lot) over this situation but not as much as the real estate agent!

The next one I bought was for a friend of mine; I decided there wasn't any point being able to purchase investment properties if you couldn't help your friends and we had a friend who needed a place to rent. So we bought a two bedroom cottage in Dinsdale during Easter 2004 for $105k. The vendors were asking $109k. We rented it to our friend for $185 per week.

Although this property wasn't being purchased at a discount (and we did try) it still provided us with good positive cash flow. It is also situated in an area which is zoned high residential, there is an opportunity to build town houses in the future on this site, so it provided us with extra development opportunities. After my friend moved on due to her health, we had no problems renting it out for $200 per week.

Pushing the boundaries

By this stage we loved our newly discovered hobby so decided to push the boundaries and we put eight offers in at once. Mostly these were sight unseen. The theory was to put in the offers, inspect the properties while negotiating and then continue with the deals if they stacked up. We ended up purchasing three properties at a good discount. Ulster Street was a two bedroom flat in a block of eight; our first offer was accepted at $15k below asking price. I was slightly angry, thinking we should have offered $20k below, but it was still a good deal. We rented this out for $160 per week to the tenant who was already living there. The second one was a three bedroom, single garage Hardiplank home in the same street in which we live. It was purchased for $16k under asking price; this place also came with tenants willing to stay, so after interviewing them, I decided that I wouldn't regret the decision as they were truly lovely. They were also happy to pay the $220 per week.

Buying this two bedroom flat in Irene Crescent made it three properties bought in a week. A great buy at $23k under asking price.

Irene Crescent was the third property purchased in one week. I had previously been through it but at that time it was on for $150k. Being a two bedroom flat, I felt it was way overpriced. Our trusty agent rang me half way through a meeting to tell me that the price had been reduced. I asked him to draw up a contract and I would send Phil for a visit on his way home from work. To date I feel that this one was our best buy, purchasing for $23k under asking, $5k under CV. We get positive cash flow for this property also, renting it out for $215 per week. This place also came with some lovely tenants who we were happy to keep on. We negotiated hard. The agent would say: 'The vendor won't go below this price,' and I'd reply, 'Well, I'm not going above this price.' I loved winning those price wars!

One day I was having lunch with some investors. I had met one at a seminar, swapped business cards and he called me, inviting me to meet him and his other business partner. I asked them what properties they had going at the moment and he mentioned he'd just bought a place in Aberdeen, in Irene Crescent. After hearing how much he paid for it, we then discovered that it was next door to one of our houses. After discussing the opportunity with Phil and the current owner, we decided it would be valuable for us to own both properties. So for a finder's fee we bought the other Irene Crescent property at $123k plus $5k finder's fee. We rented it for $215 per week also. We had to do some work to both units: we fixed some water issues in both bathrooms, recarpeted and put in new vinyl, painted and put up new curtains.

 In five months we have acquired eight properties. All the houses are within five to 10 minutes of the centre of Hamilton. This means we own over a $1 million worth of property.

It's quite mind blowing to think that we own this, and I'm only 26, my husband is 36. We love purchasing property, we love being landlords, and we love knowing that our future will be great.

Life begins

We had hoped to own over 10 properties before the end of the year. I had decided to stop at eight due to the amount of time that it takes to purchase, sort out tenancies and the like. We have also found the current market above what we are prepared to pay. We are really proud of what we have achieved.

We will purchase more properties; it's just a matter of time before we do.

I have now set up a business called Property Purchasing Consultants. I specialise in portfolio development where I help my clients find houses. I provide property and area analysis, arrange LIM reports, building inspections, valuations and rental assessments. I offer this service to everyone from investors to first home buyers. The focus is on a service that absorbs all the stress and hassle associated with purchasing property. My decision point was when our original agent quit her job and didn't tell me and didn't follow through with the final inspection or bring me around the usual bottle of wine!

My husband trusts my judgement; I haven't purchased anything that I later thought I shouldn't have.

Since starting up my consulting company, I have joined the Waikato Property Investors Association. I have met some amazing investors. I've also got my own radio show on real estate on Community Radio Hamilton.

> My life began the day I walked into the first Richmastery seminar. I haven't looked back and I am amazed at the opportunities that have arisen since I made the decision to become an investor. Whatever the future holds it will be because we made the decision to change our lives.

We now associate with many like-minded people who inspire us, support us and encourage us. I find inspiration in reading books, and I love to read the ones written by people who I admire and look up to. They include Brad Sugars, Phil Jones, Martin Ayles – to name a few.

I have also found the *Kiwi Property Investor* magazine an amazing source of information and inspiration that is at times needed if you hit a slight bump of stress while doing a sticky deal. What I love so much about being an investor is that investing isn't a competition. Investors like to help each other to become a success too. All investors love to talk about their achievements, and they are more than happy to assist with issues. While everyone else is out there thinking that they would like to become investors, I have done it. I have done it for my children, I have done it for my husband and I have done it for our future. It hasn't been hard as we have had the right tools to begin with. I encourage anyone wanting to take the step to go for it!

TOP TEN TIPS

1. Go to the Richmastery seminars. They have provided me with the correct tools to build my frame for investing.

2. Set some goals and set them a little higher than you originally want to achieve. Even if this goal isn't achieved, it is better to achieve 80% of 100 than 80% of 10.

3. Set other goals that don't have an immediate dollar value, e.g. better education for your children, holidays or retirement.

4. Join your local investors association, for motivation and access to different investors and investment styles.

5. Be creative. Find properties with a twist, subdividable sections, ones close to schools, the CBD or ones which you can add value to.

6. Invest in the Richmastery Property Analysis software; it's essential for working out the figures, and eliminates guesswork.

7. Subscribe to the *Kiwi Property Investor* magazine (available through www.richmastery.com).

8. Don't be scared to interview real estate agents to find one who is prepared to work for you.

9. To save time and money, have a family trust and a LAQC set up before you start purchasing. Work out what kind of an investor you want to be before setting this up as it affects the kind of structure you have.

10. Enjoy what you can do and what you're creating.

Chapter 32

No fear

'Opportunities arise every day. Don't let fear and a lack of knowledge slow you down.'
— **Shaun Walker,** Canberra, AUS

I attended Richmastery's three day Property Academy last year and it changed my life.

To give you a little background, I resigned my commission from the Royal Australian Navy after 15 years of service in July 2003. I'd travelled extensively into war zones and around the world. I had joined when I was 18 and felt I wanted more. When you are in the Navy you are there to do the Navy's bidding 24 hours a day.

I woke up one day and all my brothers and sisters were married with kids, I was still single with $125 in the bank. Apart from that and my Hyundai XL worth $5000 I had nothing.

It was 6 April 2001. It was the day I was given the *Rich Dad, Poor Dad* book by a friend of mine who was reading it. I felt crap and felt like I'd wasted 12 years in the Navy and all the money I'd earned. I drank it all up; I lived the high life in Sydney, in gorgeous rented houses, partying hard. I realised when I read the book that I'd been doing it wrong; it struck a chord with me. I then went looking for books on property investing in Australia but there wasn't much information around.

Saving at sea

I was then posted to Nowra and about six months later I went off to sea into war zones again. When you are at sea it's easy to save. I saved for about four months and came back with $8000. I hadn't stepped off the ship one day during the whole trip so couldn't spend it on drink.

On my return I bought a two bedroom unit in Queanbeyan for $55k. They were asking $60k; I got them down and also got $7000 of that paid for by the government First Home Owners Grant. I then rented it for $120 after putting in a new kitchen, on which I spent $2500. I rented it through a property manager. I arranged a principal and interest loan and paid it off in three years.

I kept coming back from war zones with cash I'd saved and putting lump sums on the mortgage. I know it wasn't the right way to do it but I couldn't find any information on how to invest in property and to learn how it all worked.

Looking for a better way

After I left the Navy I started a public service job in Defence Communications, based in Canberra. When I resigned from the Navy I got a lump sum payout of $50k. Originally I was going to use the money to go to university and study accounting. After realising how much it was going to cost, I thought, 'Bugger that – there's got to be an easier way!' After all I just wanted to learn how to make money and to become financially literate.

I went to one of Richmastery's Profit from Property evening seminars here in Canberra after scouring the newspapers and going to all the property seminars. I paid the $69.95 and really liked what they had to say. After being told the cost of the three day Richmastery Property Academy I was a little hesitant to part with my hard earned cash. It seemed like a lot of money to give to people I didn't even know.

After about four to five days of thinking about it, and many late nights soul searching as to what I wanted to achieve in life, I decided to contact Richmastery and sign up for the Property Academy. I attended it in Sydney in August 2003. The academy was everything I needed, and more.

One of the life changing things for me at the Richmastery Property Academy was learning not to be scared of money and how to leverage your time to good effect. This came to me while we were running around buying up property, trying to make a profit in the Property Game.

As I was calculating my profit margin towards the end of the three days, I realised that I had (on paper) around $1.5 million in property making me around $100k year! I was thinking, 'Wow, this could be real money one day.'

Kicked into action

It dawned on me that being scared of money had kept me in my comfort zone for way too long. It kicked me into action definitely; I knew there was a better way and I now I could see how to do it. If it sounds so easy, why aren't more people doing it? I can see why they're not now, as I discovered that the time and effort required is huge.

So after the Richmastery Property Academy ended I returned to Canberra, armed with the knowledge and tools that I needed to get started. Rather than setting goals I decided to get my feet wet and get in boots and all.

I moved into my Queanbeyan property and renovated it. I spent a total of $5000 (which is too much), repainted inside (it's a brick and tile house), filled in holes in the wall, got rid of the old heaters, recarpeted and put up new curtains and blinds. I lived in it for 12 months and got it revalued at $195k in September 2003. Then I rented it out at $175 per week.

I started making offers and this is when reality hit me. Although the course had taught me everything I needed, the real estate agents just would not return my phone calls, nor did they want to speak to me. It was a heated market.

Multiple offers

Time to think outside the square: using Richmastery's Analysis software, I started my own searching. Using the 100–10–3 rule I was looking at about 20 properties a night for about three months. I eventually found about 15 properties in Darwin that if bought at the right price would produce a great after tax return.

So I organised pre-approved finance and used the letter to assure the real estate agents that I was genuine in my offers. I was offering 10–15% below what they were asking. Let's just say that of the 15 properties that I was interested in, I received 14 very abusive phone calls! I have never heard an old lady (a real estate agent) swear like a dockyard worker before. But as we learnt at Richmastery: you don't kill anyone with offers, but you certainly give

Two bedroom unit in Queanbeyan bought for $55k in 2000, now valued at $195k.

a few people a heart attack. But with the 15th offer the agent even told me why the vendor was selling and what offer she would accept.

Eventually after haggling I got a three bedroom unit in Darwin CBD for $210k, fully furnished (I got the furniture for free after much haggling) and rented for $265 a week. By using the equity in my own place, I used no money of my own! Darwin has gone up 20% in value since January 2004.

I then found a good accountant through Richmastery's website and put in a 221d (a pay as you go tax return, which means you get tax taken out of your earnings every two weeks) and I haven't looked back since.

The Darwin property makes me $150 after tax a fortnight! Not bad since I didn't use my own money. I refinanced the loan against the Darwin property in May 2004 and took $20,000 in equity out of it.

Moving sideways

Realising the housing market was too hot, and having plenty of equity left it was time for a change. By this time I had a great group of people around me who also invested in property. We were invited to put up working capital in a livestock farm.

So I set up a company (another learning curve) and invested $85k in the business. My returns from September 2004 are $1000 every five weeks now, expected to be $1000 a month, for 12 months, then $5000 a month for six months, then $10,000 a month for the life of the contract (five years then onwards). Believe it or not these are undervalued numbers. We will run out of land before we run out of stock. We even have export licences to China, Japan and some Middle Eastern countries. We are experiencing some difficulty with local council approval for the business but are working through this. Once the approval is in place we will move up to $5000 a month three months after that.

No holding back

Until the farm money starts rolling in I have rented my place of residence in Queanbeyan out for $175 a week (I still have a mortgage of $66k on the property) to cover the interest repayments on the company. In the meantime I am house minding a friend's place for $100 a week and keeping an eye on his 17-year-old son. The house sitting arrangement includes all bills being paid by the owner.

> Opportunities arise every day; you just have to be smart enough to take them or not. Now I'm open to them, whereas before I wasn't. Don't let fear and a lack of knowledge slow you down.

I am currently looking into buying real estate in the United States and the United Kingdom. This is because they don't have negative gearing; the rents are high enough to cover the mortgages. Rents are a lot higher in those countries compared with the price of the property. There are bigger deals to be had, better networks and more opportunity. $Aus130k will get me a two bedroom house in Manchester, which would rent for around £120 a week.

Investing overseas is not as hard as it sounds, but I first must learn about offshore accounts and paying tax in two or three countries. I am learning and I know I will be educated in the near future in what I need to do.

I have been reading and pestering a lot of people, such as the author of the books on offshore investing for Australians, written by an Australian accountant. I contact him by email and ask him questions. He is Lance Spencer at www.tridentpress.com.au

By the time I invest offshore the company will be making a profit and six months later I intend quitting work and moving to the UK for six months to buy property.

The Houston Street, Darwin unit I purchased after three months of looking and making offers on 15 properties — I got the furniture for free.

Instead of paying tax every two weeks I now pay once a year and last year got a rebate and didn't pay income tax because of the 221d, so this year I'm paying 16 cents in the dollar tax instead of 30 cents.

Keeping positive

I now have a portfolio of $560k with mortgages of $294k, giving me $266k equity. After tax cash flow is currently around $21,000 per annum. Since January 2004 prices in Canberra have been starting to drop. Lots of people who've bought off the plan are seeing values dropping. However, as my investments are cash flow positive I will be fine – that's the beauty of the investment strategies I learnt from the Richmastery education.

Since attending the Richmastery Property Academy I've read huge numbers of books. Some of the memorable ones are Margaret Lomas' books, also Steve McKnight, *0 to 130 Properties in 3 Years*, Peter Span's *$10 Million in Property in 10 years* and Phil Jones' *Real Money Real Estate*.

TOP TEN TIPS

1. Never believe a real estate agent without double checking — salespeople are paid to be friendly; it doesn't mean that they are your friend.

2. Network, network, network. Deals aren't going to come to you; you have to let people know you're looking.

3. Never let fear and a lack of knowledge slow you down.

4. Get a good team around you: financial backers, and people you can bounce ideas off. You need good accountants, solicitors, mortgage brokers.

5. Don't forget your dream because without the desire you'll never achieve. It helps you remember why you're sacrificing now.

6. Suffer short term pain for long term gain.

7. Learn how to budget, I know where every cent of mine goes, I save every cent I can and I don't go without. Write down what you were spending. I was shouting $400 worth of beer a week; now I live on $500 a fortnight.

8. Never stop learning. If you can't afford the books go to the library. If you don't know something read about it. If you can't read about it find someone who has the answers.

9. Don't use credit cards; avoid personal debt.

10. Lead, follow or get out of the bloody way — a lot of my friends are concerned that I don't know what I'm doing, but at the end of the day it's your decisions, your mistakes, so take responsibility, learn and move on.

Chapter 33

Winning deals

'Every time I do a deal I like to win. To me the fun is in landing the deal and finding the next one.'
— **Mark Bosje**, Wanganui, NZ

M y wife Amber and I moved to New Zealand from the United States in 1996. We now live in Wanganui, a small city in the lower North Island of New Zealand, with our five children, whom Amber home schools.

I am a minister with the Grace Baptist Church and we were sponsored by a large group of churches (about 70) in the States to move to New Zealand, where I started up a Grace Baptist Church in Wanganui in 1997.

Settling in

The first property we bought was our own home in 2001. It took a long time for us to get the deposit for it. However, we weren't trying that hard because we didn't think that we could have got a mortgage as we weren't residents at that time. It took us five and a half years to get our residency. I did start shopping around before then. I looked at houses for two years before we were in a position to buy. When we moved here we moved for good, to live, so we were always on edge waiting for our lawyer to call to say it was official – that we could stay.

So when I saw our home for the first time I knew that it was a good deal. I offered $9000 below the asking price of $149k. He verbally accepted the offer but had an open home the next day that he didn't want to cancel. I didn't have finance approved but called the BNZ and asked if they would give us a mortgage without residency; they said yes but that we would need a

20% deposit. We only had $15k but managed to get the rest from other sources. We ended up calling the vendor back and offering his full price of $149k. I knew it was still a good deal; it was recently valued at $280k.

So we purchased our home in April 2001 with 20% down. It is a three bedroom family home, with a spa bath, a single attached garage plus a tandem garage and single garage out the back. It also has a large sleep-out that we are now fixing up for when my parents come to stay from America.

First renter

Less than a year later, I read Robert Kiyosaki's *Rich Dad, Poor Dad* and I mentioned to our lawyer that we were interested in eventually purchasing a rental property. He immediately suggested a two bedroom unit with which he was familiar. He was dealing with a family that was about to be asset-tested by the government and he felt it would be in their best interest to make a quick sale. They were asking $72k for the unit, but I was able to purchase it for $54k. The bank gave us a 90% mortgage on our home, so we got back half of the original deposit on our home to use as the deposit on this property. This money also covered my legal fees. I was suddenly a landlord, with a money-making property, and had not used any ready money.

I did it all wrong at first. There was a lady at our church who was having a rough time so I put her in there for two years for $100 per week, which was below market value. Once she had moved on I bumped the rent up to $130 per week.

Getting inspired

I also read the rest of Robert Kiyosaki's books, along with *Real Money Real Estate* by Phil Jones. I also read John Burley's *Money Secrets of the Rich* and *Real Estate Riches* by Dolf de Roos.

Rich Dad, Poor Dad and John Burley really convinced me that I had to do something about our financial situation – we were living week to week. With a family of five I realised I would eventually have a lot of expenses such as weddings, university tuition and other things like that.

I've always had an interest in property and after reading *Real Estate Riches* I realised that it was a reachable thing for me to pursue.

Very soon afterwards in July 2002 I was invited by a friend to attend a Richmastery Profit from Property evening seminar in Palmerston North.

Boots and all

I had felt like I was moving in the right direction, but the Richmastery seminar encouraged me to jump in boots and all. I went home and had my two properties revalued. The unit I bought for $55k revalued to $70k and my own home valued up to $165k.

I then used the equity to purchase two more houses. Wanganui was still in the doldrums at that time, and property prices hadn't moved for seven years. At that time I felt I was the only one looking at property; I had my pick of houses.

I bought the first place for $40k. It was a two bedroom stucco house and it had a sunroom, garage and shed. It was tenanted and rented for $130 per week.

The second place was a three bedroom house with a sunroom. They were asking $56k; I offered $40k and got it for $42k. I first rented it out for $140 per week and it's now rented at $145 per week, which is an 11.5% return. I recently sold this one for $72k in order to buy a better quality property.

No cash outlaid

I am very fussy when choosing tenants. I have a straight appointment form, and I call their references, their workplace and their last landlord.

Since my bank would not accept the new value of my first property until after six months, I just went to another bank. In both cases, I borrowed enough to cover the entire cost of the house as well as all of the legal fees. I now had three rental properties, all positively geared, and they still had not cost me one cent of my own money.

After six months, I purchased a fourth rental property through a private deal. I did not have quite enough equity, so I offered the vendor an extra $3000 if he would gift it back towards the deposit. After both lawyers were satisfied with the arrangement, I purchased the house for $61k. I then got

back the $3000, meaning that I had only paid $58k. This property was also positively geared. I rent it for $140 per week. So far, I had about $100 per week coming in after all mortgages, rates and insurances.

Freeing up some money

In December 2003, I sold two of my properties. The original unit was sold for $80k, giving me a clear profit of $25k in just 18 months. I also sold one of the cheaper houses, which was not in the best area. It returned a $21k profit in just 16 months.

I used this money to fix up the two rentals that I still had, to buy two more rentals, and to take my wife to Auckland for a three day shopping spree! The other benefit of selling these two properties was that the money I made went on my own home, but the new mortgages went on the rentals. My accountant made sure all the paperwork was correct, and I now owe very little on my own home. This allows me a tax rebate on the majority of the interest that I pay.

Spending again

The next rental I purchased this time was for $60k; they were asking $65k. It was a stucco house with a tile roof, three bedrooms with a sleep-out and a small garage. The couple who had been renting my unit before I sold it said they wanted me for a landlord so I got them in there. I spent $6000 on renovations: I recarpeted, repainted, using contractors, and changed the light fittings – tradespeople in Wanganui are cheap. The total rental return is $160 per week.

In Wanganui the boom pushed up rentals; it had been common for a three bedroom house to rent for $130 per week, and now it's hard to get one for $160 per week. For a house that is worth $80k, tenants would be more likely to pay $170 per week.

The next house I purchased was in February 2004 at the height of the property boom. It was a classic one of the 'D's that Phil Jones talks about – a deceased estate. It had been on the market for three years for $40k and no one wanted to touch it because the beneficiaries of the estate were scattered all over the world and the tenant had been nothing but trouble. I decided the numbers made it worth the trouble, offered $6000 less than they were asking, and nine months after starting the deal finally settled and purchased the house for $34k. The house immediately valued up to $62k, and my local real estate agent told me he had a buyer for $72k. I decided to keep it, since I had met the tenant and with a bit of work got the rent payments up to date and an automatic payment in place.

Having fun

I now own four rentals, with a net income of $178 per week. On my home and two of the rental properties I have principal and interest mortgages and an interest only mortgage on the other two. I am now having valuations done on two of my properties, and will be looking to buy two more in the near future.

I also used equity to buy our church building. We arranged a rent to buy deal and purchased the building for $195k. The deal is that the vendor rents it to us for two years and then we get all the rent back and over that time we will pay him off so in that time we will own the building.

My goal is to do it for fun. Property investment is like playing Monopoly. We don't spend the money; we put it back into the houses. Every time I do a deal I like to win. To me the fun is in landing the deal and also finding the next one. I enjoy going through the paper on Saturday and seeking out the deals. In just three years we have come from a position where we could not even raise a mortgage because we were not yet residents to having a total portfolio value of $425k and total mortgages of $310k. I would like to get my portfolio value to over $1 million.

TOP TEN TIPS

1. Don't be afraid to sell if it puts you in a position to buy a better deal.
2. Take your time. Lots of time, if necessary. One great deal can be better than five good ones.
3. Use good legal help. My lawyer is not only first-class, but he has helped me find two of my deals.
4. Keep your accounting above reproach.
5. Treat your tenants right. When things slow down and empty houses start to show up, you want tenants to want to be in one of your houses. Real estate is about people!
6. Don't be too lenient. Tenants are customers who deserve good service. They are not charity cases.
7. Pay your tradespeople immediately. This gives you an edge when you need them fast.
8. Ask LOTS of questions. There are no dumb questions. There are only dumb people who won't ask questions.
9. Ignore the critics. Many of your friends and family will feel duty bound to warn you why it won't work. Smile a lot as you walk away.
10. Have fun!

Chapter 34

Advantage from adversity

'I learned from my bad experiences ... in future I wanted to do things differently.'
— Jla (Grace) Zou, Sydney, AUS

I am a migrant from mainland China. I came to Australia 14 years ago as an overseas student when I was 24 years old. I had studied a BA in English Literature so I became advanced in the English language in China and came to Australia to do a course in business management in Sydney. Here I met my husband, Hugh, an Australian. We were married in 1990 but I became widowed in 1992 when my husband died tragically.

My late husband left me with a large debt on our joint property in Cromer, in the Northern Beaches of Sydney. I couldn't afford to pay the mortgage, so I moved out of the home and shared a rental unit with another person, while our home was rented for three years. The rent paid for the expenses.

Hard time to sell

In 1996 I began studying for my Masters degree in Interpreting and Translating. In late 1996 I fell pregnant and the father of my child left me because he was not ready to be a father. Knowing that I would be a solo mother, I then decided to sell my former home, and build a nest for myself. It took many months to sell the house – a three bedroom split level house with ocean view on the northern beach – because it was the end of the boom in the property cycle. It was eventually sold in December 1996 for $280k, and by mid 1997 the same property was worth $380k, because the market started to soar. My late husband and I had bought it in 1991 for $220k. Today it is worth more than a million dollars as it has sea views.

Bad time to buy

I was very inexperienced in the property market and by the time I was ready to get back into the market in mid 1997, the prices had gone up considerably and I could only afford a large two bedroom unit with single garage plus storage and one bathroom in Dee Why. This unit was near the beachside of the suburb and close to the town centre. I purchased it for $235k plus stamp duty and taxes, a total of around $250k. This unit is now valued at $450k. With the proceeds of this sale and with other money from my husband's estate I was able to put down a deposit on the unit of $175k plus costs. I borrowed $65k and even found getting this level of finance difficult as I was a pregnant, single woman without a full time job as I was freelancing as an interpreter. I found that experience of dealing with the banks extremely stressful. The unit has been rented ever since and now brings in $310 per week. I haven't increased the rent for the past three years (2001–2004) as I have a very good tenant, but it could potentially rent for more.

Learning from experience

I learned from my bad experiences of selling at the wrong time and buying in the boom, and I felt that in future I wanted to do things differently. So I started my self-education in property investment. I wanted to turn adversity to my advantages. I began to read most of the top property investment books available.

I read the whole series of Robert Kiyosaki's *Rich Dad, Poor Dad*. I also found Paul Clithorall's book *Making Money* very helpful, as it gave me a solid system and the foundation of a long term investment plan.

Before I became a mother I had not been concerned with making money as my job provided enough money for myself. Working as a conference interpreter I earned a very good wage and could make $600–800 per day. But with my son on the way, I was determined to build a secure future for him. He was born on the 28/08/97. Chinese people believe that eight is a very lucky number and I have found that determination and luck go hand in hand.

I accepted welfare payments for about two months but felt it was very

The equity from my first investment let me buy a new home.

demoralising so I was determined to get back to work and to be financially independent. I found a live-in babysitter to look after my son and went back to work as a conference interpreter when he was two months old.

New home

By late 1998, the value of my unit in Dee Why had risen by at least 20% and I had enough equity to buy a home for myself. I moved on and bought a two storey, five bedroom brick house on the northern beaches, with a lovely back garden, for $427k (plus $8k stamp duty) and rented out the unit in Dee Why.

I now have some boarders living in two of the rooms and they contribute board. I put down a deposit of 20% secured against the unit and borrowed the rest of the money, servicing the mortgage with my own money and help from my boarders.

Let the Games begin

Between 1997 and 2000 property prices boomed in Australia, especially in Sydney. So, in mid 2000 I began looking at property again as the value of my own home had gone up to around $600k. In 2000 I observed that there was little interest in property due to the Olympic Games and the introduction of GST. The market was settling and I snatched a rundown three bedroom brick house with 800 square metres of land in Frenchs Forest, a very good suburb on the northern beaches, for $388k, using the equity in my own home for the 20% deposit. This house had been rented for 10 years and was in need of repair. I painted it throughout and put in a new kitchen; after the renovation it revalued at $450k. I rented this out for $450 per week; the rents were very good in the Olympic Games period.

In April 2003 when the tenants moved out, I spent three months renovating the house; I put in another bathroom with a shower and additional toilet, new blinds to replace the curtains I had made myself. I repainted the interior myself with the help of friends, and put in aluminium blinds; it looked fantastic. In total I spent $20k. After doing this work, in late 2003 it was valued at $675k.

It then stood vacant for three months after I left it up to a property manager to rent and finally I took matters into my own hands and rented it to three Chinese students.

Buy and hold

I attended a Richmastery Profit from Property Retire Young, Retire Rich property seminar in Sydney that I found very helpful. I also read another book by Paul Hanson and thanks to the confidence and knowledge I gained from attending the seminar, reading all the Richmastery newsletters I received as a club Richmastery member and all the information on the Richmastery website, I was able to gain a clear understanding of how to structure a long term investment strategy. I decided my intention was to buy and hold.

I refinanced my three properties in 2001 and found I had more equity to spend on further properties. I went on to have an investment partner and together we bought another three properties with 50% ownership each. Our plan was to buy one property per year.

The first property I purchased with my investment partner was a two bedroom unit in Dee Why near the beach for $265k in 2001. We put in 20% deposit (total $80k) plus stamp duty and costs. For any deposit under a 20% you have to pay mortgage insurance in Australia so I always stick to the rule of paying a 20% deposit. We rented it immediately for $280 per week, so it breaks even. In 2004 the bank valued it at $350k.

In September 2002 we bought a three bedroom townhouse (one in a block of five) in Auburn, in Western Sydney, near Paramatta. Auburn is an up and coming suburb but still affordable. The townhouse has a nice courtyard, is double brick in good condition and eight years old. The vendors were

I used the equity in my home for a deposit on this Frenchs Forest house, which I renovated for rental gain.

asking $365k; we got it for $323k and the 20% deposit was secured against our new Dee Why unit, which had revalued at $350k. We rented it out for $310. We have to top up the strata management and council rates out of our own money.

A bad buy

In December 2002 we purchased an off the plan, split level unit in Zedland, in Sydney's eastern suburbs. This was sold to us by a company marketing a new development site. We were a little crazy at that time due to all the success we had experienced and, looking back, this was a bad buy. We bought a deposit bond of $5000 for three years. The developers said the project would be completed in 2005 and at that time we would settle the full purchase price of $520k, plus $30k stamp duty and solicitors etc. (For us this meant a deposit of 20%, i.e. $110k.)

Because the market began slowing down in early 2004, the developers rushed through the project, completing it earlier than planned. We were advised that we had to settle on the deal early, in April 2004 (although they didn't actually complete it until June 2004); we had not planned for it to be completed until late 2005. The fine print in the agreement said that we had to settle when it was finished. If we want to sell it in today's market it would fetch $480k, just 80% of the purchase price. Many of the investors in the development are of Asian background. The developers had also set up their own company to manage rentals but rents were lowered in the scramble to rent out the units.

We signed a contract with a property management company but they couldn't rent it for two months, so we eventually found another agent who rented it for $320 per week, whereas we had been expecting about $420.

Neither of us had any money in hand for the $110k plus $20k stamp duty costs to settle, so we looked at forfeiting our deposit, but even if we did that the developer could still come after us. We tried to sell the Auburn property but there were no buyers, as the market had slowed in February 2004. In the end my investment partner had to sell his home unit in Dee Why to come up with the money.

> This was a shocking experience and has taught us a strong lesson. With all our other properties we had been conservative, had done our own research, and now we know we will never again buy any property through a large marketing scheme.

Still in good shape

I now own three properties on my own, worth around $2 million. My total mortgages against these are $880k, meaning I have created equity of $1.2 million. Plus I have 50% ownership of an investment portfolio worth $1.3 million, with total net assets around $1.5 million and total mortgages of $960k, meaning a total of $340k in equity.

Even though we were hurt by our final purchase, overall our portfolio is still in good shape and our mistake won't stop us investing.

Our next step is to buy positive cash flow properties to balance our negative cash flow, as the reason for investing is to give us a passive income. But if the properties are all negatively geared that defeats the purpose of investing.

Development project management

For the last three years I have also helped manage a property development project, helping investors from China invest in property in the Coolangatta area on Australia's Gold Coast. This has been very successful and I am now investing some of my family's money too.

The first two projects were housing developments. The first was a six house development and the second was 19 houses. I get a 10% share in the profits for my part in the work. All of these projects have a 100% return and I have now invested $400k in a new project in which I stand to gain a 30% share in the profits.

This is a 12 storey, 27 unit apartment block development that will return over $5 million. We bought the land for $1.22 million in April 2004 and once the DA (development application) was approved for a 27 unit development in September 2004 the land was revalued at $2.7 million. It featured in the local paper, and we have set a benchmark in the Tweed Head area of the Gold Coast. This is situated 100 km south of Brisbane, five minutes to the Gold Coast airport, 500 metres to the beach and 200 metres to the shopping centre. It is expected to be completed by Christmas 2005.

I am bringing investors to the project and we have contracted a trusted local project management company to project manage the development and they have asked me to be part of their company. I plan to move to the Gold Coast area during this time. I see this as the future for me; I am going to go into project management.

You can do it too

I wish to share my story with young women and single mothers in particular. I always encourage people around me to start saving for their first deposit. If someone had taught me in my twenties what I know today I would be in a much better position now. Please take responsibility for your own future. If I can do it, you can too, and with help of Richmastery and the Richmastery education, you can do it better. I have passed on my knowledge by mentoring my stepdaughter on how to save, as she could not budget.

TOP TEN TIPS

1. Educate yourself and gain confidence through knowledge.
2. Have a long term investment plan; set your goals.
3. If possible buy a property that is positively geared to balance negative gearing.
4. No matter where you stand now it's not too late to start — the Chinese have a saying that a thousand miles starts from the first step, so take action for your own financial future.
5. Get mentoring from people who walk the talk and are investing themselves.
6. Use property managers to manage your portfolio. Otherwise the small things can stop you from achieving the bigger picture goal.
7. Focus on getting a good team around you: lawyers, accountants, tradespeople.
8. Always look into the bigger picture and don't let small obstacles stop you from achieving higher goals.
9. Always look on the bright side.
10. Commit yourself to your plan, don't get sidetracked, and keep going.

Chapter 35

Rebuilding

'If I buy two rentals, over time this should give me equity for four then eight and so on.'
— **Wayne Bray,** Wellington, NZ

A s a result of Richmastery's fantastic introductory presentation, the four hour Richmastery Profit from Property seminar in Wellington, I have purchased three rentals returning positive cash flow in the hand each week.

I had lost everything I had worked all my life for when my marriage ended five years ago as we had to sell all of our property. I have three children and still play a big part in my children's lives. This was a turning point for me as I realised I needed to rebuild what I had lost.

I went along to the Richmastery Profit from Property evening seminar after a friend paid for me to go along. He is a property investor and felt I could really benefit from it. I had owned rentals in the past and a 30 acre farmlet and homestead in Pahiatua (a small town in the lower North Island of New Zealand) but had to sell up when my marriage ended.

A paradigm for change

The Richmastery Profit from Property seminar gave me a paradigm for change and I realised that there are ways of achieving your goals that are more likely to work than the way I used to do it. The formulas for purchasing property and the positive cash flow model really struck me big time, and the ease with which you can achieve your goals if you do it wisely. I have always been interested in property and was glad to find out how to go about investing in it.

Some of the most valuable books I have read since doing the Richmastery Profit from Property seminar are *The Magic of Thinking Big*, *Rich Dad, Poor Dad* and *The Cash Flow Quadrant* by Robert Kiyosaki.

A new home

When my wife and I separated we had a house in Upper Hutt, north-east of Wellington. I bought her out of the house but then found that, because of the memories it held for me, I didn't want to stay there. So I sold the family home for $130k. I ended up with about $40k cash. I then used this cash for the deposits on my next two property purchases.

To find a new home for myself I targeted Timberley, a lower socio-economic area of Lower Hutt. While it was a grotty area I liked the way it looked out over the Upper Hutt Valley. I put offers on four different houses for their GV (government valuation).

All were accepted, but as each contract was conditional I pulled out of three and just purchased one, which is the house I now live in.

I got the property for $113k in June 2002; it has recently been valued at $170k. The registered valuation at the time I bought it was $125k. I originally offered $115k but couldn't get finance for the loan so I told the vendor I could only get $113k and they accepted that.

Holiday home

I wanted somewhere to go with the children at weekends so I began looking for a holiday home (bach). I discovered that Foxton Beach about an hour and a half north of Wellington was the cheapest place on the northern coast to find a bach. A lot of the beaches closer to Wellington had already risen in price and were out of my reach. I found a house at Foxton Beach for $27k and went in with my parents. They put up $13,500 and I put up $13,500. We purchased it in June 2002.

After using the $40k cash, my mortgage was $86,500. The mortgage is secured against the house so effectively the holiday home is freehold.

Two years later the holiday home was worth close to $100k (almost four times what I paid for it). It is on a full 1200 square metre site and 1.5 km to the beachfront. It had a garage on it with a shower, toilet and kitchenette. I have put in extra walls and made two rooms and insulated it and put ceilings in so it is now quite livable. Now we use it for the weekend and I have researched the cost of putting a 'Versatile' kitset house on the site, which would cost $40k.

First rental investment

I found another property there which was a three bedroom house that the vendor was asking $35k for. I got a valuer to check it out and he found out that the studs were too far apart so the bank wouldn't lend any money on it. So I continued to look around and found a two bedroom cottage on a 1000 square metre site. I offered $40k for it; the vendors were asking $45k. They didn't accept it, but eventually I got it for $43k. So in November 2002 I purchased my second property at Foxton Beach. I then rented it out for $130 per week. I did this through a local property manager from Property Brokers in Foxton.

The tenant said she wanted to stay there long term but she moved out because she got a state house cheaper. However, my mortgage broker found another tenant and now takes a 7% management fee. I have become a third party in the arrangement, which is great.

> I treat all my tenants like customers. The gas stove broke and I replaced it with an electric stove immediately and my tenant sent me a card to thank me. I look after my tenants' problems immediately because if I look after them they will look after the properties and pay their rent.

Finding value in Wanganui

I went through *Kiwi Property Investor* (KPI) magazine (available through www.richmastery.com) and saw that Wanganui (north-west of Wellington in the North Island) was an undervalued area in early 2003 so I started targeting places on the internet.

I then met a woman at the Rent Centre in Wanganui, Kathy Verhock. I told her I wanted to buy a place and was looking at Castlecliff, where houses were going for under $30k. She said not to buy there as the banks often wouldn't lend money on houses in this area. She said she would find a place for me.

A solid three bedroom house in Wanganui, returning positive cash flow. My kids helped with the tidy up.

Kathy called me to say she had found a property that was close to the hospital, shops, public transport – a nice three bedroom house. It had rimu ceilings, and a fireplace. So I got a building inspection done and it was fine apart from having a low floor; the inspector recommended adding vents to improve air circulation, which I haven't done yet. The vendor was asking $48k; I got it for $45k. It was already rented at $140 per week, and the same tenants are still in the property now.

I have built a porch on this property, a friend who is a builder helped me, and it took a couple of days. The tenants think it is fantastic, as its somewhere under cover to sit and to hang their washing. I also had to fix the front porch and renew the deck. Also I painted the roof; this work was a total cost of $750 and we did the work ourselves.

Slow to rent

The next place I targeted was Woodville (a small central North Island town near Palmerston North) because I had seen a five bedroom house there for $20k advertised in the *Trade and Exchange* (a free weekly advertising paper). I spoke to the owner but then spoke to a local real estate agent who said the house was on for $35k, so this ruined the sale. However, she did call me about four months later to say that a family was selling two or three houses in Woodville. She said the registered valuation on them was $50k each. I offered $45k for one and they didn't accept. I then offered $49k.

I was told that houses were easy to rent in the area, so I bought the place in May 2004. But then it sat empty for three months. Initially I used property

I added a garage to my Woodville property to make it more appealing for renters.

brokers in nearby Pahiatua but they didn't do anything so I went to Remax in Pahiatua and they also haven't done anything.

I advertised in the *Trade and Exchange* and the internet, and arranged finance of $6000 to put a single garage on the property as that seems to be important to tenants. I tidied up the section and took away trailer loads of rubbish, put carpet down and painted the kitchen and lounge and the exterior of the house. The house is in good condition as it has aluminum joinery and is solid.

After three months I finally rented it for $110 per week and the tenants are very happy.

Strength in numbers

My long term goal is to own 10 rentals. My theory is the rule of twos: if I buy two rentals, over time this should give me equity for four then eight and so on. I work on the rule of numbers, so if I have 10 rentals and one is vacant it won't be such a problem as if you have one rental and that is vacant; the other nine can cover the rent.

My rule is to only buy north from Upper Hutt to Wanganui as that is practical for me to do my own maintenance and check on my properties. I like to do a nice job myself. I enjoy it and it helps to keep within my budget.

I have registered as an LAQC for my rentals and I am in the process of setting up a trust for the family home and bach. It feels progressive and reassuring. The name of my LAQC is Serenity Property Management. It's an ironic name but it works for me.

All my investment properties have increased in value and are all earning me a positive after tax cash flow.

TOP TEN TIPS

1. Buy positive cash flow, and buy on the numbers only, not on emotion.
2. Buy tenanted properties.
3. Don't take advice from poor people.
4. Have trusted people in your team like a good lawyer, accountant etc.
5. I strongly recommend protection in your structure like setting up trusts and LAQCs.
6. Associate with like-minded people.
7. Always try to buy the most amount of land so you can add value by subdividing later.
8. Treat tenants as you would your best customers: look after them.
9. Take action, as action conquers fear.
10. Always try to buy property in a growing area, not an area in decline.

Chapter 36

Seeking self-sufficiency

'If I hadn't had my accident we would never have done it ... I began looking for a secure future.'
— **Joy and Brian Hamilton,**
Palmerston North, NZ

I have not made miraculous purchases of 10 houses in 10 months with $1 million in equity type, but I believe my story may inspire people with disabilities to consider property investing.

Seeking security

In 1990 I had a car accident that left me a tetraplegic and reliant on a wheelchair for mobility. I was married with three young sons at the time. Concerned about my financial future, my husband Brian and I looked around for a way I could invest so that I would not have to worry financially if in the future I needed fulltime medical care.

We were concerned as we both come from large families and we weren't going to inherit much money, so we needed to find a way to become self-sufficient in our old age, especially if I end up needing special care.

We had been living in Palmerston North for three years, we were both from here and had lived in Wellington for five years and then moved back again. When we first moved back to Palmerston North I was not working but then Brian was made redundant so he stayed home with the kids and I went back to working at my old job with the National Library.

When I had the car accident I was on a work related trip at the time. I was in the Burwood Spinal Unit at Christchurch for 16 weeks then I came home to be with my children. The boys were then four, six and eight years old; they

314

were quite little. It was 18 months before I went back to my job; fortunately they held it open for me. I still work there 30 hours a week, managing their curriculum resource service to schools.

Early successes

When we began investing in 1991, my husband and I owned a home in Palmerston North, which we'd bought for $87k in 1987; at that time it was worth $102k. Using the equity in our house my husband and I purchased a three bedroom townhouse in Maxwells Line, Awapuni, Palmerston North in 1992 that could be adapted for a wheelchair user. The purchase price was $95k, and the deposit was $20k.

The man who had lived there had been a heavy smoker and just sat at home and smoked. Brian did the renovations himself. We painted, wallpapered, replaced curtains and since then we have recarpeted and reroofed the house. We now rent it out for $220 per week. This was a great success and the tenant stayed for seven years.

We thought, 'This is easy,' and decided that we might do it again. The rent comes in and you don't have to do anything. Inspired, we purchased another property in 1995. Again this property could easily be adapted for a wheelchair user, and by now I had become conscious that there was a shortage of accommodation for people with disabilities.

This house was also in Palmerston North at Ruamahanga Crescent. The vendors were asking $110k; we got it for $103k. The grounds were overgrown and uncared for. It had been rented by an absentee landlord who wanted to get rid of it. We cleaned up the exterior and the garden and did a full interior paint and paper. We then rented it for $190 per week on a P & I loan.

Our first renter in Palmerston North, a three bedroom townhouse — a great success for us.

The bank rolled the two loans together, which we now know isn't a good thing as you need to have properties divided up when you do your tax.

Again we were fortunate to get tenants who wanted to stay: the first family stayed for five years. We currently get $200 per week for it, but could easily get $220. However, the family who are currently there have been there for three years, and we prefer to keep reliable tenants by maintaining the rent at a reasonable level. Last summer we painted the exterior and replaced guttering.

Looking further afield

Then another four years went by, we thought we're starting to get a bit of knowledge about property investment, but Palmerston North property was not doing anything, not moving up in value at all.

At the time I was learning that disabled people had such trouble finding a place to live and to get the alterations they needed done to flats through Work and Income NZ. Also we were thinking about where we could have Christmas holidays with a family and a wheelchair. Camping was difficult for me, and motels were too expensive.

So we went looking for property in Taupo, a popular lakeside holiday destination in the central North Island, in the weekends and got to know a real estate agent who was good and used to fax us down information on properties. With his help in 1999 we purchased a two bedroom property in the central Taupo area.

The asking price was $125k; we paid $115k. It had a small, easy-care section, with a double internal access garage. The property was in good condition and only needed some wallpapering and painting inside. We first rented it for $170 per week, and it currently rents for $185 per week.

Another in Taupo

In 2000 we were up in Taupo again and were reading the property papers – we look at them wherever we go – and we saw a house that had been wheelchair adapted. So in February 2002 we purchased our second property in Taupo. It is a two bedroom house in Rotokawa Street, coincidentally the same street as the previous house. It was a deceased estate and the family was desperate to sell.

One of two houses we bought in the same street in Taupo. We bargained hard on this deceased estate.

We were now becoming hard bargainers, and stuck to our first offer, and they came down to our price. They were asking $102k; we got it for $93k and when the government valuation came out in July it was $110k. It was a bonus that this property was adapted for a wheelchair.

We learnt a lesson here when we took over the existing tenants. We took over an existing contract, and we couldn't put the rent up for six months, something we were unaware of. So they continued to rent it for $150 per week and once the contract ended we were able to put it up; it now rents for $185 per week.

Rotokawa Street was a bit of a grotty street because there were lots of rented homes in it but over the years it has tidied itself up a bit; I have never had trouble renting either property. Our Taupo properties are both attractive and low maintenance.

Managing the properties

Initially we used a property manager for the Taupo properties, but we had a couple of bad experiences. The first one we used allowed the tenant to get behind in the rent, and we had to draw his attention to it when we weren't paid.

When the tenant moved out we decided to find a new property manager and we went to check on the property to see what maintenance was needed. We discovered that the bond had been given back to the tenant without a thorough inspection having been carried out. We found a window was broken and damage to a wall.

So we now manage all our properties ourselves, including the ones in Taupo. This means the occasional trip to Taupo (which is two and a half hours' drive from Palmerston North) to change tenants and to inspect the property when tenants leave, and then to sign up new tenants, but with email and cell phones, we can be quickly contacted. We have built up a list of Taupo contacts, so repairs and maintenance can be carried out quickly and efficiently.

Other than this we visit for property inspections every three or four months. Taupo is such a lovely place to visit we consider it a treat to spend a day or weekend there!

Where possible we let our properties to people with disabilities, but this has proved difficult over the years because we want tenants quickly and often there is no one with a disability looking for accommodation (to afford a market rent, people with disabilities often need to share their accommodation). At the moment we have a solo father with a disabled daughter living in one property.

Offering a good service

Because we manage all the properties ourselves, my husband Brian does all the maintenance and I manage the administrative side of things and the tenants. We have a checklist of things we ask our prospective tenants. We always do a reference check with previous landlords if we can and speak to the people on the references rather than trusting the written word.

We've been very lucky in all these years we've not had too many problems. At one stage we did have a couple who were not paying rent and you do have to act sooner rather than later when rent is not being paid. We always contact them immediately the rent payment is missed and give them the opportunity to explain and come to an arrangement for paying it back. This way we have few problems.

Our tenants always treat me with respect and we do the same to them. We have come to believe over the years that we are now providing a social service in offering clean, tidy, comfortable homes at a reasonable rent to people.

Private buy

The next house we bought was in October 2004 in Salisbury Avenue in Hokowhitu, a nice suburb of Palmerston North. It is near the river and the golf course. It was a private sale from someone I work with who was upgrading her house. It was very neat and tidy and just eventually will need a new driveway and some work on the roof. My colleague didn't want to be bothered with agents and people coming through the house so we purchased it for $160k with a $10k deposit. An agent had wanted to market it for $175k. It is renting for $220 per week.

Keen investors

Over the years we have become keen property investors. We became Club Richmastery members and now avidly read *Kiwi Property Investor* (KPI) magazine (available from www.richmastery.com) and we attend the Manawatu Property Investors Association meetings. We listen and learn from all the Richmastery CDs that have been sent with the KPI magazines, and I read property books to build my knowledge.

Just this year we have formed an LAQC company for our properties. Plus we have set up a family trust for tax purposes. Our latest property has gone into the LAQC but we will move the other properties into the trust.

Buying strategies

When we do the figures on buying a property we look at the amount they want for the property and the amount of rent we can get back and the cost to borrow that money; whatever we borrow we want to get back. We aim to only buy properties that are positive cash flow, but this is becoming more difficult as house prices have risen.

Although finding the property is difficult as I cannot always get in to view it, I find real estate agents great and have built up a wonderful relationship with some who bring deals to us. We also have a great team of advisers in our accountant and lawyer as well. I also use the internet to do research.

We are always on the lookout for more properties. We have bought five houses in 14 years and our total portfolio value is now approximately $1.088 million. We have about $680k equity in them. Our total after tax cash flow is more than $8000 per year.

Our goal from here is to have a total of 10 properties by 2010, so that's another five over five years and by then the first five properties will be paid off. We will then focus on paying off the latter five with the rent from the first five. By then we will be thinking about retiring and my husband will be 65.

Taking control of our future

Our property portfolio definitely makes us feel more secure about our financial future. If we hadn't done this we'd have this house and a family car but we wouldn't have the equity we've got now or the potential equity. It makes us feel that we have taken control of our future. We are now firm believers in goal setting, listening to motivational speakers and reading books; we are a lot more goal driven than we were and it has flowed on to our kids.

My middle son Jason is already saving for his first house and on his $8 an hour wage as an apprentice has nearly saved the deposit. He goes through all the property papers looking for suitable houses. He's just turned 20.

We love the Richmastery CDs that have come out with KPI magazine. We find great value in being Richmastery members and have enjoyed reading many books including *Real Money Real Estate* by Phil Jones, *Real Estate Riches* by Dolf de Roos, *Get Rich, Stay Rich* and *Rich Dad, Poor Dad* by Robert Kiyosaki.

We have had no problems raising finance. All our loans until the last one were with the same bank. This last time we used a mortgage broker, and changed banks, getting a very good fixed interest rate.

We are very humble about our investing and we don't tell lots of people about it. Our families think we must have lots of money, but it has been hard work and an expensive business.

If I hadn't had my accident we probably would never have done it. It was because of my accident that I started looking around for a way to a secure future. Anyone can do it but they need to treat it as a business. If you are going to manage your own properties you need to look after tenants because getting it wrong can lead to the renting disasters you read about.

I love property investment: it becomes a passion, and we look at property wherever we go now. My advice is to just do it! If you run it like a business and are prepared to stay for the long haul, you can't go wrong with property.

TOP TEN TIPS

1. Select tenants carefully, and then look after them. Speak with a past landlord if possible rather than just accept written references. Fix problems promptly.

2. Phone your new tenant when the first automatic payment goes in to let them know it has been received and to thank them. They seem to appreciate this, but also, it lets them know we are watching for the rent to go in.

3. Don't just take on friends and family of existing tenants. Always meet any prospective tenant and check them out.

4. Become knowledgeable about property investing in all aspects. Join your local property investor association. Register with the various internet property investor sites (e.g. www.propertyinvesting.com).

5. Check rents weekly, and follow up any missed payments immediately.

6. Always make sure the property is clean and tidy, lawns mowed, carpets cleaned, when the new tenants move in. This sets the standard that is expected.

7. Don't be in a rush to buy a number of properties. Do your due diligence and walk away if the figures don't add up. After the purchase, take time to bring the property up to rentable standard if necessary, select the tenants carefully, and then let it all settle down before you start to look for another property.

8. Make sure you have a lawyer and accountant who understand property investing.

9. Keep careful and accurate records.

10. Photograph any damage that has been done by a tenant as possible evidence if you end up at the Tenancy Tribunal. Have deadlocks that are keyed alike, installed on the back and front doors. Then when tenants vacate change the lock barrel. The old barrel can then be used on another property.

Chapter 37

Bumpy but bountiful trip

'We have proved that you can start with next to nothing and, with focus and determination, get into the investment game.'
— **Jeff and Maggie Vickers**, Feilding, NZ

I live with my husband Jeff in Feilding, a small town in the central North Island of New Zealand about two hours north of Wellington.

At the end of 1999 both Jeff and I had just come out of broken marriages, aged 35, with nothing other than $40k personal debt! Both of us had had a series of great jobs, and had been involved with motor sport (and its costs) for a number of years. We got together in early 2000. I'd owned my home since I was 18 but I had just kept refinancing to put more money into our motor sport.

Must be another way

I knew Boyd Gunn, the real estate agent/author, and a mutual friend had heard about his book. So I went into the local book shop to buy it. I also brought Kiyosaki's *Rich Dad, Poor Dad* and *Building Wealth through Property Investment* by Dolf de Roos. Funny, I hadn't read any books for years let alone bought any, and I read all three within a week. Soon after I met Jeff I was telling him about Boyd's book and it came to light that both of us were interested in property, wealth creation and self development. So we absorbed ourselves in our education.

Jeff had had good jobs for 20 years but when his marriage ended he got a bank statement and he had $400 in his savings account. He thought, 'I've been working for 20 years and I've got nothing. So in another 20 years I'll be in the same position.' He had his toys and that was all. That started him thinking that there must be another way.

In September 2000, we purchased a home for ourselves in Gemstone Drive, Parkdale, Upper Hutt, a suburb of Wellington. We just scraped together a minimal deposit of $13k despite still having loads of personal debt. It was a three bedroom 1980s home with a double garage. We purchased it for $126k and its market value was $123k! (We paid too much!)

In April 2001 we formed a company (Smiley Face Holdings Ltd) with the help of a financial advisor as we were determined to improve our financial future and all the books told us we could. We went to a Robert Kiyosaki evening seminar in Wellington and embarked on buying our first investment property.

Close to the wire

In May 2001, using the equity in our home which was now worth $135k, we purchased a three bedroom flat with a garage in a block of two, in Pasadena Crescent, Totara Park, Upper Hutt. The mortgage broker put us on an interest only loan. It was the third place we'd looked at and the agent said there were lots of others interested and that we should make our best offer. We ended up purchasing it for $82,500. Its registered valuation was $82k. (Once again we paid too much.) We rented it out for $160 per week.

Soon after we attended another seminar presented by Dolf de Roos because we were now property investors! However, despite having our mortgage on interest only, we were still in the mindset of paying off the mortgage and then saving up for the next one. It was our accountant at the time's advice not to make the company an LAQC. We discovered that he really knew nothing about property.

We didn't know about doing numbers. We now owned two properties both 90% financed and had more personal debt as we had paid most of the deposit on the new place on the credit card.

We were so hyped by the Kiyosaki and de Roos seminars that we thought, 'Bugger any rules!' But I suppose looking back although we made mistakes at least we got started.

House in Main Street, Marton, bought $10k under value and provides great cash flow.

In September 2001 things were very tight financially. We played landlord but when our tenant moved out we thought, 'How do we find a new one?' We decided to find a property manager. We hired the first one we found who worked for the local real estate agency. The place was vacant for six weeks before the property manager got it tenanted.

About that time we decided to move to Feilding, a thriving farming service town near Palmerston North, in the lower North Island. So we spent money we didn't have tidying up our home in Upper Hutt to make it better for tenants – more personal debt! We painted half of the inside, put in a new kitchen bench top. It was still owned by the family trust. Then we rented it out, using the same property manager. It took her two months to find a tenant. This brought us pretty close to the wire.

In January 2002, our financial position worsened as a result of both of us changing jobs, plus the moving costs and we had to find six weeks rent and bond for the place we were renting in Feilding. It was a very difficult time. For our own sanity we set a deadline for renting the house in Upper Hutt otherwise it would go on the market. Just a week before the deadline the property manager said she'd found somebody.

Just at that time we were doing Anthony Robbins Personal Power CD and learning about negative neuro-association. That is well and truly what we had with this property manager; every time we heard from her we always expected the worst.

In February 2002 we joined the Manawatu Property Association and immediately became involved; Maggie was the Vice President for 2004. We met and associated with like minded people.

Scraping through

In March 2002 I looked for an accountant in the Manawatu. We found one who was good and who pointed out some of our errors, and assisted us in correcting things. One of our criteria was that they needed to be a property investor themselves, which he was. He told us that we needed an LAQC and also chattels valuations for our properties. And in August 2002 we sold our former home in Upper Hutt from our trust to our company (now an LAQC).

We then went to a Richmastery Profit from Property evening seminar in Wellington and learned that we had done some things right and some things wrong. We realised we needed some more education. We were unable to afford to go to the three day Richmastery Property Academy the following month, but made the commitment to ourselves to attend the next one. We did purchase the Richmastery Property Analysis Software.

At that stage we were looking to buy a home in Feilding but we didn't know what we wanted to buy. Ultimately the bank made the decision for us. They said we could buy a third investment property at 70–80% finance, or if it was going to be our own home we had to spend over $100k and they would give us 95% finance on it. Because we had a minimal deposit there was only one option. The bank made it clear that they were not very happy with us, but helped us out. Our personal debt was not really reducing.

So in October 2002, we purchased a home for ourselves in Feilding under our family trust. It was a three bedroom home with a nice outlook and a single garage. They were asking $117k, we got it for $112k. It was revalued at $135k in February 2004.

Tenant troubles

In November 2002 we were alerted to tenancy problems at our old home in Upper Hutt by our former neighbour. We had said that the tenants could have pets but found out they had a horse living in the backyard and guinea pigs and rabbits in the conservatory. We kept hassling the property manager to do something about this but she did nothing. It took nearly two months before the horse was finally gone. Then the tenant's boyfriend got released from jail along with two of his mates so there were five adults and two toddlers living in a smallish three bedroom house. The ex-jailbirds ended up doing burglaries around the neighbourhood, and dealing drugs out of the house.

Two bedroom unit in Blackwell Street, Marton. We had to scurry around to finance it but it has good cash flow.

In January 2003 some members of the local gang smashed into the house after an unhappy drug deal, and they threatened the local neighbourhood kids that were watching all the action. We were mortified that all of this was happening in our old home, to which we had an emotional attachment. However, after much time, anguish and to-ing and fro-ing we managed to get the tenants out.

In February 2003 we attended a seminar presented by business expert and author Brad Sugars, in Wellington. This gave us a boost and even though we had been through a heap of problems, we stuck to our determination that investing was a good idea.

The tenants were gone but the place was a mess, which I found very upsetting because of the emotional involvement with the property. So for eight weeks during March and April 2003 we spent every weekend in Upper Hutt, repairing damage and redecorating our old home. Our personal debt increased on the credit card as we had to spend close to $10k fixing the place up.

When we were finished we were exhausted but we did manage to increase the rent by $20 and got a good tenant, who stayed for 18 months.

Determination and change of team

We felt like giving up at this point but we thought, 'No, this is our business.' We booked into the Richmastery Property Academy in May 2003 instead.

What a life changing experience! When we were driving home we were going through all of the emotions possible, from elation as to what we had learned, to comfort that some of the stuff we were doing right, to hopelessness for some of the stuff that we were doing wrong to frustration at the fact that we now knew how to do things better. We wanted to just get out there and buy, buy, buy – but couldn't because we were personally in a financial hole. We still had $54k of personal debt to deal with and every property we had purchased was bought by just squeaking into it financially.

> After the Richmastery Property Academy the first thing we did was fire the property manager. We didn't know anything about property managers then, but we now tell them what we expect. We interview them first. We also interview other members of our team, our accountant and solicitor, to ensure that they are property investors themselves, or at least understand what we are wanting to achieve. We've learnt now that people specialise in different areas. It's important to have a good rapport with your accountant, lawyer and property managers.

We found a retired accountant who manages over 200 properties. He was cheaper, does a far better job and he owns a large number of his own properties. He is brilliant and looks after both of our properties in Upper Hutt.

Also after the academy we asked ourselves what was holding us back. We made a very hard decision to sell our beloved motorcycles, which raised $12k and cleared some personal debt.

In June 2003 we began a series of discussions with family members regarding an equity guarantee so we could purchase more property. We were thinking creatively as Richmastery had suggested we do at the academy. We ended up getting an equity guarantee from Jeff's father over his home in Upper Hutt.

Back into the market

Over the next month we looked at about 30 properties in the lower North Island towns of Ohakea, Bulls and Marton, as we knew that industry was coming back to the Rangitikei area. We put offers on three places, even though we knew we only had finance for two. All three got accepted so we pulled out of one deal and in July 2003 we purchased two properties in Marton.

One, in Barton Street, Marton, was valued at $45k and we purchased it for $39k; we rented it for $110 per week. The second, in Main Street, Marton, was valued at $60k and we got it for $50k; it returned $125 per week.

These properties were fantastic cash flow and both lots of tenants wanted to stay. We found a good property manager in Marton, and we were very clear about our expectations.

We had been crewing for the Richmastery Profit from Property Evening seminars in Palmerston North, and in October 2003 we crewed at Richmastery Property Academies in Auckland and Sydney. These were fantastic events, and what a fabulous way to spend time with like minded people. We learn so much every time we spend time with other investors and it's a brilliant feeling to be helping other people with their education.

In February 2004 we became involved with the local Richmastery Personal Property Mentoring Group and are learning heaps more. We have been working hard on eliminating our personal debt, now very much reduced!

In April 2004 we found a property in Blackwell Street, Marton. We had challenges with getting finance as we couldn't prove Jeff's income (due to us taking up a business opportunity only a few weeks beforehand). It's another great cash flow property, and we were determined that there would be a way to finance it. We were turned down by several banks and mortgage brokers, but vowed not to stop trying, and finally got finance through a second tier lender, Strata Funding. The asking price was $54k and we purchased for $48k. It's a two bedroom unit in a block of four, with a registered valuation of $53k. We rent it out for $125 per week.

In early 2005 we purchased two three-bedroom units in a block of flats in Feilding that are positive cash flow.

We now have a total portfolio value of $685k including our own home, with total mortgages of $505k and have created total equity of $180k.

> We have proved that you can start with next to nothing and with some focus and determination can get into the investment game. We now have a good income stream from our properties and no personal debt.

We have also recently purchased a motorcycle, and we are thoroughly enjoying our freedom again (one more bike to get next year and we will both be extremely happy).

Well worth the bumpy ride

We're incredibly pleased with how far we've come, as we came from a place of $40k personal debt and no savings. Despite a whole heap of knock backs with determination we have made this thing work! And let me tell you, it's worth it! We are well on our way to our first million and beyond!

The education we have had through Richmastery has changed our lives. We now crew at each academy and regularly go to Wellington to either crew at Richmastery seminars, or attend seminars by international speakers. We read all the time now. We are also members of Peak Performance and Success Coach Kurek Ashley's Life Success Club and we manage the Richmastery Profit from Property evening seminars in our region. People think we're mad and that we're seminar junkies but we find that even though you've heard it all so many times, you always pick up more.

Our ultimate goal is to have over 100 income streams by the end of 2007, and have all the choices and freedom in the world. Our reward for our efforts is to spend three to five months riding motorcycles throughout the United States in 2009 – or earlier!

Financial freedom rocks!

TOP TEN TIPS

1. Get educated.
2. Get started.
3. You don't have to have money to get started.
4. Think like a business owner.
5. Work out your criteria and rules.
6. Love the numbers not the property.
7. Hire the right advisors.
8. Be patient.
9. Be flexible.
10. Be persistent.

Chapter 38

The leverage game

'Now that I understand how leverage works ... in another couple of years, I could own $6 million of property.'
— **Anthony (Sammy J) Johnson,**
Gold Coast, AUS

I moved permanently from Europe to Byron Bay on the New South Wales coast in 2001 after visiting Australia for many years and finally deciding to emigrate there. I had owned a building company in the UK and Italy and had done a few of my own renovation projects over the years. This was all great experience but I didn't have a cohesive goal or plan. I was just buying and selling. My basic knowledge was to buy as cheaply as you can and sell for as much as you can. But as my core business was building for other people investing was really not my focus.

Ready to take action

After I had moved to Australia, I was reading the paper, thinking, 'Right, this is it. I'm 47 years old. It's time to get down to making a lot of money.' I saw an advert for a Brad Sugars' seminar and the name put me straight off. But I thought I'd listen to what he had to say anyway. So I went to his three hour evening seminar in Brisbane. I was just amazed; I was absolutely captivated by the guy. He asked anyone interested in knowing more about his Billionaire in Training Course to stay for an extra half hour at the end. I was there with my partner, Sandhan. We just looked at each other and said, 'We've got to do this!' That was until we heard the price – it was going to cost $16k for both of us to do it. But we decided that if this was what it takes we would do it – we were ready to take action and felt this would give us the tools to do it.

So we enrolled in Brad Sugars' Billionaire in Training course. It was sold as business, property, shares – basically how you can use all these different asset classes to make a lot of money and how they work together. It was held at the Hyatt Regency at Coolum in May 2002 over six days, with between 150 and 200 people attending.

> Over the six days, I had just nine hours sleep – it was absolutely insane. We started at 5 am and sometimes went until 3 am the next day. What I got out of it for me was the first real hit of finding out really what it meant to be in business, all about teams and having the right people.

There was a point on the course where a lot of money was gifted to charity and it was at this point that my whole perception of making money changed. I knew that if I did have money I could do a lot more with it than just own fast cars.

Into business

Following Brad Sugars' Billionaire Boot Camp, I bought into two businesses. The first was two dining guides for tourists, one based on the Gold Coast and one based in Brisbane. They were asking $150k; I negotiated $75k and put down a $25k deposit, and said I'd pay the rest in 12 months. Four months later I sold the business for $110k to a guy who was working for me. So I made $35k in four months.

The second business I bought were two tourist magazines based in Cairns and Alice Springs. We paid $650k for them; we put in cash from England that my business partner provided to me, becoming my equity partner in the deal.

> One of the things Brad Sugars drummed into us was the need for leverage. When I did the boot camp, this was a new word for me – basically it means having people working for you to create more time.

Franchising

Brad Sugars also talked a lot about selling a business again and again, and the only way to do this was by licensing it or franchising it – there you've got leverage. So my goal was to expand a stable of tourist magazines to more locations in Australia and New Zealand and to set a franchise system in place.

So following this advice we then created the franchise system and started up two more similar tourist magazines for Port Douglas and the Cairns highlands.

I gathered information on all the businesses on the eastern seaboard of Australia, from Cairns to Adelaide, and also researched all the magazines that would be potential competitors. I then systematised everything according to Brad's way of thinking. He also talked about having an exit strategy and my aim was to exit in three years, as I needed three years to build the business. When I took it over it was turning over $700k, now it turns over $1.1 million. After three years I sold it for $1 million, and the deal settled in October 2004.

Commercial properties

At the same time as we were building the business, we bought our first commercial property on the Gold Coast, in Labrador. It was worth $1 million, and the figures were great. It was a huge tin shed and the tenant sells truck parts and repair trucks.

The difficult thing with commercial properties is you have to put down a deposit of 30% ($300k in this case). I ended up persuading the vendor, who wanted to lease the building back, to give me a year's rent in advance ($125k), which is what I used for part of the deposit. The rest came from extra money from England (from my business partner, who is my equity partner).

After 18 months the property was revalued at $1.25 million and we were able to pull our deposit money out of it. It brings in $127k a year, so it's very cash positive.

I was petrified going into a million dollar deal. I kept trying to build as much insurance into the deal as possible, so I could feel more comfortable. The first thing was the upfront rent, then I paid the mortgage company for one year too, which meant I had $65–70k cash flow out of it. I also asked the vendor to arrange to give me a six month bank guarantee of rent should they default. They are a very established company.

This deal was amazing; it was the basis of my foray into the commercial property market. Tony, the real estate agent who had helped me with this deal, became a really good friend of mine and still is. After that I bought another property through him that I also thought was a really good deal.

Reinforcing the leverage game

Around this time my business/equity partner and I decided we wanted to get more education on property investment. We attended the Richmastery Profit from Property evening seminar and thought that was great because it focused solely on property and I felt that that was where my main interest and passion lay. I love property. After the seminar we both enrolled to do the three day Richmastery Property Academy, held on the Gold Coast in December 2002.

> Even though the course didn't talk much about commercial property investment, again it was the reinforcement of the leverage game that I really got. They teach that when you buy a residential property you either do it up or add value. Buy below market value and then recycle your equity by getting it revalued and take your money out. The recycling of equity was a reinforcement of how the game is played – I was just playing with much bigger figures. From the Richmastery Property Academy, I also learnt about the strategy of not selling.

Inside three years we have come to own $3 million worth of property over only four properties. The equity we have accumulated is $900k. But I can also leverage against $3 million worth of assets.

Our first commercial property will be vacant at the end of five years but the tenant will give me one year's notice and my plan then is to knock the building down, spend $1 million and develop the site into units. The mortgage on the property is $800k. I will have to borrow another $1 million, but it will be worth about $3.1 million because it will have 2000 square metres and you can sell or rent per square metre. I estimate I can get $1700 per square metre.

If I rent all the units I build I will make another $50k in rent on top of what I already get. It's just fantastic how it all works.

At the very least I will have $1 million of equity, against which I can borrow $750k, that will allow me to buy another $2 million worth of property ... it's crazy.

Great returns

Our next purchase after the Richmastery Property Academy was in February 2003. This was 4000 square metres of land, with 2000 square metres of concrete block building, with four tenants. It was located in Andrews, a suburb of the Gold Coast near Burly. The tenants love it as it is cheap.

The vendor was retiring and selling some of his properties off. He was asking $860k for the property; I got it for $800k. The rental return was $94k. I needed a deposit of 30% (about $270k). So I borrowed $150k in equity out of the first property in Labrador, because it had gone up by $250k, and then scraped together $120k from the magazine business and bought it. This deal at that time had an 11% yield, which is a great return. The last valuation is for $1 million and it is now bringing in $98k a year in rent.

After buying this property, I had hit the wall in terms of equity and my equity partner did not have any more cash to put in to the next deal.

Two retail units off the plan

The man who sold me the first property in Labrador told me that he had a parcel of land that he wanted to develop and he was thinking of building a factory for himself. I talked him into dropping that idea as I would lose a good tenant and told him he could make more money by developing more industrial units on the block. He decided to take my advice. Then Tony, my real estate agent friend, suggested I buy one of these units. He said it's not going to happen straight away, it will be 12 months before you have to settle and all you have to do is put a small deposit down.

So I went and had a look at the block of land; it was the location that got me. It is right next to Harbour Town, which is a huge shopping centre just off the Gold Coast highway. I'd also heard that the Gold Coast council had relaxed the laws on retail premises. In the past they'd only given retail licences to properties that were fronting the main highway but they had

Units near Harbour Town that I bought off the plan. For an outlay of $2000 on them, in 12 months I made $340k in cash and equity.

recently changed this to include anything that was up to 100 metres back from the highway.

I paced out 100 metres and it came to the front of where the unit I was looking at would be situated. There was another unit on the plan beside it that would also be able to be retail too. Tony said, 'Why don't you buy that one too?' I said I didn't have any money. He convinced me by saying the rents were good. So I put my name down for Units 1 and 2, both of which could be used for retail.

So we committed to buying two of them off the plan. I told them that I would agree to buy them if I could exchange contracts immediately and only put $2000 down. We bought them for $1250 per square metre, about $750k for both units.

I said I would include a default clause that if I did default we would pay the 10% deposit in the contract, and put down $1000 on each contract. The vendor was happy because he had a sale. In the meantime the rest of the properties for sale have sold for $1500 per square metre, which means that on completion of the properties we will have approx $170k equity in them.

I have negotiated a rent with a tenant for $150 per square metre per annum instead of the $125 square metre per annum that the agent was talking about initially. Now all the other units have commanded the same price and therefore all our properties have gone up in value considerably.

The units were completed and we settled on the deal on 15 November 2004. We had to put down an $80k deposit on the two properties. I have since sold Unit 2 for $1750 per square metre, which means all of them have valued up to that. My equity partner and I got $100k each from the sale of this unit.

I then had a valuation done on Unit 1 for $800k, which we had paid $560k for. I will now refinance the unit to 70% of the value, which means I have got the property for no money down. What a deal – in 12 months for an outlay of $2000 I have made $340k in cash and equity. We rent this for $68k per year so it's totally positive.

Structure

Structure is important. I always have a trustee company and unit trusts, one for property and one for business; they shouldn't be tied up to the same trustee companies. You should have power of attorney on the property one, but the director of the property trust should not be yourself, for asset protection.

I've used a number of so-called experts. But at one point I ended up with three companies, two family trusts and a super, making eight trusts and three companies in total. Now I have simplified it all and my advice it to try to keep it basic but essential. Make sure you have a good accountant who is an entrepreneur and is looking after himself, who thinks outside the square or along the same lines as you. Take the time to find those people because they save you a lot of grief.

You can learn too much, and get paralysed from analysing too much. I have just done it and it works.

Goals

My aim now is to accumulate as much property as I can. My whole perspective has changed. When I started off I just flippantly brought out a figure at Brad's Boot Camp that in 10 years I would own $50 million worth of property. At the time it sounded mad but now I know it's not, because after three years I already own several million dollars worth of property and that will keep doubling it, so I could have a tidy sum by the time I'm 60. Now that I understand how leverage works, I can see how it can all happen.

Like Brad Sugars says, you just have to imagine what you want and now I can see that actually it's possible. I can see that in another couple of years, which would be five years from when I started, I could own $6 million worth of property, all from leveraging off other people's money.

I have also read a lot of books. Brad Sugar's books are really good. I have also read all of Robert Kiyosaki's; while he does repeat himself, they are easy to read and because he reiterates the same points, they start to hit home. Another favourite is *Raving Fan*, a little book by Ken Blanchard and Sheldon Bowles. The guy in the book is a dentist who talks about how you must create Raving Fans of your business who will refer everyone there – this is the ultimate goal in business.

I also love Anthony Robbins. He is invaluable, and his DVDs are great. I did his Date with Destiny six day course in April 2004 and found it amazing.

TOP TEN TIPS

1. Always try to buy cash flow positive so you know that even if the interest rates doubled you could still service the loan — it's like a big insurance.
2. Try to always buy in an area of population growth. If there's only a certain amount of infrastructure there then your property and land will attract a premium.
3. Do your numbers; it's absolutely essential that they stack up. Don't go on emotions. But if the numbers stack up you should stretch yourself.
4. Focus on what you want, on what it feels like to have that, and when you have that in your sight everything that you are doing is heading in that direction. Conversely, if you focus on the negative that's where you're going.
5. Get educated. You may not understand what you're getting out of the courses or books at the time but you need to keep absorbing information, and you'll always learn something important.
6. You just have to jump in and do it.
7. Don't be afraid to make mistakes; it's the way to learn.
8. Find your niche passion in the property market and get to know that market and focus on that area.
9. Repeat that same process in another area.
10. Structure is very important: get it right before you start.

Chapter 39

Attitude and motivation

'No matter what your age, it is possible to achieve financial security in residential real estate.'

— **Bob Stewart, Palmerston North, NZ**

I am an internet publisher, real estate investor, father and husband (and previously a university lecturer and professor in education, university deputy vice-chancellor and city councillor). I'm 65 years old.

My main message is that, no matter what your age, it is possible to achieve financial security in residential real estate. In particular if you are one of the baby boomer group or older, don't think you've left your run too late.

I've been a property investor on and off since my late twenties. However, the last five years, since my 60th birthday, have been particularly remarkable for me. During this time I have acquired 30 residential properties that now represent $8.5 million in value; of this the bank owns $4.5 million and the rest ($4 million) is my share (and my family's share). The properties are located in different parts of Auckland, downtown Wellington, the Kapiti Coast, Palmerston North and Rotorua. Some of my properties are strong in cash flow, and some in prospects for capital growth. About 70% of the 30 properties owned are currently cash positive. The remainder are close to being cash positive (except for the lifestyle properties, such as our home and holiday home).

Five of these 30 properties were purchased through the Richmastery Property Deals website at discount prices. I have attended the three day Rich-mastery Property Academy, and previously a Richmastery Profit from Property seminar, Retire Young, Retire Rich, which I found most useful in achievement of my goals.

> This is a little about what it took to acquire these assets. The crucial thing is your attitude. Yes you do also have to have the techniques. But if you really want the results, you will be motivated to dig out the techniques that will work for you.

The advantage of residential real estate

Early in my investing career I learnt that there is something very special about residential real estate. The banks are experts on assessing investment risk (that's their job); so what type of investment do they like? For mortgage purposes, residential real estate is the only AAA rated investment and on this they will offer up to 95% loans. Try borrowing that amount to purchase shares, businesses, or even other types of real estate!

> Residential real estate also has lots of other advantages. There is personal control of the investment, it's affordable for the majority of homeowners, a line of credit can be secured over the investment property and for over 50 years it has maintained at least a 5.7% average annual capital growth rate, over the whole of the country. It has a broad market in good times or bad – people always need a roof over their head.

Vision and goals

Let me trace for you the process five years ago that led to the purchase of my 30 properties. At that time I began doing a three year programme for business entrepreneurs that was helpful for me to create a vision of how I wanted my life to be. This programme aims to give a balanced emphasis on personal, health and financial aspects of life.

At the start of the programme we were asked to imagine that we were at our own funeral. What would people be saying about what was important to us during our life? What would we like them to say? We were then challenged to create a vision of what we actually wanted to achieve in the three major areas. Then it was a matter of developing a plan, including specific time-frames, to achieve these goals.

This provided the seedbed for me to attend the three day Richmastery Property Academy in April 2002, as well as other seminars including two weekends in Sydney with Robert Kiyosaki. These were powerful influences. They gave me the push to get back into the market again. I needed to use all the 'smarts' possible in wealth acquisition. I had the vision and the knowledge – it was simply a matter of putting it all into practice.

I set financial goals whereby my income and net assets would be doubled during the three year programme. The goals seemed almost overly ambitious at the time, yet three years later I found I had substantially exceeded them. I have now set myself a new goal by the year 2010. By this date, my goal is to have increased my family's share ($4 million) of the properties to the figure of $15 million.

Putting it into practice: key points

So how did I put all this in practice? Here are some of the key points

Positive attitudes towards money: Strange as it may seem, most people actually have negative views about money. It's not difficult to gather negative sayings about money such as 'filthy rich', 'poor but happy' or 'Money is the root of all evil'. Although not realising it, they are repelling money, rather than attracting money into their lives.

To become wealthy you have to turn around these negative attitudes, and replace them with positive empowering beliefs, such as, 'I am prosperous and comfortable with money' and 'You can do a lot of good with money.' (Bill Gates gives only a fraction of his money to charity, yet with some of this money a new strain of wheat has been developed that could save the lives of many millions of people around the world.)

Unless you have your views on money sorted out, you will repel money and lose it even when you do receive it. A good example of this is seen in people who win large sums of money in lotteries. Five years after collecting all that money, it has been shown that 80% of the winners have lost their newly acquired fortune and are probably worse off than they were previously.

Vision: Ask yourself. Are you really prepared to make the changes necessary in your life to achieve wealth? What would it mean to be comfortably wealthy? You need to be able to picture in very specific terms what you would do, where you would live, what you would own. The first step is to create a vision of how you want your life to be.

Don't go with the herd: To succeed, you are going to have to do things *differently* from the great masses of people in our society. A survey on attitudes towards investing showed that most people 18 to 24 years thought it was too early to start investing; people 25 to 44 years were too busy with children and mortgages, and those 45 years and over thought it was too late. It is only one person in 100 who will build sufficient assets for a comfortable retirement.

Opportunities to help others: Wealth can provide many wonderful chances to benefit others in need. One of life's immutable laws is that what you give out will come back to you. Some of these benefits will be your own emotional and physical health, and your own quality of life. A person with a generosity of spirit will attract the same attitude in others, and will receive back this benefit.

Assemble your team: After you have a clear vision (as I have discussed above), the next thing is to have your team. You cannot do it all by yourself. You need good professionals with whom you can work well, and who are also on your wavelength. These people include your solicitor, accountant, real estate agent (or purchasing agent); property valuer, chattels valuer, property manager and mortgage broker (if you use one).

You need to make sure that you have addressed all **risk issues**. Some of these risk issues are *insurable* (these are addressed by major medical, income protection, trauma cover, death or terminal illness, landlord protection and general property insurances). Some of the risk issues are *non-insurable* (these are addressed by separation of wealth from risk by establishment of trusts etc., cost-saving legal structures, tax effectiveness, and succession planning).

I initially found it difficult to get good advice on the best legal structure for me. I had to go through several advisors before arriving at a structure that really suited my situation. There are plenty of advisors who are happy to charge you to set up trusts and companies, but they are not so helpful on how to set up the *relationships* between the trusts and companies, and how to *manage* the structure effectively.

This Hillsborough, Auckland home leapt 25.8% in value in just one year.

Buy and hold: My intention with the properties that I buy is long term acquisition and rental income; that is, I have a 'buy and hold' philosophy in my property investment. This doesn't mean that you cannot sell the occasional property that does not measure up for retention. You should clearly set out your criteria to remain in your 'buy and hold' portfolio.

> There needs to be clear separation within your legal structure if you are also interested in trading properties, so that there is no 'tainting' for tax purposes of your 'buy and hold' activities. Properties that are purchased with the intention of profiting from an increase in value are taxable.

First things first: A key concept for me was leverage: leverage of my time and effort. Twenty percent of what you do will produce 80 percent of your results. You need to work smart, not just work hard. Everyone needs to learn to use their time, energy and resources as effectively as possible. New Zealand is a particularly good place for real estate investment. We have steady economic growth, international high rental yields and generally good tax benefits for property ownership.

How to buy the properties

If you have the vision and the team, what is the next step? You have to be smart in your property investment strategy. There are traps out there for the unprepared. So do your homework. Seminars, books and tapes can be worth their weight in gold.

Two rules in buying properties are: (1) Don't pay too much (ideally you should be purchasing the property for less than the registered valuation). When you buy the property is when you make your money, not so much when you sell. (2) Look for a twist in the property purchase. Recognise that advertisements to sell properties are often 'cries for help'. You can be the 'White Knight' who comes to their rescue.

The property cycle: Take note of the 'property cycle'. Over roughly seven years it appears that there is a general progression from 'boom' (12 o'clock) via 'downturn' to 'recession' (6 o'clock) to 'upturn' and finally back to 'boom'.

> Good buys are available at any time of the cycle, but obviously it's a lot easier to get these when there is gloom and doom all around, as there is at the bottom of the cycle. For five out of seven of these years, the newspapers and the financial advising industry will 'bag' property. So, to go out and buy at these times requires a lot of courage. During these doldrums years for property (in mid cycle), there are far more opportunities for good purchases. However, there are still good buys in boom conditions – it's just a lot harder to find them.

Different parts of the country are at different stages of the property cycle. Sometimes within one city there can be a ripple effect, like dropping a stone into a pond, whereby an increase in the market in the inner suburbs of Auckland, for example, will move to suburbs further out over a one to two year period. Waterside properties and those with desirable views will also benefit from above average capital growth.

What sort of property to buy: There is a choice to be made as to whether to go primarily for high capital growth properties or high cash flow producing property. It is a good idea to purchase four or five cash flow properties for every one high capital growth property. If you have a cash producing business or job/profession, you can concentrate more on the high capital growth type of properties.

There's also a choice to be made as to whether to focus on properties that suit the average person (i.e. 90–110 square metres, three bedrooms, own section fully fenced with its own garage), or to focus more on the housing requirements of the changing demographics of our society (such as students, Generation Xers etc).

> I like to buy a *variety* of properties (the principle of diversification). I always try to buy as much as possible below the registered valuation, and I look for a good balance between a good cash flow, and good capital growth. I prefer to purchase a large number of smaller value properties, rather than a few higher priced properties. This is also part of my diversification principle. It means less risk to me. I buy all over New Zealand using property finding services like Richmastery's Property Deals website. I try to look at demographic statistics and see where people are going. They are going north and to the big centres and for lifestyle to the coastal areas. That's very much the baby boomer generation, looking for nice living environments, like Nelson, Tauranga and the Kapiti Coast.

Even in a market that is near its peak, there are still 'good buys'. You will just have to look harder to find them. It may require patience because property is a time game. On the Richmastery Property site, better deals are now returning, and in the future they will be even better.

Purchase examples

As I have purchased 30 properties in the past few years it is not possible here to write about each of these transactions. However, here are some examples: two properties, located via the Richmastery Property Deals website.

I purchased a four bedroom home in Hillsborough, Auckland in March 2003 for $325k through Richmastery, and the market value at time of purchase was $385k. However, just over a year later (June 2004), it was revalued at $430k, representing a value increase per year of 25.8%. It is currently rented for $450 per week.

Another property purchased through the Richmastery website was a one bedroom flat in Grey Lynn, Auckland in October 2002. I paid $150k for this,

Purchased when built, this Albany, Auckland house has increased 17.6% in value per year.

and the market value at the time of purchase was $172k. In June 2004 I had this revalued at $215k, which shows a value increase per year of 26.1% per year. This is rented at $260 per week.

Another example of a property in my portfolio, but not purchased through the Richmastery Property Deals website, is a four bedroom home in Albany, Auckland that was built for me and purchased brand new in January 2001 for $402k. The market value at time of purchase was $413k. In March 2004 it was revalued at $625k, which represents a value increase of 17.6% per year. This is currently rented for $550 per week.

The value increases per year for the four examples are exciting. But what if you consider the return on the 20% deposit that was made in the case of each property. The return on the actual money put up on the deal (i.e. the 20%) is even more amazing. Taken in order, the return on the 20% deposit for the Hillsborough home is 129% per year for the deposit. For the Albany home it is 87% per year.

It pays to keep 'crunching' the numbers for your properties. I use spreadsheets to do this. You should certainly do this before any purchase. The decision process to buy an investment property is a numbers game and should not be based upon emotional considerations. There are several software programs that can assist you in this number crunching process.

Assistance and management

There's help out there: You can learn a lot from property seminars, books, property magazines, advertisements, real estate agents and membership of property investors associations.

Banks: I currently deal with eight banks. I sometimes work through brokers, but also make direct approaches to various banks who are familiar with my track record. I have no problems raising the mortgage money now – how different from the Bad Old Days!

Property management and rental agencies: Managing property is a challenging job and some agents are definitely better than others. If you choose to have an agent look after your properties, you may need to make some changes until you find the best agent to manage them for you. If you can afford it, it's good to have a rental management agent. Your main job should be looking for the next deal and strategic planning. Property management can bog you down. I regard the 6–8% of the rental that I pay to the agent as money well spent. I am currently using the services of nine rental agents in five different New Zealand cities and towns. I use landlord insurance, as it looks after the majority of damage and rent arrears from tenants, covering up to 75–85% of possible losses from rent owing.

So my message is: Go ahead, you can do it!

There are three major mistakes people make:

- Lack of clarity about what they want in their life.

- Procrastination over starting important tasks through fear of failure.

- Not persisting in the face of challenge and uncertainty.'

TOP TEN TIPS

1. Take charge of your life and avoid blame and denial. Blaming others for one's difficulties may be satisfying in the short term, but in the long run it is very disempowering.

2. Develop a very specific vision of what sort of person you would like to be: your personal life, your health and your financial life. Are you really committed to achieving success?

3. Ask yourself what specific strategies will help you to move toward this specific vision.

4. Be focused. Probably only about 20% of your actions will help you toward your specific vision. Concentrate your energies on this 20%, and not the remaining 80%.

5. Look at a lot of properties (or have someone do this on your behalf, i.e. use property finding services).

6. Do analysis on the possible investments and pick the best.

7. Diversify. Buy some cash flow and some capital growth properties, buy different types of properties, in different locations and spread your investment around (i.e. buy more lower priced properties rather than fewer higher priced properties).

8. Buy when people are selling, and sell when people are buying.

9. Time is your friend in real estate investment. Although there is a place for other strategies, a buy and hold strategy has a lot to commend it.

10. Allow yourself to make mistakes.

Summary

You have just read story after story from 40 people just like you that **MASSIVELY** transformed their lives through real estate investing. So I guess the big question is ... **what are you going to do now?**

If you're like 95% of the public you will DO NOTHING. Incredibly, 95% of people who read a book do nothing with the information in it. They invest their time reading it and money buying it and then do ... NOTHING! Most won't even avail themselves of the 4 FREE BONUSES mentioned in the next couple of pages or listen to the attached audio CD. And they wonder why they are broke or don't have enough money and stay on the 'work wheel' for the rest of their lives.

This book was not written to tickle your ears so you could do nothing! It was written to encourage, inspire, motivate and jolt you into taking ACTION and becoming a Real Estate Millionaire. The lives of the people in this book changed because they took ACTION. Remember that in life *nothing happens unless you make it happen!*

Success does NOT come to those who wait; it comes to those who take it! So I ask you again: What are you going to do now? Success is in the follow through!

Here is the Richmastery formula for getting rich:

Education + Action > Resistance = Riches

Your **Education**, and the **Action** you take with it, must be greater than your **Resistance** (to do NOTHING) for you to create **Riches**.

No one ever becomes a Wallaby or All Black when they can't get off their butts and go to training. And, consequently, *no one will ever get rich if they are not prepared to invest in themselves with a decent real estate investing education and then put it into action.*

In chapter after chapter of this book you have heard how investors' lives were significantly transformed by attending the Richmastery Property

Academy. The academy was the catalyst for many to turn from average to exceptional. The approximately $3000 course fee has reaped graduates millions of dollars in wealth. The only question that remains is: will you attend the academy so it can do the same for you?

A privileged few

Each year this book will be read by *thousands of people* but each year we only run one or two Richmastery Property Academies for the first few hundred individuals who take ACTION and book to attend.

The academy is not about the number that attend, it's about the quality outcome each person receives and how it dramatically and significantly empowers their lives to achieve a whole new financial level. For this reason the numbers of people who attend each academy are strictly limited.

The Richmastery Property Academy is a three day journey that will reward you for the rest of your Life. So conquer your *Resistance* and take *Action*: go to www.richmastery.com or phone 0800-006-000 (in New Zealand) and 1800-888-686 (in Australia) and book your seat for the next academy now.

Your passion for an outcome drives your outcome

If you are not passionate about being rich, if you would rather slave on the 'work wheel' for 60 years to retire for seven before you die then this book will not change you, because only you can change you!

There's an old saying, you can lead a horse to water but you can't make him drink. You can lead a man to knowledge but you can't make him think.

You just watched 40 investors pass you on the wealth highway in this book and that should make you think long and hard about what you have achieved in the last three years and what you could achieve in the next three years with the right education and tools.

Wealth is created by putting education into action. If you don't have the education you can't put it into action.

Thank you for spending your valued time reading this book. My hope is you will become passionate about all life has to offer and share the gems you have learnt in this book with others.

I look forward to seeing you at the academy and if you do nothing else, go to www.richmastery.com and register for our FREE newsletter and FREE online forums for investors. We are here to help and support you and would be honoured to be of assistance through those services on our website.

Successful investing

Phil Jones and the Team at Richmastery

P.S. Remember: If you always do what you have always done, you will always get what you always got and life will never change. Step up and do something with your life, attend the Richmastery Property Academy and celebrate the financial rewards for a lifetime.

A Special Reward

To help you get the most out of this book we provide you with the following four Special Rewards. Please make sure you use them and enjoy them.

The goal in providing you with these free additional resources is to encourage you to continue the positive real estate investing journey you have started by reading this book.

1. FREE Bonus Chapters

In addition to this book there are at least five bonus chapters that are available for you to read or download from our website. These chapters are essential reading and will further equip you with an array of powerful tools to help polish and improve your investing. To access these bonus chapters go to: **www.richmastery.com/getrichbonus**

2. FREE Online Investor Support

We invite you to join the Richmastery Forums at our website **www.richmastery.com**. This is a live, fun internet meeting place used by thousands of other investors (and many of the investors in this book) to meet, chat, support, share information and help one another achieve investing success.

We strongly recommend you participate in this investing community, which is designed to help support and further your investing results.

3. FREE Property Analysis Software

The number one tool that EVERY successful investor should be using is Property Analysis Software. It's a critical decision making tool that can save you thousands and make you thousands. To download a free 14 day trial of the software many investors in this book use and recommend, go to: **www.reviq.com**

Note: Many of the investors in this book refer to the Richmastery software; this software is now known as RevIQ.

4. FREE Live Event

We want to give you two tickets valued at $79.90 to Richmastery's four hour How to Profit from Property Live Event so you can build on the exciting knowledge you gain from this book. If you would rather watch the DVD of this evening, we have arranged $20 off the price of this for you. To get your FREE tickets and DVD discount go to: **www.richmastery.com/getrichbonus**

SPREAD THE SUCCESS

SPREAD THE SUCCESS SPREAD THE SUCCESS

· ·

We are currently compiling a book of success stories about people who during their lives have sought help and inspiration through books, seminars, coaches and the like in order to achieve their goals. The degree of success may vary and we are open to including all stories that in some way have had a positive outcome.

We would love to hear about **your** story no matter how small. This could include anything from stopping biting your fingernails to improved health and relationships or business, sporting and financial success.

Our book is designed to inspire and encourage others through your **real life** experiences so that they too can realise their dreams and enjoy the same sorts of successes you have.

To contribute:
Visit **www.spreadthesuccess.com**,
answer a few simple questions and we will contact you about an interview. (Just for doing this you will receive a free eBook and be entered in the draw to win $600 of success products!)

Share your story and spread the success!

Phil Jones and Amanda Craddock

About the authors

Phil Jones

After starting with just $25,000 in 1999 Phil Jones has accumulated a multimillion-dollar property portfolio. Along with his business partner, he founded Richmastery in 2001 to empower and educate other investors.

Richmastery has now trained over 45,000 investors in New Zealand and Australia and Phil has become a respected and sought after speaker at key educational events including Brad Sugars' Five-Day Entrepreneurs Bootcamp.

Phil founded the *Kiwi Property Investor* magazine with his business partner and built it to be the number one selling magazine in the Business Category in New Zealand before transferring his interests in the magazine to his business partner in October 2004.

He is the co-author of the best-selling book *Real Money Real Estate* and the pioneer of the world's first property analysis software, called RevIQ, with the ability to download live real estate information. This software product is endorsed by international accountancy firm BDO and Australasian data specialists RP Data.

Phil's wife Corinna Jones is now an active co-partner in Richmastery Ltd. They have two children Cheinnelle and Jack. Phil's passion for real estate and his wish to help equip others to use property as an investment vehicle to achieve financial freedom is the driving force behind the success of Richmastery Ltd.

Andrea Crabb

Andrea Crabb carried out all interviews and research for this book, bringing to the task more than 10 years' experience in the media industry. After completing a BA in English Literature and a Diploma in Journalism, Andrea worked as a television researcher, freelance print journalist, broadcast journalist and radio producer before working as a researcher and assistant producer on numerous international television documentaries for renowned networks such as National Geographic Television and Discovery Channel. She also worked as a public relations consultant and in television communications before joining Richmastery Ltd. Andrea is currently the communications manager for Richmastery Ltd.